MW00425142

I AM

Love

conf #
3875 7698 450

I AM
Love

From Nothing...to All Things

by

Reimar A. C. Schultze

CTO Books
PO Box 825
Kokomo, Indiana 46903 USA

All Scripture quotations are taken from the King James Bible unless otherwise noted.

Published by:
CTO Books
An outreach ministry of Call to Obedience
PO Box 825
Kokomo, Indiana 46903 USA
www.schultze.org

To purchase additional copies contact:
BookMasters, Inc. USA toll free 1-800-247-6553

Publisher's Cataloging-in-Publication
(Provided by Quality Books, Inc.)
Schultze, Reimar A. C.
    I am love : from nothing-- to all things / by Reimar
A. C. Schultze. -- 1st ed.
      p. cm.
    LCCN 2006936524
    ISBN-13: 978-0-9724411-1-7
    ISBN-10: 0-9724411-1-5

    1. Schultze, Reimar A. C. 2. Clergy--Biography.
3. Children of interfaith marriage--Germany--Biography.
4. Holocaust, Jewish (1939-1945)--Germany--Personal
narratives.   I. Title.

BV660.3.S38 2006   280'.092
                        QBI06-200091

Printed in the United States of America.

CONTENTS

Foreword

The first time I met my father was in the fall of 1962. His 6' 4" frame towered over my tiny form as I gasped for breath in an incubator. I weighed 3 pounds and 14 ounces. He and my mother had already given me to God.

And giving things to God, I confess, has been my father's habit. He keeps giving tragic things to God, and God does amazing things. And he had been doing this long before I was born. He had a rather tumultuous start. Being born part-Jewish in Hitler's world, he spent his childhood under the shadow of the Nazi terror. He and his family endured a harrowing flight from Germany, only to be interned in a detention camp. His father and baby sister perished.

What happens when a man gives unspeakable human tragedy to God? This book is the miraculous unfolding of that story. It is so much more than an historical account of the *Mischling* (part-Jew) experience during the holocaust. It chronicles the transformation of tragedy into glorious purpose and meaning. And such a transformational experience could change all of our lives. While many survivors of tragedy go through life with bitterness and regret and a horrible sense of being cheated of something that could and should have been theirs, my father is full of wonder and joy that the hand of God has redeemed his experience.

Once, while giving a radio address, he proclaimed with astounding joy, "The Nazis hated us, the British and Americans bombed us, the Russians drove us out of our home, the Danes put us behind barbed wire, and the Jews did not accept us because we were not Jewish enough...and I forgive them all!" My father is a free man. And this book contains the pathway to that freedom for all of us. There is no tragedy that God cannot redeem.

Back to the struggling babe in the incubator. My father gave that babe to God, and now I am here to write this foreword. It was an incredible experience to have been raised by a WWII refugee and Holocaust survivor who had surrendered himself truly to the living God. My earliest memory is kneeling beside my very tall daddy and giving my life to his even bigger God. And his God has become my God. How wonderful it has been.

I remember the Rocky Mountain adventures in the summer, camping at 8,000 feet in an old olive green tent with my parents and my three siblings. We thought it was the vacation of choice, not knowing we were too poor for anything else. Daddy would pick a mountain to climb and then all six of us would hit the trail if there was one. If a raging mountain stream was in the way we would either pick our way gingerly across on a fallen tree or my father would strip a sapling pole and hold it horizontally with a child clinging to each end. Then we would inch our way across the snow melt stream like a six-legged animal. I would occasionally lose my footing against the swift current, but my daddy's feet were firm, and disaster was averted. My mother would stand with her hands over her mouth saying, "Reimar...Reimar!" But Daddy believed in taking calculated risks. And he taught us responsibility, faith, teamwork and perseverance in those mountains. We learned to keep our eyes on the goal, and to overcome our fears and every obstacle. Complaining or giving up were not options.

At home, I remember waking up to the sound of my father praying. He seemed to have a great time with his Maker, and that didn't hurt my opinion of prayer - or of God. He rarely watched TV, and neither did we. We were too busy living real life rather than passively watching the imagined lives of others. And Daddy took the time most fathers give to the little box of flashing colors and gave it to the higher work of loving his wife, his children and his God. Family night was a highlight each week. Sometimes when we were small, my tall daddy would lie on the floor like an alligator. Who would dare to touch the sleeping fiend? Peals of laughter marked those evenings. There were games in the living room, trips to the library, ice cream cones, and long talks about whatever was on our minds. Never once do I remember our father raising his voice at us. He was a rock, unwavering in his integrity and pursuit of the true Kingdom of God.

Now I live in a village nestled in the Appalachians. I still climb mountains and cross streams. Not just the ones that surround our village, but also the exhilarating peaks of God's purpose and destiny. The view up here is glorious! Our children are by our sides, holding on to the sapling of truth handed down by my father. My father's adventure fanned a spark into a flame within his children. Now that spark is igniting the third generation.

My father's life and suffering now makes sense. In the furnace of affliction, God forged a man of purpose, integrity and courage. His legacy of joy and redemption he offers to you in this book. This is more than a story; it is a light on a path seldom traveled, a path across raging streams and up glorious mountain peaks where we become all we were born to be.

Esther Schultze Morey

Introduction

It is indeed challenging for me to cover seventy years of my personal history, spanning such a vast era in space and events, from Nazi Germany to a walk with my Creator now in prosperous America.

As you follow me through these annals, you see a little boy whose everyday life was a challenge, whose family was uprooted several times, and who was given no answers as to the purpose or destiny of life.

It is only very slowly that my soul was awakened, first ever so dimly through divine light filtering through the morning mist hovering over human misery, and then, finally, breaking out in full brilliance at noonday, through the divine Son of all sons, Jesus the Christ.

In this writing, when it comes to a conflict between historical data gathered from the archives of the Holocaust and my experience as a part-Jew in the midst of it, I let the "but I was there" overrule the words of the scholars and historians who were not there.

It is a well-known fact that six million Jews perished in German-occupied territory. But what is not well known is how the part-Jews fared under the Nazi repression. This book gives the reader a little window on their fate, which was not so much governed by law as by the whim of the Gestapo. As a whole, the full-blooded Jews' destiny was unalterably fixed, while the part-Jews were forever living in a twilight of uncertainty.

The Jews and part-Jews who went through the twentieth century's unmitigated catastrophe are mostly deceased by now. Hence it is up to their children to keep the story alive above the clutter of tens of thousands of documents on this period of human tragedy.

I am one of those many children, and I have chosen to put my story on paper. Yet, perhaps the main difference between my story and that of others of like experiences is that my story, rather than ending with the same gloom and doom by which it started, ends with the great commanding theme that *the world is not fair...but God is good.*

However, we will never see God's goodness and love with our fists clenched in His face, but only as we humble ourselves in obeisant surrender to His mighty power, wisdom, and everlasting compassion.

Reimar A.C. Schultze

I AM
Love

CHAPTER ONE

"I Love You, I Love You..."

I was thirteen years old when I rode my bicycle into a forest near Hamburg, Germany, wanting only to escape the rubble of the city, that was once my boyhood home but had since been destroyed by British bombs. I had no tent or blanket to bring with me, so as night fell and the temperature cooled, I covered myself with pine branches. I slept soundly until early morning, when I was rudely awakened by ants crawling up my legs. As I jumped up and stomped my feet to rid myself of those unwelcome visitors, the golden beams of the sun broke through the birch trees, and the song of a nightingale disrupted the hallowed silence.

Then a voice spoke to me and said, "I love you, I love you; I AM love. All the destruction you see about you is not of My doing but is the result of man's inhumanity to man." It was the first time I heard the voice of God, and it was also the first time in my whole life, ever, that I was not in the presence of death, destruction, or human misery.

It was 1949, just four years after the end of World War II, when I spent that night in the forest and heard the voice of God speak to me of His love. I was four years old when the nightly bombings of Hamburg, the second largest city in Germany, began in 1940, and those terrifying nightly air raids were my first childhood memories. Our family of five lived on the fifth floor of an apartment complex at the time. Two or three times each night, we were awakened by the somber sound of the warning sirens, and we clearly understood the message: "Death is on the way!" We quickly scrambled out of bed to get dressed, while my father grabbed a flashlight. We were not allowed to turn on the electric lights, since we were under blackout orders to make it difficult for the enemy aircraft to find the city. My mother frantically helped us younger ones as we joined with the other families scurrying down the five flights of stairs, with nothing but a few flashlights to illumine our way.

On those steps, body was jostled against body, especially as traffic increased with each lower level; families clutched the railings and one another, careful not to miss a step and stumble. The occasional shriek of a frightened child pierced the otherwise relatively silent but hurried descent of a people who did not know if they would be burned alive, asphyxiated, or buried in the next few minutes. Mothers did their best to comfort their sobbing little ones, whose fathers were off fighting either the Allies in the west or the Russians on the eastern front.

About halfway down, as if we needed a reminder, the final siren began its deafening sound with one long, loud, deep tone. This put a ghastly exclamation mark on the pre-alarm siren, which we had already heard. This ominous siren did not warn us that the bombers were coming, as had the first siren, but rather it declared, "They are here!" At that sound we nearly catapulted ourselves into the basement bunker where a dim light revealed our terrified faces. A man wearing a white armband at the bunker entrance was the only one who spoke, instructing us to hurry and to stay close together.

As I recall, the bunker was equipped with a box of sand, a shovel, a pickax, a fire extinguisher, and a first aid kit. Once we were all corralled into that living casket (which is exactly what became of 78 percent of the bunkers in Hamburg), a smothering silence enveloped us as all ears strained to pick up the sound of any nearby explosions. Eventually, another siren sounded, telling us that once again we had escaped death or injury. We then scrambled back up those dark steps to our apartments, where we tried to get some sleep before morning. The whole scene was repeated over and over again, night after night, until finally my parents were too tired to take us downstairs any more, and chose instead to take our chances in our little apartment. Overall, our family survived hundreds of bombing raids in that city.

At one point the situation in Hamburg had become so dire that the city officials arranged for trains to take thousands of children into the country in an attempt to spare them from potential death by bombs. Along with thousands of other children, my siblings and I tearfully waved goodbye to *Mutti* (Mother) as the train pulled out of the station, not knowing if we would ever see her again. We were placed in foster homes in little villages for a short while, but eventually the program was abandoned because it was too stressful for the families. As a result, the city was full of children whose lives were constantly in danger.

As damage from the air raids increased, my oldest brother, Eckart, would come home from school with reports of smoking rubble on the ground here and there in the neighborhood, and of the ambulances and fire trucks having difficulty getting through. We had no idea at the time that before the war was over our entire block would be leveled, though by the grace of God we would be spared.

Although these actual air raids began when I was four and continued until we escaped Hamburg when I was six, I continued to be "bombed" in my dreams for another thirteen years after that. It wasn't until I was a nineteen-year-old freshman at the University of Wisconsin that I was finally free of those horrible nightmares. Until then, each night I dreamed of a bomb falling through the roof of our fifth-floor Hamburg apartment. The bomb would then break through the ceiling of the fourth floor, then the third, the second, the first, and then the roof of the bunker, where it hit me directly on the bridge of my nose. I would awaken from these nightmares absolutely horrified, with a cold sweat on my back. But at the age of nineteen, when I had known Jesus Christ for three years, I finally said, "Jesus, could you stop the bombings, please?" And He did. I have never been "bombed" since. That was my first experience with an instant answer to prayer.

The story of civilian suffering during wartime receives little attention. We hear a lot about the military casualties during battle, but little about the 600,000 civilians that became casualties to Allied bombings in Germany alone. On July 27, 1942, Hamburg experienced the heaviest assault in aerial warfare history. The Royal Air force called it "Operation Gomorrah."

Shortly before midnight, 739 aircraft attacked our city. This "firestorm" created a tornado-like inferno, a huge outdoor blast furnace with winds up to 150 miles per hour and temperatures of 1500 degrees Fahrenheit. Street asphalt burst into flames, people were cooked to death in air raid shelters, and pedestrians were sucked off the sidewalk like leaves into a vacuum cleaner. Eight square miles of the city were incinerated. That night alone, there were 40,000 casualties.

What do you do when so many are killed in one night? Where do you put the dead? Where do you bury them once you dig them out from the rubble? The cemeteries aren't large enough; the roads are blocked with bricks and steel. Who will wipe away the tears of the thousands of young mothers and children?

Think of it. Forty thousand civilians killed in one night! Civilians, not people in uniform. These were mothers, children, and old people. We mustn't reduce them to statistics; they were persons created in the image of God. They were Heidis and Juttas, Giselas and Renates, Elses and Hansis, Friedrichs and Johanns and Günters and Klauses and Siegfrieds. Oh, there were tears enough after that horrible night in Hamburg to make a river! The pain of that monumental tragedy lingers with its survivors to this very day.

But it wasn't the air raid bunkers alone that forged my first childhood memories. Our partly Jewish family faced the added menace of the Nazis and Hitler's diabolical plan to exterminate God's chosen people. In addition, we faced the horror of the brutal Soviet invasion, followed by two years of deprivation in a detention camp, then life in the rubble of post-war Germany, and finally, freedom—both within and without. Through it all, I learned gradually, yet ever more intensely, that though *the world is not fair...God is good.*

Through the ages people have looked around at the suffering and evil in the world and asked, "Who is responsible for all this?" God Himself gave me the answer, clearly and beautifully, when He spoke to me on that sun-streaked morning in the forest outside Hamburg: "I love you, I love you; I AM love. All the destruction you see about you is not of My doing but is the result of man's inhumanity to man." It has become more and more obvious to me from that time on, though I did not clearly recognize it at the moment, that salvation is nothing other than God delivering man from his own inhumanity.

Vati
"I always wanted to marry a Jew."

1929

Mutti
"God has a plan."

CHAPTER TWO

My Grandparents and Parents

In order to do justice to the goodness and faithfulness of God in my life, I must begin with the story of my family, a Jewish/Gentile blend that resulted in the emergence of the man God purposed me to become from before the creation of the world.

Maternal Grandparents

My grandfather on my mother's side was Jewish, and yet he was a Hebrew Christian because he had been baptized by the Jerusalem Church in Hamburg in 1897. So then, was he a Jew or was he a Christian? If being a Jew or a Christian is a matter of faith, then Hans Benningson was a Christian. If it is a matter of race, then he was a Jew.

To the Nazis, Jewishness was strictly a matter of blood. In the New Germany, Hitler's Third Reich, it was not what you believed or how you worshipped God that made you a Jew, but how you were born racially. The Nazis believed there was something about Jewish blood that produced inferiority, uncleanness, deceitfulness, and weakness. To the Nazis, Jewish blood was like a cancer to the superior German race; if it was not removed, it would eventually destroy the whole nation.

So my grandfather Hans was racially Jewish: his parents were Jewish, his grandparents were Jewish, and so forth. They had been loyal Germans for many generations, but their sin was that they were German Jews, and Hitler's goal was that not one German Jew would remain alive in German-controlled territory—or anywhere else in the world, for that matter. Ridding the world of Jews was what the German *Führer* referred to as the "Final Solution."

Hans Benningson was tall, handsome, and charming, and he never met a stranger. He liked to wear fancy shoes and walk with a nice cane—not because he needed it for support, but because it was in style. Hans was also a gentleman and a disciplinarian. *Mutti* (Mother) told us that during dinner her father would walk about the dining room table with a switch behind his back, and if any of his three daughters slouched even the least bit, he would swat them on their back. On the other hand, as his little girls became young ladies, he never failed to greet them in public with a tip of his hat.

In addition, Hans was quite brave. One day he took *Mutti*, who was still a little girl, to a sidewalk café. When the traffic would not stop to let them cross, he simply held up his cane in front of the oncoming cars and walked his pretty daughter across the boulevard. That was Hans, willing to tread where most would not. He had few fears, and many of his traits were also evident in my mother.

Hans was bold, openhanded, and confident, an entrepreneur who could go from one job to another as easily as a bird could switch trees. Once he ran an auto garage and another time he was a locksmith, while yet another time he ran an orphanage. Even when unemployment in Germany skyrocketed to 25 percent, Hans, with his charm and salesmanship, was never without work. He was willing to try anything and to tackle any job, and his attitude served him and his family well.

Grandfather Hans, the German Jew, married Frieda Nattke, an Aryan, considered by Hitler to be a pure German, in 1904. My grandmother was a quiet woman, in every way the opposite of her outgoing and sociable husband. While Hans took much pleasure in a hearty laugh, Frieda often appeared to be on the edge of tears. Hans was generous in spending, while Frieda, out of necessity, became an expert in making things go a long way, a trait my mother acquired from her and later utilized during the hardships of the war and post-war years. My grandmother often complained that her husband had more fun giving away money to the poor and needy than saving it for the good of the family. Each Christmas, Hans would go to the skid rows of Berlin and collect drunks, derelicts, and the poorest of the poor—the homeless—and invite them to Frieda's Christmas dinner.

Hans, like most German Jews of that era, never thought of himself as a Jew but as a German. Consequently, he and many others wore the swastika in the first years of the Reich, simply out of a sense of national loyalty, solidarity, and pride. Also typical of most Germans of that time period, Hans had no interest in material things. He was happy with the basics of life, such as a walk in the park or a game of chess.

Personally, I have no recollection of having seen Hans or Frieda until I was twelve years of age when, after the war, my family and I visited England, where Hans had fled in the late '30s to escape the Holocaust.

Paternal Grandparents

My father's parents were both Aryans. This grandfather, whom we called *Opa*, was a quiet man. He came from a family of tradesmen that went back hundreds of years. I have no recollection of *Opa*, since I was very young when our family left Hamburg, and by the time we returned from East Germany and the detention camp in Denmark, he had died.

Lotte, or *Oma*, our paternal grandmother, was a meek woman, who willingly put herself out for everyone. When her son Heini's family of four was bombed out of their apartment during the war, she invited them to stay with her in her tiny, one-bedroom apartment. Then, after the war, she added our family of five to the already crowded conditions. That made ten persons in a tiny one-bedroom apartment, a situation that lasted for several months. *Oma* was the cog in the wheel, and she kept everything running as smoothly as possible, regardless of the circumstances. Her epitaph could have been "She did what she could."

All four of my grandparents were honest, hard-working people. Yet, for me, the single most life-changing, determining factor was that one of them was a Jew. To a great measure, everything that happened during the first years of my life stemmed from that fact. It is because of the pressure put upon us by the Nazis that we left Hamburg, but had we stayed we would have been killed in the bombings of 1943. From Hamburg we moved to East Germany, and later made a miraculous escape from the Red Army. Because we fled Hamburg, we qualified under the Refugee Relief Act of 1953 to emigrate to the United States in 1955. Miraculously for us, our grandfather's Hebrew Christian heritage brought us blessings of life instead of death in the middle of despair, darkness, and chaos. It is remarkable that the entire life of a family could be so much predestined through the racial identification of one single person.

My Parents

Ilse, or *Mutti*, as we called my half-Jewish mother, was widowed by the time she was thirty-eight. She truly had her hands full as she worked to pull all five of us children through the most heart-rending situations of World War II, as well as the tough post-war years. *Mutti* fought this battle for survival patiently, courageously, and relentlessly, such as when she slipped behind the Iron Curtain shortly after the war to reappear three days later, triumphantly carrying a bag of potatoes to keep her children fed for another two weeks. If anyone deserved the Iron Cross for bravery in motherhood, *Mutti* would have been a noble contender.

Mutti was an institution: she was a library, she was an encyclopedia, she was a Prussian general, and she was an embodiment of humility in the skin of a roaring lion. *Mutti* was a constant source of inspiration, a resource for everything when there was nothing, an optimist in a world of pessimists, a catalyst to revive things that were not, able to kindle a fire in things that did not burn. She stood about five feet, eleven inches tall when she was not overly excited. (She always seemed to grow to immense proportions when agitated.) She had black, wavy hair, easily blown about by the wind. Her pitch black, sparkling, inquisitive eyes complemented her almost always positive expression. *Mutti* frequently joked about her big, ugly Jewish nose and long legs, yet the fact is, prior to her engagement to my father, she had been accepted as an actress in the Hamburg *Schauspielhaus* (theater).

My mother had it in her to tackle widowhood, the Nazis, the hours of the British and American bombings on our city, the threat of the Soviet invasion, the challenging flight from East to West, and the deprivation of a detention camp without ever accumulating the slightest bit of bitterness or self-pity. Above all, she was able to supervise and subdue her four surviving but strong-willed children.

Perhaps *Mutti's* spirit can best be portrayed by an incident that took place at a bus station in Milwaukee many years after the challenges of World War II. *Mutti* was in her seventies by then, when a hooded youngster approached her and demanded her purse. Rather than being frightened, *Mutti* was furious. The young man grabbed her purse, but *Mutti* refused to let go. In the ensuing battle, the robber got the purse, but *Mutti* kept the handle. Later on, laughing uncontrollably as tears rolled down her cheeks, she declared,

"But I got the handle." That was *Mutti*! She lost all kinds of things, but she always held on to something. Even in the direst circumstances, when the bread was green from mold and the soup had no solids, she found some element of incongruity that sparked laughter in her. Often only she knew the cause of the laughter, but she usually carried everyone around her into it. Yes, *Mutti* always held on to the handles of life.

Of course, *Mutti*, who was raised by a Jewish father and a Gentile mother in Berlin, also had her serious moments. There was within her a consciousness of an eternal, wise, and sovereign God, who was never to be questioned or argued with, and who was "never off the telephone line," although, at times, there were long days of silence.

In her early years, *Mutti* took a serious interest in Bible study; later, as she became self-sufficient and energetic, God took a back seat in her life while she raised us children. Visible Christianity was as good as absent from most of her life with us. To *Mutti*, religion was something never to be discussed, and so we were raised without it. We did not attend church, except occasionally on Christmas Eve, and we did not talk about Jesus or read the Bible. In fact, for years I did not even know there was such a thing as the Bible. One of my first memories of my mother having a copy of the Scriptures was when she opened them one Christmas Eve in the detention camp and read the Christmas story. Never having heard it before, I did not understand it, nor did it occur to me to ask questions about what else might be in that little black book, printed in 1913. But years later we learned that, as life got tougher, *Mutti* turned more and more to that old book in which, unknown to us, she underlined passage after passage in a concerted effort to build her faith in her Maker.

Mutti has gone down in my memory as a woman who did not know the word *impossible*. Her faith was a mixture of belief in an all-wise God and in the power of the human will. If anyone ever believed the words of the Apostle Paul, *"...all things work together for good to them that love God,..."* (Romans 8:28), *Mutti* was one of them.

But as surely as my mother's influence left its mark upon my life, the memory of my father, Alfred, whom we called *Vati*, is more like a fleeting shadow. I know I spent time with him, but I remember very little in the way of specific instances. The vague memories I do have of *Vati* were from the time when we all lived in eastern Germany, such as his occasional presence at the dinner table or the time he took us children on a walk in the deep of winter and my nose felt as if it would freeze off. But as a rule, when I got out of bed in those days, my father had already left for work. When he got home in the evening, I had already gone to bed. This went on seven days a week until he died of a combination of tuberculosis and malnutrition when I was nine years old.

Unlike *Mutti*, who was well educated, *Vati* had only a grade-school education. He came from a simple but honest family of hard-working craftsmen who spoke what was known as "Low German," a provincial German dialect spoken in the north. But just as the type of car a man drives or the size of the house in which he lives tells us nothing about his character, so one cannot deduce a man's intellect by how much education he has.

Vati, as soon as he was married, quickly employed *Mutti's* help and learned to speak High German. He soon became an accountant, and by the time of his death at age thirty-nine, he had reached the peak of his career by having become the chief accountant of a large company.

Vati was a tall man—six feet, four inches—and he was slender, though extremely agile and strong. He had sparse blonde hair, massive protruding cheekbones, and large blue, serious, piercing eyes. Although not having expressed any religious faith, he was miraculously healed from an otherwise incurable disease soon after he and *Mutti* were married.

From my faint recollection and *Mutti's* descriptions of *Vati*, I can say my father was a man who was highly respected and considered a person of integrity by all who knew him. He had great courage, as this unfolding story will relate, and he was truly the kind of man my mother needed to fend off the Nazi pressure on our Jewish family.

CHAPTER THREE

I Always Wanted to Marry a Jew

In 1926, seven years before Hitler came to power, and before my mother met my father, my mother, *Mutti*, became acquainted with a man named Rudi, the son of a wealthy industrialist. The relationship between *Mutti* and Rudi deepened until one evening after a performance at the *Schauspielhaus* (theater), Rudi asked *Mutti* for a future together.

Though happy at the prospect, *Mutti* had reservations. She was concerned about Rudi's possible reaction when he learned that her father was a Jew, but when she told him, he graciously dismissed her revelation as unimportant. What he didn't tell her, however, was that just that morning he had received a letter from his parents informing him they would gladly accept as a daughter-in-law any woman he chose to marry—so long as she wasn't Jewish.

Rudi's parents had many Jewish customers in their business, but since Rudi was the oldest child and the apparent heir, and because the winds of political unrest were already blowing and no one knew what the future might bring, they did their best to discourage their son from marrying his Jewish sweetheart. Although Rudi was more in love than he was interested in politics, he finally succumbed to his parents' pressure and broke off his relationship with *Mutti*.

Mutti and Rudi had been young and in love and, for the

most part, oblivious to the growing anti-Jewish climate in Germany. *Mutti* saw no distinction between a German Jew or a German Catholic or a German Protestant. All had fought and died for their country in the First World War. All had contributed to the arts and sciences, to philosophy, medicine, and the betterment of their country. When *Mutti* realized she had been rejected by Rudi and his parents for no reason other than her Jewish heritage, she fell into a state of despair and made her way to a bridge across one of the canals, planning to jump into the arms of death. It was only her deep-seated conviction of the sacredness of life that prevented her from executing her plan. Shortly thereafter, as if by divine providence, *Mutti* met Alfred, who would one day become my father (*Vati*), and her life took a definite turn for the better.

After they had gone out together night after night for several months, *Vati* asked *Mutti* for a commitment. This time, like an experienced chess player, *Mutti* carefully and ever so slowly introduced her Jewish heritage to *Vati*. She related her painful experience with Rudi and how it had almost driven her to suicide. *Vati* listened patiently without interrupting and then embraced her as he exclaimed, "I always wanted to marry a Jewish girl!"

Mutti was amazed and thrilled that the very thing that had been a liability with Rudi was an asset with *Vati*. Now she had a friend, someone who filled her loneliness with companionship, someone who loved her and cared for her. She later related that she felt as if heaven had suddenly been filled with angels playing the most beautiful music on violins. Life was wonderful, and *Mutti* often found herself humming an old German folk tune that included these words: "*To know one loyal heart is the highest of fortunes.*"

At this time in 1926, only three years after Hitler had made his first attempt to seize power but still seven years before he was elected Chancellor, his frequent anti-Semitic talks at Nazi gatherings had begun to make their first deposits in the minds of his German listeners. Jews, though still considered business partners, customers, and good neighbors by many, were slowly beginning to be viewed less as Germans and more as Jews. In other words, they were gradually being identified racially, with ancestral roots that were inferior to the rest of the Germans. At the time, practically no one thought that Hitler, with his few noisy followers, would ever gain any significant political momentum, but as Propaganda Minister Goebbels said years later, "If you say something often enough, and loud enough, people will eventually believe it." This new psychological weapon was used by the *Führer* over and over again to promote the four main pillars of the Nazi Party: Anti-Communism, the Versailles Treaty, *Lebensraum* (Room to Live), and Anti-Semitism. Let us examine these four pillars individually to get a better understanding of how Hitler came to power.

Anti-Communism

We will begin with a little German history. World War I was brought about by the policies of the German Emperor Kaiser Frederick Wilhelm II. When the Germans lost the war, the Kaiser abdicated his throne on November 9, 1918. Germany's first democracy, the Weimar Republic, was born soon after.

The Weimar Republic was unable to pull Germany out of the miserable social and financial consequences of WWI and was therefore strongly challenged by the Communist Party. Although well-to-do pre-war Germany rejected Communism, as poverty and hunger stalked the nation, now the Communists began to make significant inroads. Hitler was strongly anti-Communist and actually associated Communists with the Jews, marking both of them as part of an international conspiracy to destroy the German nation. So the first pillar of the Nazi party was Anti-Communism.

The Versailles Treaty

The Versailles Treaty was the peace treaty signed at the end of WWI. This treaty made unreasonable and punishing demands by the victorious French, British, and Americans against the already defeated and devastated German nation. It included the requirement to abolish compulsory military service and to make extensive financial reparation to the victor nations in the form of ships, trains, livestock, and various national resources such as coal and iron. Germany also had to give up 27,500 square miles of territory that it had held before the war, and surrender all its colonies.

Hitler used this treaty to resurrect Germany's animosity toward its former enemies. In addition, the Great Depression piled misery upon misery and nearly destroyed the entire middle class of the German Republic, further demoralizing the downtrodden nation and making its residents especially vulnerable to Hitler's propaganda. It was as if the loss of WWI and the demands of the Versailles Treaty knocked the Germans flat on the ground, and then the Great Depression came along and ground its heel right into the face of the defeated nation as it lay helplessly in the mud. Under these circumstances, a "messiah" was welcomed and easily found a loyal following.

It might well be, if the victorious allies had treated the German nation fairly and mercifully at the end of WWI, Hitler would not have found a platform for his Nazi Party and there might never have been a WWII. Rather, Germany would have become a friend of the Western world twenty-seven years earlier than it did, when the Americans learned the lesson of "love your enemies" at the end of WWII. At that point in history, instead of punishing Germany again,

America helped rebuild it through the Marshall Plan; since that time Germany has been one of the United States' staunchest allies.

The Apostle Paul said, *"Therefore if thine enemy hunger, feed him; if he thirst, give him drink: for in so doing thou shalt heap coals of fire on his head"* (Romans 12:20). As long as we meet hate with hate, we will have war; if we meet hate with love, we can beat our swords into plowshares. How much trouble could be avoided even today if the world's political leaders would read the Bible and follow its wise directions?

Lebensraum

Another pillar of the Nazi Party was *Lebensraum*. *Lebensraum*, meaning "room to live," was Hitler's agenda to incorporate all German-speaking territories into one nation, the Third Reich. This policy gave rise to the Nazis' annexation of Austria, the Sudetenland (a Germanic part of western Czechoslovakia), and the invasion of Poland, which ultimately triggered WWII.

Anti-Semitism

Now we will focus briefly on Hitler's view of the Jews. From 1924 to 1926, while Hitler was in prison for instigating an uprising, he wrote "the bible of National Socialism," *Mein Kampf*, meaning "My Fight." In it, he began to develop his racial doctrine that the Germans were superior and the Jews inferior. To Hitler, the Jew was sub-human and lacked "original intelligence." He believed the Jew had just enough intelligence to imitate and be used by the superior non-Jews, though the inferior Jew would try to rise above and control his betters through a united international confederacy of Jewry. Hitler and his scientists also tried to prove the sub-human status of the Jew and other ethnicities through anthropometry (the collection and study of precise measurements of the human body).

Hitler believed the Jews were conspirators during WWI. He blamed them for having robbed the German banks through international Jewry in the world's financial capitals. Hitler wrote about the danger of the Jew not only to the Germans but also to the whole world. He suggested that a day of reckoning would eventually come when this Jewish threat would have to be eliminated. What exactly Hitler meant by "elimination" at that time is not clear from his book, since *Mein Kampf* is not a book of plans and definite programs but of ideology. Seven years later, however, when he was elected Chancellor, he began to implement his plans to drive the Jews out of Germany through an economic boycott and other abuses. When that failed, he came up with the Final Solution, the systematic destruction of the Jews by mass murder and genocide.

Of course, the truth is that the Jews are God's chosen people, and they have given more to the world in the fields of music, art, industry, science, literature, religion, politics, and philosophy than any other people in the world. Obviously, had the Nazis been chosen by God, they would have lasted longer than a pitiful twelve years. However, the Jews have been with us since Abraham, and they will be with us forever.

Most Germans appreciated Hitler's nationalist views and simply dismissed his anti-Semitism as harmless, but his rantings worried the Jews. Thus, when Alfred exclaimed, "I always wanted to marry a Jew," *Mutti* was ecstatic. But when she finally broke the news of her engagement to her mother, Frieda was less than delighted. In fact, she violently objected and wanted *Mutti* to reconcile with well-to-do Rudi because *Vati* came from a poor family of seven brothers and several sisters. The effects of WWI and the Great Depression still had a strong hold on the German economy, and neither *Vati* nor *Mutti* had any money to be able to afford a life together. Frieda warned *Mutti* with an old German proverb, "If misery looks into the window, love goes out the door." Hans, *Mutti's* father, was also disappointed in my mother's choice, but once he got to know *Vati*, he enjoyed his company and looked forward to their visits.

After their engagement in 1927, it took my parents three years of hard work and saving to finally be able to rent an apartment so they could live together as husband and wife. Prior to the marriage, *Mutti* was a secretary and *Vati* was still developing his skills in accounting to earn higher pay. In those three years, they saw each other daily, but most of the time their dating was outdoors, even in the rain, since they could seldom afford more than a once-a-week cup of coffee in a restaurant.

Of course, it wasn't just *Vati* and *Mutti* who had it rough financially. Inflation was so bad at the time that the story was often told of a woman who, after leaving her home to go shopping, suddenly remembered she had left a million marks in a wicker basket in her unlocked house. In a panic, she hurried home to find the wicker basket gone but the million marks still there. In those days, when you stood in line outside the store, waiting to get in, a pound of sugar might have cost 2 million marks, but by the time you reached the counter, it could have risen to 4 million. Paper money was virtually worthless.

Although *Vati's* two younger brothers had served in apprenticeship programs, they joined the ranks of the 25 percent of German citizens who were unemployed. *Mutti* found a room near her future in-laws so she could walk over to their apartment to have dinner with them, and of course, she paid for the meals.

Mutti walked to work, which was a pleasant half-hour stroll through the botanical gardens, and *Vati* used his bicycle. On Sundays, the two often walked hours together through this city of one and a half million. During these walks, they began to see little groups of marching men, sporting swastikas as they moved down the beautiful boulevards. Yet nobody took them seriously, considering them to be only one of many small splinter groups of Germany's more than thirty political parties. It seemed everyone had a different idea of how to save the country.

In 1930, my parents, after having walked hundreds of miles together in three years, finally got married, but their happiness was quickly threatened. Only two years after their wedding, *Vati* was sent to a hospital with an unusually high fever. After several weeks of observation, during which he was reduced to nothing more than a skeleton, the doctor said my father had contracted a germ they could not identify, nor did they have any medicine that would help him. In fact, the physicians told *Vati* he would die. When *Mutti* heard these words, in one of her rare spiritual moments of the time she said to herself, "If God wants to bring him through, He can." She believed in God as the Master over life and death, and at this moment of crisis she found herself strangely confident. And then, three months later, against all human reasoning or medical understanding, *Vati* suddenly recovered and returned home in full strength.

The next year, *Mutti* became pregnant with her first child and quit her job. *Vati* had found a better apartment for his growing family, and life seemed positive and promising. But outside their happy home, strange things were taking place. The marching bands in the streets became larger and louder as, nervously and with mixed feelings, the Germans watched the rise of a new man.

The Weimar Republic had done everything possible to jump-start the economy and rebuild the nation, but after fifteen years of effort, almost nothing had changed. Perhaps two of the things that fledgling democracies need is money and unity. However, both of them were in short supply.

German soldiers returned from Russian prison camps but found no work to support their families. The German people were demoralized and humiliated; Communism continued to spread; and there began to be upheaval, unrest, and occasional outbursts of violence among various splinter groups. People were so disgusted with the government that they even rejected its flag.

This new man gave them back the old German Empire's colors in the banner of the Nazi Party. These old colors appealed to them, and the new man promised work for everyone. He promised new factories, the *Autobahn* (federal highways), and luxury ships that would take the workers to the Mediterranean for vacations. He also promised a car for everyone—the *Volkswagen*. He talked of unity, of dignity, of self-respect, and of honor and glory.

This new man, Adolph Hitler, was a visionary. He had a plan, and he had explanations for why Germany lost World War I. It was not that the Germans were weak, Hitler explained, nor that the soldiers did not fight valiantly. It was because forces behind their backs had destroyed their fighting power. Hitler's message resonated with the downtrodden people: Germans were good; Germans were strong; Germans were a superior race that needed only to be purged of destructive parasites within.

Slowly, ever so slowly, Hitler worked his way into the hearts of the people, one sector after another: the labor parties, the press, the churches, the youth movement, the educated elite, and the industrialists. Yet, in spite of Hitler's successes, when presidential elections were held in 1932, the incumbent 85-year-old President Paul Von Hindenburg received 53% and Hilter only 36% of the vote. But through deceit, manipulation, and bullying, Hitler left the 85-year-old Hindenburg no choice but to appoint him to the chancellorship in 1933. Hitler immediately outlawed all other parties. A year later, Hindenburg died.

~ Grandfather Hans belonged to a group of active soldiers at the end of WWI. On the lapel of their jackets, they had worn the colors of the old German Empire under Kaiser Wilhelm—red, white, and black. They stood for these colors and what they meant. Now Hitler took over this group of German military men, which had never followed any political line, and made them wear swastikas. Everybody complied, including Hans, for the law was the law, and none better understood law and order than the Germans. Since most men had families who lived on bare essentials at best, the prospect of bread on the table and a good job drew more of their attention than a strange crooked cross. Germans were tired of long lines at the employment offices and soup kitchens, and the swastika seemed a minor issue compared to this fight for survival.

Ordinary Germans did not consider themselves wise or educated or trained enough in political matters to question authorities. After all, the only democracy the country had ever experienced was during the fifteen years following World War I. And yet they had plenty of doubts about the new leader, and many hoped his radical rhetoric and strong new laws would soon fade away. While Hitler ran for office, most considered his extreme anti-Semitic attitude to be a personal grudge against the Jews, which Germans assumed would be tamed and controlled by the government. But while the vast majority of Germans were captivated by Hitler's promise for a better life, slowly and carefully he turned from spouting anti-Semitic rhetoric to introducing anti-Semitic legislation. Among this legislation were the Nuremberg Laws of 1935, which became the foundation of the entire anti-Semitic program of the Nazi apparatus. By those laws, all Germans were racially defined as either Aryans (pure Germans), Jews, or *Mischlinge* (Mongrels, meaning people of mixed race).

In 1936, my mother's sister, Aunt Hilde, came home early one day from her nurse's job at a state hospital. In compliance with the Nuremberg Laws, the hospital required every staff member to sign a paper saying they were of Aryan descent. Hilde refused because she was classified as a *Mischling*. Her supervisor encouraged her to sign anyway because they needed her, and even promised she would protect Hilde. But Hilde's mind could not be changed. She was proud of her Jewish heritage and therefore resigned her position, left the hospital, and went home. She then applied at a Jewish hospital in Hamburg where, with her high credentials, she was immediately accepted.

A few days later, under the Nazi flag, Hilde proudly marched through the streets with the *Bund Deutscher Mädchen*, the girls' equivalent of the Hitler Youth, with her hospital badge attached to her blouse, telling everyone in big letters that she was working for the Jews. At this time no one dared to attack her, but most around her felt uncomfortable. Others felt ashamed, yet few knew how to respond, for many had Jewish neighbors, friends, doctors, lawyers, and teachers who were dear to them. A wedge had been driven between Germans and their Jewish friends for no good reason, and Hilde's stand was a reminder of that tragic fact.

Many Germans and Jews alike began to be concerned over where this division would lead, but none dared to discuss it openly for fear of being arrested. Immediately after Hitler assumed power, tens of thousands of political dissenters were put into makeshift concentration camps before Dachau, Oranienburg, Esterwegen, or Sachsenhausen were built. By the end of the war, millions of Germans—all who, by conduct, association, or speech, were found not to be in harmony with the values, aims, and aspirations of the Third Reich—were put into concentration camps, along with thousands of Gypsies, those considered "mentally unfit," Jehovah's Witnesses, and

Christians. A total of six million non-Jews were killed in this manner. In simple language, from the beginning of the Nazi period, the State—and not the individual—was supreme, and from birth every German existed only for the State and the dictates of the *Führer*. Anyone who disagreed even slightly was "removed."

By 1934, some 23,000 Jews had left the country, but 10,000 of them returned in early 1935, when conditions improved temporarily. But by 1936, arbitrary terror and discrimination had once again escalated to a frighteningly high level, though it was mild compared to what lay ahead. Many Jews who had returned to Germany in 1935 quickly regretted their decision, when Jewish book-burnings, the boycotting of Jewish businesses, the dismissal of Jewish doctors and nurses from hospitals and Jewish lawyers from their practices, the restriction of no more than five percent of Jews admitted into German schools and universities, and the dismissal of Jews from all civil service jobs became a reality by 1936. Jews could no longer raise the German flag, intermarry with Aryans, or have Aryan maids. As conditions worsened, Hilde seized the opportunity to emigrate to England, where she immediately found employment in a hospital.

Hitler's first plan to cleanse Germany of the Jewish problem was through an economic boycott, designed to drive them out of business and deprive them of employment. When this failed, he began to employ increasingly harsher measures against them. Another plan was to resettle them in Madagascar, an island off the coast of South Africa, but when the British took the island, that plan was no longer possible. It was not until early 1941 that the *Endlösung*, the Final Solution to the Jewish problem, was conceived: the gassing of millions of Jews in concentration camps specifically constructed for that purpose.

The original plan to eliminate Jews through an economic

boycott did not work because most Jews were too German to leave their beloved Fatherland where their roots went back hundreds of years. Most could not and would not believe that their own government would continue its anti-Semitic actions. They hoped Hitler's hatred and rage against them would be temporary and his regime would soon pass. Some believed it was just a bad dream, while others, despite seeing tragedy befall their Jewish friends, clung to the hope that it would never happen to them. Why should a chief surgeon of a pediatric ward of a hospital, who had worked there for twenty or thirty years and had treated German soldiers in WWI, think he was no longer wanted? Tragically, those who refused to believe that Hitler's Final Solution applied to them and therefore did not leave the country in time paid for their foolish decisions with their lives, many ending up in the concentration camps' gas chambers.

There was now only one voice and one opinion in all of Germany, and it was that of Adolf Hitler, who took full control of the mass media. There was no longer a free press. There was no liberty for anyone to express themselves in any way. *Mutti* once told us, "It was even dangerous to think in one's own way. One might talk while sleeping...."

So Hans wore a swastika, and *Vati* and his brother Heini joined the *Sturm Abteiling*, the S.A., which was the paramilitary arm of the Nazi party. In retrospect, a Jew wearing a swastika seems rather ghastly. But at the time, it seemed the only choice Hans and the others could make.

It must be noted here that during the whole period of the Holocaust, the vast majority of Germans had no idea what was happening to the Jews when they were taken away. Until 1940, the Nazis had no plan to kill the Jews, and with rare exceptions, the gassing and killing of the Jews was not known to most Germans until the war was over in 1945. It was only natural for German Jews to be Germans first, to believe the best of their government, to believe that inequities would soon be resolved, and that reason and good will would prevail. It seemed obvious that once Hitler listened to the various Jewish agencies, as well as to the voice of international law and of interceding foreign governments, he would reverse his oppressive policies. After all, if there are any people in the world with a record of faith and hope in the direst circumstances, it is the Jews. Since the time of Abraham, the first Jew, Jews have always endured to see another good day. They had no reason to believe it would be otherwise now.

Mankind has been trying to get rid of the Jews for thousands of years, but has never succeeded. No one can truly begin to understand the Jewish people without reading their history in both the Old and New Testaments of the Bible. For governments to dictate their policies to the Jews without having read their history is the utmost folly. God said to Israel through his prophet Isaiah 700 years before the coming of Jesus Christ,

> *For a small moment have I forsaken thee; but with great mercies will I gather thee. In a little wrath I hid my face from thee for a moment; but with everlasting kindness will I have mercy on thee, saith the LORD thy Redeemer. For this is as the waters of Noah unto me: for as I have sworn that the waters of Noah should no more go over the earth; so have I sworn that I would not be wroth with thee, nor rebuke thee. For the mountains shall depart, and the hills be removed; but my kindness shall not depart from thee, neither shall the covenant of my peace be removed, saith the LORD that hath mercy on thee* (Isaiah 54:7–10).

It is this messianic promise and hope that causes the Jews to leave an empty chair at their table each Passover meal, expecting Elijah to come at any time to prepare for and usher in the age of the Messiah. It was this messianic expectation that enabled many Jews to sing the "Ani Ma-amin (I Believe)" as they were driven into the gas chambers:

"Ani Ma-amin (I Believe)"

Yes, I do believe,
Yes, I do believe,
Yes, I do believe,
Yes, I do believe,

With a perfect faith -- believe
With a perfect faith I believe
In the coming of Messiah,
Oh, in Messiah's coming,
Yes, I do believe.

Although he linger,
Yet I do believe.
Though he linger,
I do believe.[1]

The Jews will never go away, for God will not let it happen. When you visit Israel, many a guide will ask, "What is the greatest proof for the existence of God?" If no one in the tour group knows the correct answer, the guide will answer himself. "It's the Jew. The continued existence of the Jew is the strongest proof of the existence of God."

Historically, the Jew is an eternal optimist. The Scriptures tell them to be so, despite the dire consequences they may endure from time to time for their disobedience. So then, in the midst of all the turmoil in the early days of the Nazi takeover of Germany, the majority of Jews believed that somehow, someday, things would turn around for them. It had been deeply ingrained in all Germans, including the German Jews, to be loyal. Germans were therefore willing to be somewhat forgiving of the evils of their government. After fifteen years' experience with democracy that brought them nothing but misery, they were willing to give any strong leadership the benefit of the doubt. And, of course, their fear of appearing disloyal or un-German in this threatening environment forced the German Jews to do their best to cooperate with the new system in order to protect themselves and their families.

It was in this environment that my mother gave birth to me, on what was probably a rainy day in the month of May in Hamburg, Germany—one more mixed-race "mongrel" child beginning life amidst the dangers and chaos of a country dominated by a government sworn to soon eradicate every vestige of Jewish blood from the land.

CHAPTER FOUR

The Birth of a Mongrel

I was born on May 10, 1936, which was both a Sunday and Mother's Day. I was the third child, following a brother and a sister. A few years before my birth a law was passed that allowed every German family to get ten marks monthly for any newborn. With the expansion of Germany on his mind, Hitler encouraged childbirth, and mothers who had five or more children were even decorated with medals by the Nazi Party.

My mother was delighted with this law, and when I was born she quickly applied to receive the much-needed extra income. She already received the check for Eckart and Renate, my older siblings, and obviously expected one for me. But several weeks after she filed the application, *Mutti* received a postcard telling her to appear at the government office. When she arrived, she was told that because her father was a Jew, she did not qualify to receive the extra income. This was one of our family's first personal encounters with Nazi anti-Semitism, the first dark cloud that began to settle upon our precious young family. Now the word "Mongrel" *(Mischling)* appeared on my birth card. The official identification of *Mutti's* family with the Jews was, in itself, not a problem, for *Mutti* was proud to be of Jewish heritage. But the implication of the designation in this anti-Semitic environment was deeply disturbing. Since I had one Jewish

grandparent, I was classified as a "Second-Degree Mongrel."
My mother, having a Jewish parent, was a "First-Degree
Mongrel." An ominous air of uncertainty began to permeate
our home and our hearts.

When *Mutti* first received this bad news at the government
office, she burst into tears, but after a few moments she
gathered herself together and went home, where she promptly
opened her Bible, turned to Psalm 91, and read verses 11 and
12: *"For he shall give his angels charge over thee, to keep thee
in all thy ways. They shall bear thee up in their hands, lest
thou dash thy foot against a stone."* Next to these verses she
wrote, "Reimar 9.8.36" (my name and that day's date, August
9, 1936). Looking back upon the horrible years of suffering
and the wonderful deliverances our family experienced since
that day, I often think of those prophetic words, *"...he shall
give his angels charge over thee, to keep thee in all thy ways."*
The Lord has certainly been true to His Word.

From then on, my siblings and I were treated differently
than our Aryan friends, being denied government child
support and being without legal rights. When the Hitler
government came up with the Nuremberg laws to classify
the Jews and Mongrels as *Untermenschen*, or "sub-human,"
we were indeed relegated to the world of sub-humans.

Conversely, Aryans—pure Germans—were rated as
Übermenschen, or super-humans. They were considered the
elect, a superior race, and it was the mixture, or the corruption,
of the super race by Jewish blood that Hitler blamed as the
primary cause of all of Germany's troubles, from the loss of
World War I to the collapse of the economy that followed.
Hence, the elimination of all Jews from German-controlled
territory became Hitler's priority from which he never
departed, right up until he committed suicide in his Berlin
bunker in 1945.

In addition, in 1936 all Nazi paramilitary, or *Sturm*

Abteilung (S.A.), men were required to be party members. My Aryan father was in the S.A., and my mother clearly remembered when he came home from one of the meetings and informed her that he had been asked to resign because he refused to divorce his Jewish family. *Vati* was the only man on the block who was never again seen in uniform, which put a stigma upon him of not being "one of us" anymore. This was the second blow to my parents, increasing their fear of what lay ahead. We were now clearly conscious of our second-class status and aware that justice from the government was no longer on our side.

By this time, membership in the Nazi apparatus was very helpful in gaining and keeping employment, as well as getting advancement in the workplace. The 25 percent unemployment figure drove many to join the party. Because *Vati* was no longer in the S.A., he was fired from his job the next day. Fortunately, a Catholic lady hired him shortly afterward, which enabled him to continue to support his family.

It was becoming increasingly difficult for Jews to have any sort of occupation. Jewish department stores were confiscated, and the name "Isaac" or "Sarah" had to be added to the business name of all Jewish businesses. This prevented anyone from being able to say, "I did not know that was a Jewish shop, so I purchased my goods there." The anti-Semitic propaganda machine, run by Hitler's right-hand man, Joseph Goebbels, made it clear that Jews were traitors, deceivers, liars, unpatriotic, and dirty. Anyone who associated with them was frowned on for "siding with the enemy."

The music of the famous Jewish composer Felix Mendelssohn was soon banned, and in 1938, Jewish businesses were attacked and synagogues burned, and Jews began to disappear from neighborhoods. You would walk down the street and suddenly notice that your Jewish neighbors were no longer there. The children weren't outside playing in the yard, the mother wasn't walking down the sidewalk carrying her shopping bags, and their car was no longer parked along the curb. No one in the neighborhood seemed to know what had happened. All anyone knew was what filtered through the grapevine, which was that the Jews were being transported to the east where they would be settled together to help with the war effort. After the war, of course, the Germans learned the truth: the Jews had been moved to concentration camps, some of them dying on the way but most of them perishing after they arrived. The closed trucks that came to pick up the Jews by night often had their exhausts redirected into the back of the truck where the passengers were then gassed to death in transit, long before they reached the camps.

In 1938 Hans, my Jewish grandfather, got terribly sick, after which his whole life changed. None of us knew exactly what happened, though we understood that he had received some sort of information that suddenly caused him to break all connections with his friends and acquaintances. His dinner table, formerly filled with guests each Sunday, was now empty. Instead, Sunday after Sunday, Hans and Frieda left their home and came to eat with *Mutti* and *Vati*.

Soon a plan was devised to save Hans from the Nazis. Miraculously, he was able to obtain a visiting visa for a short business trip to England. He had to purchase a round-trip ticket and carry only light luggage. To avoid suspicion, only *Vati* went with him to see him board the ship, although the whole family wanted to go along to bid him farewell. Of course, Hans never came back. He stayed in England as his daughter, my aunt Hilde, had done, and sent a note back to his wife stating that he had fallen sick.

Vati and *Mutti* and we four children moved from our home to Frieda's because it was a larger apartment and it would save everyone money. Frieda especially needed all the help she could get now that she was without her breadwinner. Hilde, who worked as a midwife in London, sent what little money she could from her meager monthly income.

One day a gentleman came to the door asking for Frieda. He said the government knew she received money from England, and they wanted an explanation. Frieda broke down and, nearly hysterical, called for *Mutti* to come and give a reason for the transfer of money. *Mutti* was able to explain the circumstances without revealing that her father was a Jew. A few days later, however, *Mutti* was summoned to the Administrative Office where, in the presence of his secretary, a high official began to question *Mutti* severely. It was a frightening experience for my mother, and in the end she was forbidden to receive any further money from England. This grumbling, angry official warned her of severe consequences to the whole family if they received any more payments.

When *Mutti* finally left the office, the same official met her at the main entrance, only this time without his secretary. Mother thought surely she was about to be arrested, but to her surprise, the officer offered her a friendly smile and explained that he also had a wife and children and that he had to act the way he did in the presence of his secretary. He then told *Mutti* not to despair, that things would improve, that one of Hitler's generals was also of Jewish descent, and that things could not continue as they were.

To celebrate the good news that there were dissenters in Hitler's government, *Vati* and *Mutti* went to the *Schauspielhaus* (theater) that night. It was the first time they had gone out together in their nine years of marriage. The play was Franz Grillparzer's <u>Medea</u>, a Greek myth with racial implications that showed the triumph of love and justice over prejudice. When the play was over, the audience applauded with exceptional, deeply felt enthusiasm. It was obvious, from this and other instances, that the German people innately knew things were not right with this government. Most Germans dragged their feet at the repressive Nazi measures, even most of those within the Party apparatus. Hitler noticed the reluctance of the *Volk* (people) in following these measures. Consequently, he would pass an anti-Semitic law or promote a brutal action and then wait to see how the people responded. If the response was negative, he would wait a while before passing the next anti-Semitic law or promoting the next action against the Jews, thus giving the people time to absorb and accept the most recent change before being confronted with another. These periodic respites from oppressive measures caused a number of Jews who had left Germany to return, thinking perhaps the situation was improving, only to discover otherwise and later be arrested and killed in the gas chambers.

-- Although more and more measures were gradually initiated, the German people were left in the dark as to the final purpose and outcome of Hitler's actions. There was no publicized anti-Semitic plan stating that if the Jews could not be driven out of the country by economic boycotts, expropriation, repressive laws, or brutality, they would eventually be killed in concentration camps. Therefore, the timing of anti-Semitic policies was closely watched and manipulated by Goebbels. Even when anti-Semitic attitudes began to be ingrained in society, most of the German people were not willing to act against the Jews by illegal means, nor were those who supported the Jews willing to act illegally against the government. This was a country of law and order, and the due process of law was first used by many groups: the press, the church, the unions, and even the Jews themselves, in an effort to maintain or regain their freedom. In no way did anyone suspect what was in the back of the minds of Hitler and his loyalists. When Germans voted for Hitler, they did not vote for the extremist positions of the Nazi Party but rather for its plan for economic revival.

A few months after Hans had safely joined his daughter in England, Frieda was also able to escape and rejoin her husband. The primary agency to help get Hans and Frieda out of Germany was a wonderful, Jew-loving church in Hamburg. This church also ran a hospital and had the most hazardous name any church could possibly have in Nazi Germany: the *Jerusalem Gemeinde* (Jerusalem Church). Since its inception in 1850, this church had successfully aided thousands of persecuted Jews leave the European continent to emigrate to Great Britain, the United States, and South America. It was this very church, with its sweet, white-hooded assembly of deaconesses, that eventually helped our own family to emigrate to the United States. Now, decades later, Hitler is gone, as is his Third Reich, but the Jerusalem Church, though destroyed by bombs, stands rebuilt today as a beacon of a great truth uttered by Jesus: *"...upon this rock* [the confession that Jesus is the Christ] *I will build my church; and the gates of hell shall not prevail against it"* (Matthew 16:18).

According to the Nazi stance of the day, I was born a Second-Degree Mongrel, but I have never been offended by that. In fact, I wear that name as a badge of honor, for as with Nathaniel of the Bible, I also am a true Son of Abraham— well, almost. In that capacity, I would like to make some observations about anti-Semitism and God's chosen people.

If you think Hitler's attitude was an isolated dark spot in history, you might also believe such a thing could never happen again. However, in the context of history, anti-Semitism existed long before the days of Jesus, and it will continue to exist until the end of time as we know it. Indeed it is now as powerful as ever in the Middle East, as well as in parts of Russia, Europe, and elsewhere. Though anti-Semitism may not be actively expressed in every place, it does quite frequently show up in very subtle forms.

Anti-Semitism did not begin with the election of Hitler to the Chancellorship in 1933. Its roots actually go back as far as the Jewish Exodus from Egypt in 1500 B.C. and the rule of the Persian King Ahasuerus in 500 B.C.; it also appeared in ancient Greece. The Greeks considered their polytheistic religion superior to the monotheism of the Jews with all its strange dietary laws and sexual restrictions. The Roman emperor Claudius I considered the Jews a plague throughout the world. The early Christian Church, once it moved from being persecuted to receiving favor from the government, also turned against the Jews in the fourth century. The Jewish people have indeed been the most universally hated and persecuted ethnic group in all of history.

At the ecumenical council of Nicea in 325 A.D., the professing church for the first time formulated an anti-Semitic policy. There it was stated that the Jews must continue to live "in seclusion and humiliation" for "the sake of Christianity." Both of the great Roman Catholic scholars, Augustine and Thomas Aquinas, believed that Jews were to be confined in locked ghettos and rendered servile, being permitted only such rights as were considered necessary to human life.

The misinterpretation of the Holy Scriptures contributed to anti-Semitic legislation, expulsions, pogroms, and massacres of hundreds and thousands of Jews in every century from the beginning of the Christian era. The message of the professing church, although not of the true Church that Jesus founded, has been throughout all of time: Jews, go away!

Here are just a few dates when anti-Semitism reached it heights: in 1290 Jews were expelled from England, in the

1350s from Germany, in 1394 from France, in 1492 from Spain, in 1496 from Portugal, and from the Papal States in 1569. Even Martin Luther, the founder of Protestantism, although at first favorably inclined toward Jews, later condemned them to ill treatment and expulsion from the country. John Calvin, the sixteenth century Church reformer, stands out as one of the few influential churchmen who were gracious toward God's covenant people.

Considering these facts, it is obvious that Adolf Hitler found little opposition from the Vatican or from the state-run church of Germany against his anti-Semitic agenda. It is likely that, had the churches taken a pro-Jewish stance, the Holocaust would never have happened. Germany, where practically everyone is baptized into either the Roman Catholic or the Protestant faith, would have followed an official position of loving the Jews, had the churches promoted it. Indeed, the theological positions of many churches of Christendom, even to this day, are either subtly or openly anti-Semitic, with some espousing a "replacement theology" that claims God is done with Israel and Christians have become the "new Israel," replacing the Jews as the covenant people of God.

Here is the truth: Jesus was a Jew, all His apostles were Jews, and the first people to receive Jesus Christ as the Messiah were Jews. God, through Abraham, made an everlasting covenant with the Jews, a teaching that is reiterated by the architect of Christian theology, the Apostle Paul. In fact, almost all the teachings of Christianity were given to us by the Jews. In short, Judaism is the root system of Christianity. Jesus said, *"salvation is of the Jews"* (John 4:22). Yet, this does not leave us gentiles out of the equation. When we obey God we also become His chosen people (1 Peter 2:9).

The Church is in great need of repentance toward the

Jews, who indeed provided the foundation of the Christian faith and gave us the Book of all books, the Bible. It must be remembered that God, in His first words to the first Jew, Abraham, put a curse on anti-Semitism when He said to him, *"and curse him that curseth thee"* (Genesis 12:3).

The trail of Jewish tears runs deep and wide throughout history. These trails of suffering inspired the Jewish journalist Theodore Herzl to publish a pamphlet in 1896, advocating the establishment of a Jewish state, which is now a reality in Israel. But the tears of Jews continue to water the Holy Land as they are murdered in buses, restaurants, discos, homes, and hotels—blown up by Palestinian terrorists in the Jews' own country.

Even here in the "land of the free," the hatred for Jews lurks just below the surface in many a heart. I could hardly believe my ears when, after coming to the United States, I was sitting in a cafeteria at the University of Wisconsin campus when a student said to me, "Hitler made only one mistake."

"Vat ist dat [What is that]?" I asked in a strong German accent.

"He did not kill all the Jews."

On another occasion, while I was hiking in the Rockies, a Jewish staff physician from a Florida hospital confided to me, "I have served faithfully in this hospital for over twenty years, but I have never been promoted to a senior position because I am not one of them. I'm a Jew." So it is clear that anti-Semitism was not born in Nazi Germany, nor did it end there. It merely escalated to unprecedented levels, culminating in the mass executions and gassings of six million Jews in German-occupied territory.

Until 1938, the Jews had faith in the international community. The repressive anti-Semitic laws and actions of the Third Reich were publicly known by the whole world. An international conference was held at Evian, France, in 1938, during which the leaders of thirty-three nations, including England, France, and the United States, represented by President Franklin D. Roosevelt, met to address the "Jewish problem." Allowing the Jews to emigrate to other countries was proposed as a solution, but each nation believed the Jews should go somewhere other than their own country. Hope for the Jews to receive help from the international community soon died, for it was not only Germany that seemed to have no room for the Jews, but the whole international family of nations. There is no doubt in my mind that the conference at Evian gave Hitler the "green light" to proceed toward genocide of the Jewish people. He saw that no nation of significant influence cared enough about the Jews to stop him, and the infamous *Kristallnacht* (Crystal Night) massacre occurred only four months later.

And so it was in 1938 that Hans and all his Jewish relatives in Berlin saw the inevitable "handwriting on the wall." Hans escaped to England, while his relatives fled to South America. In that same year, Germany annexed Austria and immediately imposed the full range of anti-Semitic laws on the Austrians that Germany had already implemented. The Austrians raised almost no protest at all, as their 200,000 Jewish citizens were abruptly plunged into repression.

In summary, it can be said that the pre-war anti-Semitic measures peaked at three specific points:

1. The economic boycott of April 1933 with its legislation restricting Jewish businesses, professions, and civil servants;

2. The Nuremberg Laws in 1935; and

3. The failure of Evian in 1938.

The aftermath of Evian resulted in a rapid and relentless program to humiliate, ridicule, punish, imprison, and ostracize the Jews.

Yet, in the midst of all this darkness there was the tiny nation of Denmark, which stood out heroically in the saving of the Jews. In 1943, the Danish people learned that all of their 7,500 Jews were to be deported to concentration camps. Quickly the Danish people did their own roundup and helped all their Jews escape to neutral Sweden.

By 1938, 150,000 or about one-fourth of German Jews had already left the country. After that it was nearly impossible for Jews to get out of Germany, and anyone who made even the slightest legal protest on the Jews' behalf risked being sent to prison or the concentration camps. The majority of the Jews who remained in Germany at that time eventually perished by the time the war ended.

CHAPTER FIVE

East Germany

By 1942 the Reich government was pursuing a full, relentless war effort on three fronts: with the Allies in the west and south, the Soviets to the east, and the war against the Jews in all of German-occupied territory. Massacres in territories seized from the Soviets continued through mass executions of Jews by the *Einsatzgruppen*, or occupation groups, which were special troops that followed the advancing army. They rounded up Jews, stood them in front of large open pits and ditches, and mowed them down with machine guns. The concentration camps were also working Jewish slave labor to death as they manufactured war materiel and other goods.

And then, in the early part of 1942, the Final Solution was implemented. Thus began the mass transportation of Jews from Belgium, France, Holland, and Germany to the gas chambers at Auschwitz, Maidanek, Treblinka, Sobibor, Belzec, and Chelmno, all of which were in occupied Poland. In 1943 Germany was the first country to be declared *Judenfrei*, meaning "free of/purified of the Jews," but other countries soon followed.

The number of Jews killed during WWII came to a total of six million: three million were gassed in concentration camps; one and a half million died at the hands of the *Einsatzgruppen* and in other massacres; another one and a half million died due to horrible living conditions, such as the half-million who perished in the Polish ghettos. Of the half-million Jews in Germany proper, half fled the country, while the other 250,000 were exterminated. As mentioned earlier, another six million non-Jews were also eliminated: confessing Christians, political dissenters, Gypsies, mentally handicapped, and others. That makes a total of twelve million people murdered by the Nazis.

Again, while all this was going on, the German citizens were kept in ignorance. Eventually, the completely subservient media told the public that Jews were being "resettled" in occupied Poland, which was partly true, in that all the death camps were in Poland, and that the Jews were "resettled" in slave labor camps, gas chambers, and mass graves.

Vati, no longer in the *Sturm Abteilung*, was called in several times by the draft board. Each time, miraculously, he was able to convince the officials that he worked in a defense-related industry. By that time, due to high casualty rates, even seventeen-year-old boys were being drafted to operate the air defense artillery, known as Flak, so the pressures on *Vati* to be drafted intensified. Likewise, *Vati* was increasingly pressured to desert or divorce his "Jewish" family.

Finally, in late 1942, the day before *Vati* planned to leave Hamburg to follow up on a job offer in the province of Pomerania, another draft notice arrived. *Vati* knew he was running out of time and options, so he made the decision to move the whole family east as quickly as possible. He knew the *Gestapo*, the secret police machine, did not run as efficiently in the east as in the west, and so a move meant buying more time, more safety and togetherness, and longer life for the Schultze family.

We packed and moved east during the night to Lauenburg in Pomerania, which is now Poland. It was a large town of perhaps 50,000 people, with wide, tree-lined streets. The homes were either stucco houses with red tile roofs or condominium-style duplexes, all with overflowing flower boxes adorning the balconies. There were no high-rise apartments as in Hamburg, so we soon found ourselves living in a condominium. Our ample front yard was surrounded by a beautiful stone wall decorated with cross-shaped openings. We children used to peek through those openings and watch the German guards as they kept a close eye on the captured Russian soldiers working in the potato fields.

This was quite a change for us, but again, had we not left Hamburg when we did, it is certain that all of us would have been killed in one of the bombing raids, because our entire block was leveled just a few months after we left. For the Schultzes, what man intended for evil, God used for good, and our family was spared.

It was about this time, when I was seven years old, that I first remember hearing Hitler speak on a radio broadcast. His speech made quite an impression on me, even at such a young age, because I recognized there was something unusual, sinister, and even devilish about the way he spoke and the things he said. Hitler normally began his speeches in a low voice, speaking rather slowly, and then ended up almost screaming in a high-pitched tone. The thing I remember most about his speeches was his talk about a "Thousand-Year Reich." When I heard this, I was deeply disturbed and asked myself, *Why only 1,000 years? If it is a good Reich, why not forever?* I was troubled and wondered what corruption there might be in Hitler's Reich to cause it to fall after a successful 1,000 years. How could Hitler know it would last 1,000 years, rather than 500 or 1,500 years? What I didn't understand at the time was that something within me was looking for an everlasting kingdom, a kingdom I later came to know as the Kingdom of God. I was turned off by Hitler, but I wasn't sure why at the time. Now, in retrospect, I know that everyone is born with an innate knowledge of good and evil, and that knowledge enabled me to see the evil of Hitler's life and purposes.

Soon after we moved into our new home, we observed thousands of German soldiers and their military equipment moving through our city toward the Soviet Union. We boys enjoyed listening to the singing of the marching troops, and later found plenty of spent machine gun shells in the nearby forest, left behind from military drills. But our experience with the bombings in Hamburg made us question our country's invincibility and whether Germany could win the war or those marching soldiers would ever return.

Hitler had started his campaign into Russia with practically no preparation, so when he did attack the Russians they were caught unaware, having been lulled by the *Ribbentrop* treaty in which Germany promised not to attack Russia. Hitler assumed the Russians would be defeated quickly and easily, like most of the rest of Europe, particularly since he considered the Slavic people *Untermenschen* (sub-humans).

So, on June 22, 1941, German troops poured into Russia, and the Russians had no choice but to retreat, trading space for time. They let the Germans spread themselves thinly from Leningrad in the north to Stalingrad in the south, and then the Russians barricaded themselves into these and other fortified cities, built up their armies, and waited for the deadly Russian winter to fight for them. Russia had been through this twice before: with Napoleon in 1812, and with the German Kaiser Wilhelm in 1917.

The Battle of Stalingrad (Volgograd) resulted in a disastrous loss of 300,000 German troops and 1,700,000 Soviet troops. The Battle of Leningrad (Saint Petersburg), with its 900-day siege, produced nothing but lost time and supplies for the Germans, and the ultimate death of 1,017,881 Soviet troops and 125,000 German troops. *Vati's* brother Rudi miraculously lost only his thumb at Leningrad and was sent home to Hamburg as a survivor. (The overall casualties for World War II for the German military were 3.25 million, and the civilian casualties were 3.8 million. For the Soviet Union, the casualties were 13.6 million troops and 7.7 million civilians, while the United States suffered 295,000 military casualties and a minute number of civilian casualties. If you transfer these figures from statistics into fathers, orphans, and widows, you end up with a broken heart that only God can repair.)

As time went on, the huge high school across the street from our home was turned into an army hospital. Once, when I was eight, I walked through the hallways of this hospital, only to find room after room crowded with the wounded and the halls almost impassable due to stretchers lining both sides. Large red crosses were painted in white circles on either side of the hospital roof to let the approaching Soviet aircraft know that it was a hospital. Of course, an enemy would never bomb a hospital since it would need such facilities after its conquest for its own wounded. At times, while playing in our sandbox, I would look up to see the beautiful glitter of airplanes against the sun, bombers headed west to Berlin with death in their bellies. A few days before the Soviets took our town, medical personnel dumped arms, legs, and other body parts into an area just outside the hospital, then enclosed the area with a picket fence.

By 1943 everyone was experiencing the hardships of war. Food became scarce. Breakfast was limited to oatmeal and dark bread, but we were thankful for it and became so used to it that we still enjoy it to this very day. Supply trains, powered by mighty steam locomotives, came back from Russia with heavy coats of ice, so women began to knit socks for the soldiers, and the government ordered furs and woolens for them. But it was much too late to help the freezing soldiers on the front lines. Everything possible was done in Germany to keep the war machine going in spite of the loss of most the country's factories to allied bombings.

Surrender never entered Hitler's mind, and those who dared to suggest it were severely punished. Once, while dining in a small restaurant, *Vati* overheard someone suggest that perhaps the war could be lost. Immediately a plain-clothes secret service agent came to the table and arrested the man. It is likely that his family never saw him again.

As the war continued, the German people were told only what the Nazis wanted them to know about the battles, the victories and defeats, and the Jews. The Allies knew by now about the ghettos and concentration camps because they had taken aerial photographs and had seen the smoking chimneys in the death camps. In addition, every now and then, someone would miraculously escape one of these camps and tell the story to foreign officials. And yet the stories of the atrocities were not published on the front pages of the newspapers in the free world since they were considered too horrible and unbelievable for the general public to see. The prevailing attitude among the Allies was this: let us first defeat Germany, and then we will see what we can do to help the Jews. Nevertheless, little by little, my parents began to discover that their government had been lying about its treatment of the Jewish people.

For example, one night, in the summer of 1943, *Vati* was restless, tossing and turning and unable to sleep. *Mutti* thought he might be sick, but when she questioned him, he finally told her what was bothering him. That afternoon he had seen a group of *Schutzstaffeln* (SS) men leading a large company of prisoners—almost all with the identifying yellow star of the Jews—into the big open space in front of *Vati's* office. These highly trained troops were Hitler's right-hand men, used in intelligence work, for political surveillance, in human blood stock control, as shock troops, as overseers of concentration and work camps, and as Hitler's terrorists. Once they had the prisoners in the open space, the soldiers began chasing the prisoners around the field. When an old man fell down, a soldier beat him. All the employees watched from the windows, and one young lady even took a picture of the activity. An SS man spotted her and came in and took her camera away. He then screamed at her and asked if she wanted to join the assembly outside. Later, after the soldiers and prisoners were gone, the men and women who had witnessed the barbaric actions and were ashamed of it opened up to each other about the horrifying atrocity. It was then that *Vati* first learned that Jews were not sent to the east for resettlement but were instead being imprisoned, though he did not yet discover that they were actually being sent to concentration camps and killed.

A few weeks later, on a lovely August evening, a neighbor lady brought my sister Renate home. The lady was noticeably upset, and *Mutti* invited her inside. This neighbor began to pour out her concerns, explaining that while she was visiting relatives in a nearby town and waiting to cross a railroad track, they had to wait while three heavily loaded trucks passed by. An elegant skirt, covered with blood, fell off the back of one of the trucks, and our neighbor had cried out, "What is that?" An SS man laughingly tossed it back on the truck with a pitchfork, saying, "Oh, these are only Jewish rags." Shocked, the lady noticed all the trucks were full of the bloody garments of men, women, and children. "This cannot have a good ending," the lady said. "God will punish us for that."

Later that fall *Mutti* allowed Eckart to visit a friend in another part of town. A half hour after he left, a neighbor lady came to the door and accused Eckart of having just broken her basement window. She insisted our family would have to pay for it. *Mutti* kept her composure and said her son was not home and therefore could not be the culprit. This was an obvious and deliberate false accusation, and *Mutti* was suspicious and deeply troubled that it might have anti-Semitic motivations. Was this a trap? How many people knew she was of Jewish descent? By now, if any ill-willed person brought a charge against a Mongrel to the Gestapo, it was possible the Mongrel would be sent to the concentration camp. Eckart was now of Hitler Youth age, but because of his Jewish background he was not allowed to join any activity where the "action" was. He was the only boy of that age group in the neighborhood who, like his *Vati*, was not "one of them," so he was viewed with disdain and suspicion. As outsiders and misfits, we were always concerned for our safety.

When *Vati* came home that evening, *Mutti* told him of the accusation, and immediately his long legs bounded up four flights of stairs to the neighbor's apartment. *Mutti* listened with a violently beating heart as *Vati's* voice escalated to a pitch she had never heard before. Because of the distance to the fourth floor and the high echo, she could not distinguish his exact words, but when he came back down, he said, "You don't have to be afraid to talk to people because your father is a Jew. Even if you are really wrong, I will always stand beside you. In my eyes, you are always right. You are my wife, and I will protect you, come what may."

In light of *Vati's* loyalty and willingness to defend his Jewish wife, is there any doubt that *Mutti* married the right man? What if she had married Rudi, that son of the wealthy industrialist? Would he have stood with her, or would he have given in to Nazi pressure and divorced her, leaving her defenseless? In *Mutti's* case, a strong defense from an Aryan husband was the greatest blessing imaginable.

Mutti's concerns came to a head when *Vati's* sister Maria died. Right away *Mutti* planned to go to the funeral in Berlin. However, traveling to another city was much more difficult during the war than it had been before. Hitler was suspicious of everyone, and constantly had trains, buses, streetcars, and highways checked. As a result, *Mutti* had to get special government permission for her trip. Of course, she was frightened, but she knew she had a husband who stood with her, and that made a difference. *Vati* got the necessary forms to apply for the permit, which was given only in emergency situations. He filled out all the details, but she had to sign the forms. Since her experience in Hamburg, she had retained a horror of entering any administrative office, but she understood that she had to personally hand in the application, which she did.

The next day she was called to the government office where she expected to receive permission for her trip, which she needed right away because it was a full day's travel by train. But once the door of the office was closed and she was introduced to the highest official in town, he screamed at her that she had given the wrong information.

"Are you a Jew?" he demanded.

Because of *Mutti's* Jewish heritage and also in the interest of their children, she and *Vati* had closely followed all the developments of the Nuremberg laws in order to keep track of *Mutti's* legal status. They both loved their children more than anything else and did not want them to be hurt. According to the laws of 1935, *Mutti* was not to be considered a Jew, as she had only two Jewish grandparents and had never been a member of a Jewish community. Now, confronted with an "enemy," her cowardice vanished. Clinging to that law, she stretched herself as tall as she could and quietly but firmly responded, "According to the definition of the Nuremberg Laws, I am not a Jewess."

The red-faced, excited official gasped, stared, turned around, and went to the shelves at the side of his office. He pulled out an edition of the laws in question, became very quiet as he scanned them, and later turned and faced her again. Seemingly relieved, he said, "You are perfectly right. You get the permission to go to Berlin immediately." Then, to *Mutti's* surprise, he added, "If you ever need help, I am at your disposal."

In light of that incident, it is worth noting that many German officers, even some of the *Gestapo* and the SS, had by this time ceased to be loyal Nazis, at least in their hearts. They no longer loved, revered, or respected Hitler for his policies, but in order to save their lives and the lives of their wives and children, they continued to pretend loyalty to the Reich. Some of the officers were told that if they showed any disloyalty, their wives and children would be shot. For example, this disloyalty was revealed in the treatment of the Hebrew Christian Pastor of the Jerusalem Church, who was arrested and imprisoned by the Gestapo, but the day before he was to be sent to a concentration camp, two SS officers secretly helped arrange for his escape to Ireland. This was not an isolated incident, and many Germans, both Jewish and Aryan, owe their lives to German officers.

On that day, *Mutti* thanked the officer for the permit, and then she left, overjoyed to have received the paper that would allow her to go to the funeral of her favorite sister-in-law. She also realized that another man might have acted differently and sent her to a concentration camp, and that neither *Vati* nor she could have done anything about it.

That night she told *Vati* about her experience. He paled and said, "We must beware. The authorities know why we left Hamburg." From then on, my parents never knew if they had another day to live, or what might happen to their "Mongrel" children.

On January 20, 1942, at the first meeting for the Final Solution, held in Berlin, the question of how to treat Mongrels was discussed at great length. Up to that point, the concentration camp was the solution for all unwanted people in the Reich. But, as a death sentence was placed on all Jews, the question of how to deal with the Mongrels became the main point of discussion. The Nazi Party wanted all Mongrels killed with the Jews, but the civil servants, the bureaucrats who created the Mongrel status in the Nuremburg laws in 1935, objected. Therefore, the issue was unresolved at that time.

At the third such conference, it was decided to implement a sterilization program for the Mongrels "without further ado." If the Mongrels were sterilized, Germany could be free of the Jewish race completely within a generation. Dr. Joseph Mengele was assigned to immediately develop a cheap, cost-efficient method of sterilization for Mongrels. Consequently, experiments for sterilization of women began with Jews in the concentration camps. These experiments led to horrible disfigurements and even death for thousands of young women. Eventually the effort was stopped because it wasn't cost-efficient, though it was continued in Auschwitz until late 1944. Adolf Eichmann was in charge of the Final Solution and focused on the mass killings of the Jews, planning to kill Mongrels later to ultimately cleanse Germany of every drop of Jewish blood.

Of course, these discussions and decisions were not shared with the public. Mongrels continued to live in constant fear of being deported. The German citizens, for the most part, continued to believe the Jews were still being sent to the mysterious east for resettlement in order to help the war effort. In the final analysis, however, the fate of all Germans—Jew, Mongrel, or otherwise—was not a matter of law but of the whim of the Gestapo, who were essentially above the law.

For example, the Gestapo could and occasionally did make exceptions for Jews if they happened to be married to

Aryans, or even, on some rare occasions, if the Jews were not married to Aryans but were simply considered valuable to the Reich. In that case, papers were forged, giving the Jews Reich citizenship and Aryan status. Tens of thousands of Jews and First degree Mongrels received the gift of life from the Gestapo in this manner.[1]

On the other hand, the Gestapo had the power to arrest Mongrels, who were not legally defined as Jews, if they were reported to have anti-Nazi attitudes or if they looked too Jewish or befriended Jews, such as full-blooded Jewish relatives. Furthermore, the local informants, the *Sicherheitsdienst* (security service), often did not know the laws and could, through their personal prejudice and ignorance, arrange to send someone to a concentration camp, regardless of legal status.

It was in the midst of this climate of fear and uncertainty, while we lived in Lauenburg, that *Vati* reached the peak of his career as chief bookkeeper for a factory of a thousand men. And yet, even as the threat of death hung over us, new life was on the way. *Mutti* became pregnant with her fifth child, and we all hoped for a sister for Renate, who already had three brothers.

But as we eagerly awaited the latest addition to our family, we also lamented the fact that we saw *Vati* less and less. His job in nearby Stolp required a one-hour train ride each way. Between his exhaustion from the long hours of working and commuting, and the severe food shortages that we all suffered, *Vati's* health was failing. Though she hated to see the family separated, even temporarily, *Mutti* finally agreed that *Vati* should take a room in Stolp during the week and return home on weekends. Unfortunately this did not help *Vati's* health because his new landlord cheated him of food ration coupons, and at the end of each week, *Vati* returned home thinner than the week before.

Finally, there came the unforgettable day when *Mutti* brought *Vati* home from the railroad station, and he was so weak he could not hold a cup straight. He was shaking all over from a fever, and *Mutti* quickly put him to bed. On Monday *Mutti* called the doctor, but it was several weeks before the doctor was able to pinpoint *Vati's* problem. Finally, in June of 1944, *Vati* was diagnosed with tuberculosis and immediately sent to the hospital. All this time, even though pregnant, *Mutti* had slept next to her husband and had often eaten with the same spoon. Now, she wasn't about to let a diagnosis keep her from her husband's side. She continued to spend time with *Vati*, going to the hospital three times every day, though as a precaution she did not allow us children to visit with him.

One morning, while tending the garden, *Mutti* suddenly realized that everyone, including her husband, was made from the earth and would one day return to it. She felt alone and forsaken by the thought, but as *Vati's* symptoms improved and his fever lessened, they both began to hope that he would recover, as he had before.

Then, one Thursday, *Mutti* was stung on her leg by a bee. It swelled so badly she was unable to walk, so she sent my brother Eckart to visit *Vati*. Renate went the following day. On Saturday morning the hospital sent for *Mutti*, which she knew they would not do unless *Vati* had taken a turn for the worse. She rushed off, still limping badly and praying all the way that he would still be alive when she got there.

The doctor met her as she walked in and told her there was no hope, but she refused to give up. She had witnessed a miracle in *Vati's* life before, even though the doctors had predicted otherwise. *Mutti* spent all day with *Vati* on Saturday and then returned to the hospital on Sunday morning while a neighbor took us children to the woods. *Vati* seemed better on Sunday, and *Mutti's* leg had also improved.

Mutti was encouraged and even managed to get *Vati* to eat well that day. It was July 23, 1944, and my parents discussed the attempt on Hitler's life, only three days before, thinking perhaps there was hope in that arena as well. It was obvious there were at least some officers in Hitler's inner circle who wanted to get rid of him.

At noon *Mutti* went home to prepare dinner for her children. She was in a hurry and did not bother to set the table in the dining room. While we children ate in the kitchen, the doorbell rang. It was *Vati's* nurse, dressed in black. *Vati* was dead. According to *Mutti's* memoirs, we children screamed. In her grief, *Mutti* wanted to take all four of us to the hospital, but the nurse went to the neighbor and asked her to take care of me and my younger brother, while *Mutti* took the two older children with her. At the hospital they looked into *Vati's* white face and saw his silent mouth and closed eyes. For the first time, there was no response or comfort from their precious *Vati*, only silence.

Vati's parents, a brother, and a sister came to the funeral, which was well attended. *Vati* was taken to the cemetery in an open hearse with five-year-old Wolfram, the youngest of us four children, walking behind with a bouquet of flowers. At the grave, though *Mutti* was obviously grief-stricken, she didn't cry. As a girl, she had always wept easily. Something as simple as a frown from someone could set her off. But now, instead of collapsing, *Mutti* focused on her blessings, went daily to the graveside to "talk" with *Vati*, and began to quietly and privately rely more upon God. Yet we children were totally unaware of any spiritual awakening within her.

Coping with daily life became an ever-increasing challenge without *Vati*. As a half-Jew, *Mutti* was not legally allowed to employ a non-Jew, so her housemaid had to be let go. The neighbors tried to be kind and help in small ways, bringing firewood or helping with childcare. My grandfather in England, who sent several boxes of food to us, admitted that if *Mutti* had been the one to die, we children would have had it much worse, as *Mutti* was the one who always seemed to find a way to hold things together.

Many kind acts were done for us in secret because people were afraid to be seen as being too friendly with a Jew. The doctor refused to give *Mutti* permission to deliver her baby at the hospital, so a neighbor found another doctor who was courageous enough to care for her. The family dentist once sent ten eggs, which meant two meals for us. Upon receiving an overdue book notice from the library, *Mutti* went in to return the book and pay the fine. The librarian turned silently away without taking the money, another secret kindness from one who understood our financial situation.

While grateful for each kind act, *Mutti* also experienced cruelty where she least expected it. While *Mutti* was in labor, the midwife, who had known *Mutti* for months, left her alone and uncomforted while she went into the next room to visit with other nurses. Their loud talking and laughter was easily overheard in *Mutti's* room. Though we all feared the ever-nearing Russian advance, we also had to fear the enemy among our own countrymen, regardless of how long or how well we may have known them.

After *Vati* died, we received a small monthly Social Security check, but it was not enough to pay the rent since *Vati* was only thirty-nine when he died and had worked at jobs that paid low salaries. To help make ends meet, *Mutti* began to go door-to-door to collect insurance premiums. She also arranged to take in two schoolgirls from the country as boarders. They slept with Renate in one room, while the rest of us slept with *Mutti*.

Mutti enjoyed having so many children to work with, even helping them with their homework. Without a maid or husband, the workload of seven children in a five-room apartment kept *Mutti* so busy that she dropped into bed at the end of the day and promptly fell asleep, having little time to grieve or feel lonely.

Unfortunately, this respite did not last. As the winter advanced, floods of refugees came from the east, mostly peasants with heavy horse-drawn wagons and sledges loaded with household goods. Everyone was trying to escape the approaching Red Army, which was coming to reek vengeance on the German people. Prior to this, the Germans had created havoc in the Russian villages and cities. On their retreat from the Russian front, Hitler ordered the *Wehrmacht* (German Army) to kill all cattle and horses, and to burn villages, factories, churches, and hospitals, which would make the progress of the Red Army more difficult. Therefore, when the Red Army advanced, they did so with torrential rage, and their atrocities were reported throughout the German media. The first German village (Nemmersdorf) conquered by the Soviets was left with dead and raped women nailed to barn doors, children shot dead, and civilians crushed and smashed. From then on everyone who was able to flee the Soviet advance did so, either by train or horse cart. Practically no cars or buses were left for civilians, as all motorized vehicles had already moved to the west.

About five million refugees were riding on the crest of horror towards the west. Everyone and everything was utilized to help house these masses of people and to send them farther on their way westward. The schools were closed and used to provide shelter for the refugees, so our boarders were sent home. Soon the schools were overcrowded and refugees were assigned to citizens' homes. We were assigned a mother with two teenage girls. It was amazing to see how ordinary people pulled together during this difficult time. Most of these refugees were cheerful and courageous in spite of their fears and losses.

As this sea of humanity continued to sweep westward, we wondered if we should join them. Two days prior to our departure from Lauenburg, *Mutti* had asked a captain of the German army if the people would need to evacuate the city or if the Germans would be able to hold it. The captain had replied, "We will hold; I guarantee it one hundred percent." Hitler had ordered his officers never to admit defeat or announce evacuations until twenty-four hours before they were sure a city would be lost. As a result, there was never adequate notice of the need to evacuate. The situation in Lauenburg would be no exception. By the time we realized the city was about to fall and we needed to flee, the Red Army was nearly on our doorstep. Streets quickly became jammed with people trying to flee. Roads out of the city were soon clogged, and towns in the flight path were inundated with refugees. The weather was still very cold, and the snow had not yet melted. In fact, new snow was falling when we abandoned our home.

By that point, in spite of Hitler's assurances to the contrary, we all knew that only divine intervention could save Germany's people. Even three-month-old Elke, the little sister we had prayed and hoped for and who had been born in the aftermath of *Vati's* death, folded her hands for prayer when *Mutti* picked her up and said, "May the Lord keep and guard you." Eckart had come in just days before with the report that the frozen bodies of dead German soldiers were stacked like cordwood in the schoolyard, possibly a thousand of them. With such large numbers of refugees and dead, it was obvious to everyone that Germany couldn't possibly be winning the war.

Then came that unforgettable afternoon when God's promise, *"He shall give his angels charge over thee, to keep thee in all thy ways,"* became our mainstay once again.

Mutti had received word via radio that a Red Cross train of wounded soldiers was halting at the station to take on refugees. Since everyone was trying to escape the city and the space on the train was limited, the city government decreed that only those families who had at least three children who were orphans or half-orphans, plus one infant, would qualify to get on the train. Because Elke had been born just three months earlier and *Vati* had died six months before that, our family met the qualifications.

Often we complain to God for not having cared for us. Frequently we doubt His love under such circumstances, and often we judge Him before we know all the facts. How much better it would be to cultivate the attitude that says, "I don't know why God allowed this, but He knows, and that's good enough for me." Oswald Chambers once said, "The greatest of all of man's sins is the suspicion that God is not good." Throughout our ordeal, *Mutti* never wondered, *Where is God?* By this time she knew that God could be trusted, and He had become her refuge. She believed the words of the Apostle Paul *"All things work together for good to them that love God"* (Romans 8:28). *Mutti* loved God. Through this experience she drew nearer to Him, and as she did, God drew nearer to her.

My father had to die at age thirty-nine in order to save his family. Little Elke had to be born at this seemingly most inopportune time in order to get us out of the closing grasp of the Communists. Within a day of our departure from Lauenburg, the Red Army took our city, and most women hid in the forests to escape the lust of the soldiers. Eventually they were all found, either in a forest or when they returned for food and warmth. None of them escaped the humiliation they had so desperately hoped to avoid. Many of the women were put into work camps where they worked all day and were abused every night. Had *Vati* been alive, he would have died trying to protect his beloved wife. He always kept two loaded revolvers handy and wouldn't have hesitated to use them. It is easy to see that had the circumstances been at all different, every one of us would have suffered terribly.

In those last days in our city I would often walk to the main street to hitch a little ride on the back gliding rails of the big sledge wagons as they drove through town. What else was there for a nine-year-old boy to do, since the schools were filled with refugees? By the time the hospital train arrived in Lauenburg, most of the streets were almost impassable with traffic jams of these farm people, mostly women, children, and elderly, awaiting their gruesome fate the next day. Overall, the millions of refugees with tractors and horse-drawn carriages had to cover up to twenty-five miles each day just to stay ahead of the advancing enemy. Many of the exhausted horses pulling heavy carriages could not keep up with that pace, so the people in those carriages were overtaken by Soviet troops and suffered the cruelties they had tried so hard to escape. In addition, 1944-45 was one of the coldest winters with the heaviest snowfall in years. One of our neighbors who stayed behind told us later that wounded German soldiers were taken out of a hospital by the Soviets, laid on the snow and ice-covered streets, and run over by tanks.

So it was on the eighth day of March in 1945 that *Mutti*, a young widow, stood in the middle of our lovely living room, holding little Elke in her arms and surrounded by her four older children. She had just heard of the hospital train and she asked us, "Shall we stay or shall we go?" With a single voice, as in a chorus, we responded, "Let's get out of here." *Mutti*, who had been accustomed to following authorities all her life and who had never had to shoulder responsibility on her own, was even now seeking direction. She said later, "I took the voices of my children as the voice of God." In addition to baby Elke, there was Eckart, eleven, Renate, ten, Wolfram, five, and, of course, Reimar. I was nine years old, and once again our family was about to leave home and run for our lives.

ullstein bild/The Granger Collection, New York

Ruined street in Hamburg, 1945.
600,000 Germans were killed by Allied bombings.

CHAPTER SIX

The Great Escape

I t was March 8, 1945. *Mutti* bundled up little baby Elke, put her into the baby carriage, and pushed her through deep snow toward the railway station. The rest of us carried what we could in our hands. In my ambition, I tried to load a featherbed on my back, but quickly lost my balance and fell backward. It was the last laugh we all had for a long time. The featherbed stayed in our home for the Russians to enjoy, along with everything else we left behind. Our neighbor told us later that when the Russians came the very next day, they loaded onto trucks everything they found in our abandoned homes and then transferred it all to their boxcars—even the garbage cans—to ship them back to their country. They had lost so much in the war, including 13.6 million military personnel, so anything they found was considered valuable to them.

The flight began the moment we heard the dreaded announcement, "The Russians are coming!" There was no time to linger, no time for emotional temper tantrums, pity parties, or tears. There was no time to go to the bank. It was simply a matter of grasping for the essentials and hurrying away. We knew it was our only opportunity to escape the crush and destruction of the Red Army, and we were also concerned that if we did not get on this train quickly enough, others would get ahead of us and we would be left behind.

When we arrived at the railway station, we had to wait eight hours throughout the night, while wounded soldiers were loaded and properly attended. We did not dare leave our place during that time, lest the train depart without us. It was bitterly cold and snowed heavily throughout the night, and there was no place for any of us to sit down.

Mutti was unable to do anything for Elke, but the baby remained quiet. Though she had been born healthy, she had not developed as well as the rest of us children. *Mutti* did not have enough milk, due to the lack of adequate nutrition that was taking its toll on all of us. Also, *Mutti* hesitated to give Elke a bottle, since she had been raised to think that bottles were unacceptable.

And so we huddled together and waited—eight long, freezing cold hours. Finally, we boarded the train. Former passenger cars had been converted to hospital cars, with three lengthwise rows of triple bunk beds in each car. Between the rows of bunks was standing room for the refugees, and sometimes we children were able to lie down on those narrow bunks next to the less severely wounded soldiers. Occasionally I shared a bed with a soldier who had lost one of his legs.

Mutti had to sit on the floor or stand the entire time. The train trip from Lauenburg to Danzig (Gdansk) was normally just over an hour's ride on a slow train, since the distance was only fifty miles, but we were crammed into that train for three days and three nights, accompanied by the moaning and occasional screams of the wounded. The locomotive was constantly shifting and stopping, going forward and backward, as the battle lines between the Soviets and the Germans continued to change. The Russians were bombing the tracks in the area of Danzig, and artillery had begun shooting into the city from the outskirts.

Often when the train stopped, *Mutti* would go out to

"wash" diapers in the snow, all the while keeping an ever-watchful eye on the wheels of the train to be sure they didn't start rolling and separate her from her children forever. A few people who got out were actually left behind when the train suddenly jerked to a new start. All of us ate snow to quench our thirst from time to time.

Next to me on the bottom bunk a soldier had died. His head was bandaged, with only his nose showing through, and he lay there, unmoving, for twenty-four hours until he was put out into the snow. Of course, the stench of all those bodies—some injured, some not, but all unwashed throughout the ordeal—was terrible. There was blood on the beds and on the floor, and there was nothing anyone could do to clean it up. There was a nurse onboard, but she had practically nothing to help the wounded. On some of these trains they even used rough toilet paper to bind up the men's wounds because there were no bandages.

When we arrived in Danzig, now the Polish port city of Gdansk, we were loaded into open trucks and brought to a church where we all slept on the hardwood floor. As far as *Mutti* knew, the soldiers on the train were left behind unattended, since all facilities were overcrowded and all aid personnel were exhausted. After two days in the church, *Mutti* was assigned to a small apartment, which the owners had left for fear of the bombings. Because there were not enough beds in the apartment, I slept on three straight-backed dining room chairs placed next to each other.

The situation in Danzig was no better than in Lauenburg. The city was a heavily fortified pocket, with forty German divisions protecting the bay and harbor. Stalin, in spite of his headlong push to reach the prize of Berlin, ordered his Army Chief of Staff, Marshall Georgi Zhukow, to take Danzig. So just about the time we arrived seeking safety, the Russians swung north out of their path to Berlin and surrounded

Danzig on the east, south, and west. They began to bomb the city indiscriminately, awakening old and fearful memories of the bombing of Hamburg. But this time there were no warning sirens because German reconnaissance planes were no longer available to warn us of incoming attacks, and we were too close to the front to be alerted of incoming aircraft by any other means. Three million people, both refugees and locals, were quickly jammed into an ever-diminishing area, trapped with our backs to the Baltic Sea.

The German *Wehrmacht* tried to take its last stand at the edge of Danzig, but supplies to the troops had been cut off weeks before. Ammunition, gasoline for the tanks, and food were rationed. Although Stalin had assumed that those forty divisions could threaten his advance to Berlin, without adequate food and fuel the German tanks could do nothing but stay on the defensive. When the final attack came, Russian tanks outnumbered German tanks about ten to one.

Hitler hated the Russians nearly as much as he hated the Jews. He knew of the Allied plans to partition post-war Germany and give the eastern portion to Russia. Because of that knowledge, Hitler did one of his few good deeds and ordered a mass evacuation effort to bring as many trapped residents and refugees as possible from Danzig to the west. The *Führer* still hoped to rule a non-communist Germany after negotiating peace.

Consequently, from March 1945 to the end of the war, about 2 million people from the immediate Danzig area were evacuated by sea in the largest planned naval evacuation in history (ten times larger than the evacuation of Dunkirk). Most of the *Kriegsmarine* (German Navy) had been destroyed, but there remained a few minesweepers and cruisers in the Baltic Sea area, as well as a number of freighters, barges, and luxury ships, all of which headed our way.

One afternoon, Eckart and I went to look for some wood or

coal to heat the small stove in our apartment. To our delight, we discovered a big ship in the harbor, loading up refugees. The boat would try to take people to a western German harbor, either Lübeck or Kiel. When Eckart told *Mutti* about the ship, she reacted just as she had in Lauenburg, unsure of what action to take. How she missed the clear leadership of *Vati*! With her beloved husband gone, she now carried the responsibility of the lives of five little ones. She had already heard of the sinking of two of the refugee ships, so she had visions of her family drowning in icy waters, entombed with thousands of others inside a sunken ship.

The *Wilhelm Gustloff*, formerly a luxury liner, had been converted to a hospital ship. It had been filled almost to bursting with nearly 10,600 refugees and wounded when it was sunk by a Russian submarine in fourteen-degree weather. The result was more than 9,300 casualties, the largest and most horrible naval disaster of all time, greatly dwarfing that of the Titanic, and yet the history books seldom mention it. The *General Steuben*, with 3,000 refugees, wounded, and medical personnel, was also sunk by a Russian sub.

But again, as in Lauenburg, we children nudged *Mutti* to leave. We knew nothing about the sunken vessels or their casualties. All we saw was a beautiful big ship in the sunlit, glittering sea, and the spirit of adventure wooed us. Of course, this was also coupled with the fear that drove us earlier to say, "Let's get out of here!" We knew the Russians were coming, and we knew we were still not out of the range of danger. So, again, *Mutti* let us children decide what to do.

After we stood in line for a while, we boarded the *Kreuzer Hektor*, an auxiliary cruiser that served as a converted merchant vessel. Once on board, we lay down in tight rows, filling every square foot of space on that riveted steel floor, which was the way all evacuation ships were packed. Wolfram, Eckart, and I were assigned to one hammock. I ended up in the middle, and I really got "close" to my brothers on that journey. In order to use the restroom at night, I had to wiggle my feet between the bodies of those lying on the floor. *Mutti* soon gave up her own space on the floor to an elderly lady. Those were the days when the younger were still trained to give preference to the older, and children or youth would automatically offer their seats on a train or streetcar to adults.

Our ship was escorted out of the harbor by a minesweeper. Then it moved slowly and cautiously on its own toward the west and, hopefully, toward freedom. At the front of the ship, sailors manned long poles. When they saw water mines, they used their poles to gently push the mines out of the way. Occasionally Eckart saw streaks of red fire coming from the artillery on the shoreline, but fortunately we had moved far enough away from the land that none of the shells hit us.

Throughout this difficult time, baby Elke grew weaker. There was no fresh milk on board the ship, though everyone else was well cared for by the sailors. Even though they knew the ship could be blown up at any moment, the sailors joked with the children, attended to the wounded, and cared for the refugees as much as they were able. Finally, the ship arrived in a port—not in Hamburg, Kiel, or Lübeck, but in Copenhagen, the capital of Denmark. The western German harbors had already been mined shut, and Copenhagen was the only nearby harbor that remained open.

We later learned that by the time the naval evacuation was over, 25,000 refugees and wounded had drowned in the icy waters of the Baltic Sea. But in light of the fact that about 2 million people made it safely through those torturous waters, the overall operation was considered a naval success. Germans had grown accustomed to much greater casualties, though the death of loved ones was always a terrible burden.

The Lord had delivered us from the British and American bombs, from the Nazis, the Soviets, and the perils of the sea. The words my *Mutti* gave me at the time of my birth were more meaningful than ever: *"For he shall give his angels charge over thee, to keep thee in all thy ways"* (Psalm 91:11).

And now we were in Denmark. The next chapter of our lives would be marked by two years behind barbed wire, but it was there that I saw the first brilliant glimmer of a new reality.

The Schultze Flight

➡ **1943**   ▶ **1945**   → **1947**

1943 - Escape from Nazis and bombs,
        Hamburg to Lauenburg.

1945 - Escape from the Soviet invasion,
        Lauenburg to Denmark.

1947 - Return to Hamburg.

CHAPTER SEVEN

Barbed Wire and Green Bread

When we arrived in Copenhagen, we did not know we would spend the next two years in a detention camp with 36,000 other refugees. Upon the recommendation of the ship's doctor, Elke was immediately put into a hospital, where she died a few weeks later. On April 6, 1945, little Elke became the second casualty in our family in less than a year. Starvation had taken Elke, along with thousands of other babies who died during the harrowing escape from the advancing Red Army. This time, *Mutti* allowed all of us to go to the hospital to have one more look at our beloved family member. I still remember my sweet little sister's face, her black hair, her tiny, lifeless body in the crib, and her hands folded as in prayer. In fact, that is the only recollection I have of Elke.

But *Mutti* again managed to find the positive side of this tragedy. She understood that the baby had been given to her to enable us all to leave Lauenburg. Elke lived long enough to save our entire family from the humiliation, suffering, and possible death we would have experienced under communism. When *Vati* died, God lent Elke to us for a season in order to fulfill His purposes for the Schultze family. Had the loss been one of the other children, it would have been a much greater grief. All the rest of us had already developed personalities of our own and were strong reminders of a happier past. *Mutti* also realized that, as a widow, she would soon have to work to feed her children, and the baby would have made things more difficult. She always looked at the big picture. These thoughts gradually brought *Mutti* out of the valley of tears. Elke was a tiny human being who, in less than one year, fulfilled the life mission for which she was created.

How many go to their graves after ten, fifty, or even eighty years without ever having fulfilled the divine mission for which they were born? How much waste can there be in a human life that never engages itself in God's purposes? People waste their lives pursuing their own plans and ignoring God, and then when something goes wrong, they accuse and blame Him. Sooner or later we will all realize that it is better for a person never to have been born than to have lived without serving God.

And so baby Elke was buried in the spring of 1945, along with thousands of other infants, in a cemetery near Copenhagen. These little ones all died from starvation, cold, or disease, and then were buried five to a coffin and laid to rest under the Nazi flag. While *Mutti* stood grieving at Elke's graveside, another young mother ran from row to row, screaming, "They can't even bury them together!" This poor woman had lost her only two children within a matter of hours, and she was heartbroken that they had not been placed in the same coffin.

After arriving in Copenhagen, we stayed in a school where, once again, we slept on the floor and occasionally heard gunfire in the distance. Because of the recent German occupation, the Danes had good reason to feel uncomfortable with German refugees in their midst, and they rightly kept us under guard. The war was not over, and our benefactors had no way of knowing for certain what pro-Nazi elements may have existed among the 36,000 refugees.

While we were still held hostage in a school there were

days we survived on little or no food. On one particular day many of us children were gathered together in a school hallway when a Dane told us he had one apple to give away. He said he would throw it up in the air, and whoever caught it could have it. We were all hungry, but because I was the tallest child there, I easily caught the apple. But as I looked at the disappointed faces of my classmates, I could not bring myself to eat it, and so I gave it away.

A few days later, all refugees were loaded into freight cars and brought to a former army training center. The train ride took several hours, and since we were in boxcars, we could not see anything outside. I was nearly exploding with curiosity by the time the train finally stopped and the sliding doors were pulled back. My first sight was of armed Danish troops, with German shepherd dogs at their sides. Just past the troops and their dogs, I spotted a compound enclosed with barbed-wire and a very large watchtower rising above it. I quickly learned this would be our new home for an unspecified period of time.

But despite the ominous surroundings, we were happy. True, we would be confined and our living restricted, but by the grace of God we had not been taken to a concentration camp. Although the Danes were cautious, they treated us as humans, assigning us to barracks and providing the bare necessities of food, shelter, and minimal medical assistance. They even provided peat for our little iron stoves, and we were free to move about the camp, which was located in a forest.

In addition, all 36,000 of us were Germans. We had experienced similar miseries and losses, and although some feared the Russians might still catch up with us, we had everything we needed to function as a community: doctors, nurses, teachers, engineers, farmers, accountants, truck drivers, and architects, though most of the residents were women, since all able-bodied men were still fighting the Allies and the Soviets.

For the first year of our stay in the camp, there was no incoming or outgoing mail. For that whole year, we did not know whether our relatives were dead or alive, if our fathers or uncles or brothers had been made prisoners of war, or if our neighbors had been killed in the bombings or had frozen or starved to death. At the same time, our relatives, including our grandparents, Hans and Frieda, did not know whether we were dead or alive. There were no newspapers or radios; all we heard were rumors.

Mutti and her four remaining children slept together in two bunk beds in barrack F-10. Five ladies, six children, and one elderly gentleman shared this single room with us, making seventeen people living in a very small space. When we entered the door to our room, we would spot the peat-burning stove in the right corner. Straight across from the door was a window that looked out on some trees and another barrack not far from our own. Around the room were the bunk beds, and in the middle was a large table and wooden chairs. That was all the furniture we had. There were no dressers or cupboards, and only a communal bath down the hall where we could take cold showers.

And yet, it is amazing how we all got along, as if total strangers had suddenly become one family. In those two years, there were no arguments or fights between us, though each word spoken was heard by everyone in that room. The most amusing member of our "family" was the elderly gentleman. He had a slight case of psychoneurosis, and often came up with the strangest ideas, such as trying to invent a cup for seventeen people to drink from hygienically.

When we wanted privacy or needed to change our clothing, we hung a blanket on each side of our bunk beds. The only floor space allotted to our family of five during those two years was the 2 ½ x 6-foot space between our two bunks. Our bedding was straw, which was never changed the entire time we were there. Once you lie down on straw, it becomes flat and hard, and after two years, there wasn't much straw left at all.

We did have lots of little friends, however: bedbugs, fleas, and lice. When the room's only light bulb was turned off for the night, the bedbugs came out of the cracks of the bed frames and walls. They crawled up the walls onto the ceiling and then used their heat sensors to detect when they were above a warm human. They would then drop down and have their breakfast, lunch, and supper, all in one big banquet.

"For he shall give his angels charge over thee, to keep thee in all thy ways." Does that include protection from bugs? Sometimes. Of the seventeen people in that room, I was the only one who never had a bedbug drop down on me. But I, like the others, had lice. We did everything we could to get rid of them. At times, we took whole bed frames apart to find and kill the bedbugs. Other times, we boiled water in a basin and stuck our heads into the water up to the scalp, but our little friends always came back.

In the first few weeks, we boys just ran around in the forest that was within the borders of the camp, climbing trees and building tree houses in the branches, and doing whatever else boys do to entertain themselves. But shortly after our arrival, someone carved some chess figures, and for a whole year, I spent almost every day from morning till night playing chess. Now, when people ask me what I did with my life, I say that for one year of it, I played chess.

In the second year, we learned through the mail and the Red Cross that all our relatives were alive except for one of my father's brothers, who had been killed in an automobile accident. Grandfather Hans was well-settled in a Christian community in England, and he had English missionaries contact Danish friends through whom we were able to receive little gifts from our *Opa*. We then shared those precious treats with everyone in our room.

When we first arrived at the camp, we were inoculated against any infectious disease that could possibly trouble us. I remember being vaccinated on my arm, my chest, and my back. Nonetheless, a number of people died from some of those diseases. In the second year, when Renate became terribly sick with a high fever, she was quickly diagnosed with diphtheria and placed in an isolation barrack behind barbed wire. In order to visit her, I had to stand outside the fence and shout to her where she sat at the window. *Mutti*, of course, was deeply concerned, wondering if she would lose yet another member of her family, her only remaining daughter. But God spared Renate, and she recovered.

Food at the camp was simple: bread and soup, though there never seemed to be enough of either. For some reason, the soup was called "Blue Henry," and its consistency was more like broth than soup. A few "eyes" of fat showed on the surface, but there was nothing solid floating beneath. The bread wasn't much better. By the time it arrived in the camp, it was green with mold and had a mushy consistency, as if it had been soaked in water. But it was whole wheat bread and provided most of the nutrients we needed. When the bread truck arrived at the camp distribution center, some of us boys would try to fetch a loaf that had fallen to the ground as it was passed in a chain from one person to the other from the truck into the kitchen. Occasionally we succeeded, though not often.

I shall never forget the first Christmas season at the camp. Late at night or early in the morning, when I was asleep on the top bunk, beautiful, blonde-haired, ten-year-old Renate labored hard to sew a soccer ball for me, making it out of an army uniform she had found. What a labor of love and care that was! It was the only Christmas present I or anyone else in that room received. However, that wonderful soccer ball had a very short lifespan. When I took it outside the next day, a dozen boys quickly gathered for a game. In minutes, Renate's sewing had come undone, as strips of cloth flew in all directions.

During the first year in the camp, once we heard the war was over, we waited daily for our release to go back to Germany. By the time the second year rolled around and nothing had happened, the parents, not knowing how much longer we would be there in the camp and not wanting their children to miss another year of education, decided to start a complete school system. Enough people had died in the camp during that first year that there were now some empty barracks, and so the camp leaders allowed us to use them for an elementary school, a high school, and even some university classes.

To say our supplies were limited is a gross understatement. We had a few scraps of paper, but no textbooks or notebooks. However, we had good professional teachers and university professors among us, and many of them offered free classes in their field of specialty to anyone who wanted to come. There were classes in psychology, in calculus, in bird watching, in various languages, and so on. *Mutti* enrolled in classes to improve her English and French, and all of us children went to elementary school. Eckart particularly was glad to find out that there was more to history than Adolf Hitler.

Early on, we had to memorize the most famous German hymn, *"Ein Feste Burg Ist Unser Gott"* ("A Mighty Fortress Is Our God"), written by the great German reformer, Martin Luther. Now, this may sound strange to the average American, but in Germany, as well as in most of Europe, the church and state (both then and now) work together for the common good of the people. Religion supports the state, and the state supports religion, and so we children were exposed to the teachings of the church.

I was ten years old at the time, and as I lay on the top bunk, memorizing Luther's great hymn, I found myself wondering, *Who is this mighty God? Where does He fit in to this life? Can He be known?* It was the first time I remember having such thoughts, and that experience opened a new window of possibility for me. I was like the little boy Samuel in the Bible, who was awakened three times by someone calling his name, but he didn't know it was God speaking to him (see 1 Samuel 3:4–8). I began to sense that there was an entirely different world out there, just waiting for me to discover it, but I had no idea how to take even the first step of such an awesome journey.

Mutti also began to turn more and more to God during this time, though we children didn't discover that until much later. She started reading her German Bible occasionally, going to Sunday church in one of the barracks, and attending a weekly Bible study conducted by a Danish theologian, who poured out the compassion of Christ on the poor refugees. Yet, again, she never invited us children to go along. Her religious beliefs continued to be totally private. A few other refugees also attended Sunday church, but only a very few went to the weekly Bible study. The Germans were only used to Sunday services and did not care for additional religious activities, nor did they like what they considered to be "splinter groups." Methodists, Baptists, and Pentecostals are still considered sects in Germany, even to this day.

And then, in the midst of *Mutti's* renewed interest in God, after almost two years in the camp, the Lord reached down and moved us out of that cluttered little room. He sent us on our way, back to a city that had once been our home but was now reduced to acres and acres of rubble.

CHAPTER EIGHT

Return to Hamburg

The war officially ended on May 9, 1945. During the winter of 1946–47, the news spread that refugees could go home, provided they had a place to stay when they got there. Through the mail we had finally received, we learned that most Germans fared far worse in Germany than we did in the camp. Many had frozen to death, and others had died of starvation as their beloved country lay in ashes. Yet we all wanted to go home. Freedom has an attractive ring in people's ears, and we were all ready to rebuild our country, with our bare hands, if necessary.

And so, in January of 1947, our train rolled into Hamburg. Our first impressions were absolutely devastating, and we were speechless for days afterward. The entire metropolis of over one million people was in ruins, with rubble piled upon more rubble underneath the snow. We spotted an occasional apartment building jutting out of the ruins, some with only one wall standing all the way up to the fourth floor. People had hung bed sheets to make up for the missing walls, and had tried to survive in that cold wintry weather, waiting for spring to come. Over three-fourths of the city was demolished, and our hearts were heavy for weeks.

When we arrived at the station, we were still wearing much of the same clothing we had worn for two years in Denmark. We made our way through the rubble to *Oma*

Annamarie's apartment, shocked at how difficult it was to find it with all the landmarks gone.

Oma Annamarie, *Vati's* mother, was a widow now, as *Opa* had died soon after the war ended. She welcomed us with open arms, even though she had only a small living room and kitchen, one bedroom, and a very tiny bathroom. As mentioned earlier, my uncle had lost his home in a bombing raid in 1943, so he and his family were already living there when we moved in.

Uncle Heinrich and Aunt Gretel slept with their two children in the small bedroom. *Oma* had moved her bed into the living room. We joined her there, making a total of six in that one room, with three chairs placed together serving as my bed. The kitchen was the only place that could be heated (with coal), and it was the only place where all six of us children could play. Of course, there was no school, as practically every school had been destroyed.

We were more crowded in *Oma's* little apartment than we had been in the camp we just left, and we still didn't have enough food. With many of the roads impassable and most of the stores destroyed, the little food that was brought into the country was difficult to distribute to all the people of Hamburg. Uncle Heinrich scavenged the harbor each day, looking for a fish or two to bring home for us to share.

Feeling we were an imposition to *Oma* and her family, *Mutti* applied to the government for living space of our own. As a result, we were soon moved back into barracks, along with millions of other refugees. But for the first time in two years, the five of us had a room to ourselves, consisting of two sets of bunk beds, one desk, one chair, and one large bowl to be used for washing. It was March of 1947, and it was still so cold that we stayed in bed all day, except for one hour when we boys went out to search for firewood and get our food.

We collected branches that had been broken off the trees by the strong spring winds that swept over the wide Elbe River nearby, and then used them to heat our little stove to get some warm water to wash ourselves. But as soon as the fire went down, we went back to bed. Thankfully, this routine lasted only a few weeks.

We received our meals from a simple camp kitchen, and spent much of our time longing for warmer weather, rejoicing if the temperature rose even one degree each day. We did not regret that we had left the camp in Denmark, but we experienced more extreme cold during those first weeks in Germany than we had during our entire two years in the Danish camp. And yet, we no longer felt like prisoners, and we were hopeful that the future would be better.

We learned to get through the hardships by taking every day as it came. We had survived the bombings, the Nazi terror, the Red Army, and two years behind barbed wire. Things had to get better, even though the land was barren and desolate. Our beautiful cities had been turned into rubble; trees had been cut down for fuel; gardens, where beautiful flowers, radishes, and fruit trees once flourished, had disappeared.

Mutti soon began to receive a small Social Security check each month, and though it wasn't much, it was adequate to pay for the rent required for the barrack room and for a little bit of food from the camp kitchen. Immediately, she began to resume her household responsibilities. She managed to find a needle and thread so she could make a little money mending clothes. Often her hands were so stiff from the cold that she had to lay aside her work and slide her hands under our covers while we were still in bed. But as soon as possible, she would return to her task. We had nothing but the clothes on our backs—no books, no radios, no toys, and no outward stimulation—nothing but ourselves and our memories. But we had made it through the war, and we were together.

After a few weeks, *Mutti* was finally able to locate a home for her family—a small apartment in the basement of a little farmhouse several miles away. It consisted of a living room, one storage room, and a small cooking area, with an outhouse in the yard. It was only five minutes to the village school and a one-hour walk to the high school in the next town. We moved there in April of 1947.

I liked our new home in the village of Neuengamme. Though we still had no furniture and slept on straw on the wood floor, we thought nothing of it, as we were already used to such accommodations. After the deprivations of the past years, we felt as if we had found heaven on earth. We were in the country on a raised cobblestone road, much like a levee or dike, next to a canal. The farmer had some chickens, and he allowed me to have a rabbit and a guinea pig. We children thought life couldn't possibly be any better! Though there was no bus service in our area, we could walk for an hour on top of a dam to the closest town, which was Bergedorf, a lovely place that had escaped the bombings that had destroyed so much of our country. There was something about seeing a town totally untouched by war that soothed my inner wounds, and yet I knew that a fifteen-minute walk in the opposite direction from our home would bring us to the former Neuengamme concentration camp.

Soon after moving into our new home, we children were finally able to resume our education. I went to the village elementary school but soon came to the age when I had to make a decision about my future. The educational system was set up in such a way that, by the age of twelve, children had to decide what they wanted to do with the rest of their lives. They could continue in elementary school until they were twelve, leave elementary school and go to high school for four years, or apply for entrance at the *Gymnasium*, a six-year preparatory course for university studies.

To enter high school or the *Gymnasium*, young people had to be at or near the top one-quarter of their class in elementary school. Then they had to pass a six-day oral and written examination and come out in the top one-third or so. The standards varied a little from time to time, depending on the vacancies in the schools. With so many schools having been destroyed in the war and five million refugees swelling the population, there were far too few classrooms for the many students who wanted to enroll. As a result, only the best of the best were able to go to the *Gymnasium*.

Mutti, however, made sure that I was one of them, and so I had to walk one hour each day on top of the cobblestone dam and then across asphalt to attend classes in the little town of Bergedorf. It wasn't long before I flunked out. I had started attending this school in late summer when it was still warm. *Mutti* insisted I wear shorts, and I was very tall and had long, spindly legs. She made me walk barefoot to save my shoes for other occasions. By the time I got to school, my feet were black from my toes to above my ankles. I felt so ashamed as I sat among these beautifully dressed children who had no war experience that I simply could not think about anything else. After a few weeks, realizing my grades were woefully inadequate, I withdrew and entered the four-year high school. By then, it was getting colder, and I was allowed to wear shoes and socks.

Overall—and for good reasons—I was not *Mutti's* favorite child. I reminded her too much of her Jewish father, Hans. I had a similar personality and mannerisms, and whenever I did something she did not like, she called me "Hans." I also had a lazy streak and spent far too much time thinking and not enough time helping. From her perspective, I had to be reminded more often than the other children to "get with it."

I will never forget the day I was on my way to school and ran into the worst thunderstorm I had ever seen. In a matter of minutes, I was drenched from head to foot. The storm was so bad I actually thought the wind would blow me off the dam. I decided I needed to turn around and go back home, but after I arrived in the living room of that little basement apartment, *Mutti* seemed to telescope herself into a ten-foot tall dragon. As I stood there with water pooling around my feet on the hardwood floor, she told me what she thought of me, and it wasn't good. She called me a lazy, good-for-nothing person who would never amount to anything if I didn't change my ways. She told me I was always full of excuses, and that she did not consider getting wet to be a valid reason for not going on to school. In other words, she would rather have me die while performing my duty and pursuing education than live as a lazy bum. Of course, that was only her emotional sentiment at the moment, and I now know not to take anything too seriously that people say in emotional states. At the time, however, I was crushed.

After her vitriolic lecture, I went to our closet-sized bedroom, lay down on the straw, and began to think. Before long, I came to the conclusion that *Mutti* was right, and immediately I decided to make every possible effort to never again be the source of someone's complaint. I pulled myself together and vowed to press ahead for whatever was good and noble and right, whatever the cost. Lying there on the hard straw, with my cold, damp clothing clinging to my body, I began to get the message and vision that *Mutti* wanted for me. I started to see that I was indeed a terrible son and certainly more trouble to her than all my siblings put together. It was the beginning of my transformation into a new man. When *Mutti* went to the makeshift basement kitchen to fetch a rag to wipe up the puddle I had left on the floor, she did not realize until years later that she had wiped away a lot more than she could ever have imagined.

Over the many years since, I have heard people complain about the things they can't do: "I can't pray"; "I can't get myself to read the Bible"; "I can't get myself to sit in church for an hour"; "I can't stop overeating." The truth is, when we say things like that, we are just making excuses for something we *can* do—we just don't *want* to.

Everything begins with a vision. *"Where there is no vision, the people perish"* (Proverbs 29:18). Once we have a vision for something, it is easy to get our will behind it. Many people in America who say they can't sit for an hour in an air-conditioned, cushioned sanctuary can easily sit for hours in the cold or rain or burning sun on the hard bleachers of a football stadium, screaming, yelling, and having a good time. Tragically, they have a vision for football, but they have no vision for God. Much of this has to do with a lack of contemplation. Few people take the time to think deeply about life, death, or the afterlife. Their pursuits are shallow, shortsighted, and lacking in eternal perspective. We need to pray and ask God to stamp eternity into our eyes so we do not fall prey to empty and pointless thinking. If we will just take time to meditate and ask God to help us get a vision of the things that really matter, He will do so.

Too many parents use time as the excuse for their children's laziness, immaturity, and disobedience. They say that "time will take care of them" or "someday, he/she will grow out of it." We let the excuse of "time" waste our time! Time will no more make a man out of a boy than space will. True maturity comes only from making wise decisions and sacrifices, practicing self-denial, and, ultimately, surrendering to God.

Mutti was not one to let "time" waste her children's time. She wasn't about to abdicate her own responsibilities in hopes that somewhere down the line we would suddenly and inexplicably begin to act responsibly. In my case, the day of the thunderstorm was the day for me to begin to act responsibly. *Mutti* gave me a good talking to at that young age of eleven, and I became a more responsible person within minutes. In fact, immediately following that day, I began to excel in a number of areas, and I have been so grateful to my mother for the lesson she taught me. It was a big part of my overall preparation for a fruitful adulthood and marriage.

With the war behind us and both *Vati* and Elke gone, *Mutti* was determined to raise the rest of us up from the ashes of war to make something of our lives. That was the single goal from which she never departed or deviated, even when she had opportunities to marry and get another breadwinner to make things easier for all of us. A few months later, in particular, when she had met and become acquainted with a certain gentleman during our visit to England, she asked us if we wanted another father. This gentleman wanted to marry *Mutti* and be the new father to us four children, and he would take us out of the rubble of Hamburg and give us a splendid new life in his lovely country. We all said no, which confirmed her own deep desire to trust in God and tough it out without a husband. She knew no one could ever take the place of the man who had been willing to sacrifice his life for us, and we all felt good about the clarity, simplicity, and purity of that decision for the rest of our lives.

While still living in Neuengamme, *Mutti* accepted a cleaning job, for which she received the very low hourly wage of thirty-five marks per week and by which we were able to buy some potatoes, beets, or carrots. She was later able to get a job tutoring children who needed help in their education. At other times, she took in sewing and embroidery. There were times she spent all night knitting sweaters under a 15-watt bulb in order to bring in extra funds. Once she even disappeared behind the Iron Curtain in an attempt to trade some English tea from her father for some much more practical potatoes. It took her three days, from morning until night, going from farmhouse to farmhouse in East Germany, until she finally found a farmer who agreed to the trade. She returned the next day, triumphantly carrying her bag of potatoes.

Just down the lane from us lived a farmer who raised tomatoes. Next to his farm was a big pile of rotten tomatoes, unfit for the market. He told us we could eat them if we chose, so whenever things got short, we enjoyed rotten tomatoes until the next great feast of beets, potatoes, and carrots came along. I did not mind that. I was so happy to be free and in that beautiful countryside, enjoying my rabbit and guinea pig and listening to the croaking of the frogs in the nearby canal. We children often caught tadpoles at that canal and then placed them in our landlord's aquarium, where we watched them grow into frogs. Our previous years of hardships had taught us to appreciate these simple pleasures.

And then there was Happy, my friend who lived on the other side of the canal. Happy had a couple of goats, and were they ever fun to watch! Happy also had a canoe, and the two of us sometimes took it down the canal to pick water lilies to sell in the market for a few marks. One time we both pulled on the lilies on the same side of the boat, and we capsized. We made it safely to shore, dragging the canoe behind us, but we were scared of the consequences when our parents found out. Facing *Mutti* in wet clothing, covered with mud and with the stench of algae hanging over me, was too terrifying to consider, so we laid our clothing out on the meadow grass, begging the sun to dry them—quickly. Though I was yet irreligious, that may have been the first time I ever prayed. Unfortunately, I prayed to the sun, but the sun refused to listen. As a result, both Happy and I were forced to face the wrath of our parents. I never did find out how Happy fared when he got home, but I received another powerful lecture from *Mutti*. I got over it quickly, though, justifying the incident in my own mind as an "occupational accident" that came with plucking water lilies for profit.

And then, after living in Neuengamme for approximately one year, my grandfather Hans was able to make arrangements to bring us all to England. From there he hoped to help us emigrate to Canada or the United States. This sounded wonderful to all of us. Oh, how magnificent it was when we got on a British boat on the North Sea and ate some real food! Every bite we consumed at that dining table tasted delicious after so many years of having so little.

When we arrived, we were told we could stay in England for one month. Since my grandparents had a tiny one-bedroom apartment, we were not able to stay with them, so we children were parceled out to foster parents. None of us except *Mutti*, could speak a word of English, but these foster parents not only took us into their homes, they also sent us to school. Can you imagine sitting in a classroom without understanding a single word that is said? But our hosts were very kind and loving, and they began to teach us English.

My foster parents were the Lillys. They were so kind to me, and I truly felt loved and pampered. It was part of my healing process, and I enjoyed every minute of it. I even had my very own bedroom, with three or four pillows on my bed and a thick box spring mattress. It was the first time I had slept on a pillow or mattress in three years. I also had lovely curtains and drapes on the windows, plush carpeting, fancy dressers and mirrors, and all kinds of trinkets sitting around the room. The Lillys bought new clothes for me, including socks and shoes, and they even got me a professional haircut.

I especially enjoyed Elaine, their twenty-year-old-daughter. Each morning she and I sat across from each other at the elaborate breakfast table. Everything seemed so elegant, as if we were in Buckingham Palace. The dishes were expensive bone china. The silverware appeared to be real silver. The ornate white silk napkins looked too beautiful to use. Elaine would look at me with her big dark eyes, point to an item on the table, and then say a word in English for me to repeat. I cannot recall how many times I had to push my tongue to the front of my teeth to try out the "th's" for thanks, the, that, this, thought, and other such words before I stopped saying *tanks*, *de*, *dat*, *dis*, and *tought*. But Elaine did not give up. She pointed to the cereal, cup, saucer, furniture, and windows, gave me the English word for each, and waited patiently as I repeated them. Little by little, I began to understand. I learned and learned, and when I eventually returned to Germany, after being gone for an extended three months, I was able to converse in English.

Oh, how I loved England with its lovely homes and beautiful flower gardens! The double-decker buses were fascinating to me. Each day, on my way to school, I tried to be the first one to board the bus so I could hurry up the spiral staircase to sit up front. From this heavenly throne I could observe the sights below me as the bus worked its way through the narrow streets and sharp turns of the old neighborhoods. Then one day, after school, I went with some boys to a French fry place. I had never heard of nor seen

French fries, but once I took a bite, I could not get enough of them. Yes, England was like paradise after all we had been through the previous years.

Unfortunately, as much as Hans tried to make arrangements to get us to Canada or the United States, he was unsuccessful. We were told we had to go back to Germany because Canada and the United States had refused us entrance. Returning to Germany was like returning to nothing, but the God who said He would give His angels charge over me, even before I knew Him, looked after us. And so we returned to Neuengamme.

However, very soon after our return, the Americans established a processing center in the Bergedorf area through which thousands of displaced Germans were able to emigrate to the United States. The Americans were looking for a stenographer who was adept at both German and English shorthand, and *Mutti* qualified. We quickly moved into a better place in Bergedorf, with two large rooms and a front porch that had a little gas stove for cooking. Suddenly we were able to get cheese and hard rolls every Saturday, and milk to drink. What a treat that was!

Now that we had a larger place to live, *Mutti* assigned chores to each of us. Renate was to do the general cleaning and the laundry; Wolfram was to go to the bottom of the hill each day to get fresh milk, since we had no refrigeration; and I was to start a fire in the coal stove and keep it going all day every day. Eckart, who was then fourteen, quit school to take an apprenticeship in tool and die making in order to supplement the family's income.

It was while we lived in this new home in Bergedorf that the day came when I rode my bicycle into a forest, covered myself with pine branches, and fell asleep. I was thirteen years old, and when I awoke to the golden beams of sunlight streaming through the trees, I heard those wonderful words: "I love you; I love you. I AM love." My life would never be the same.

Left to right: Wolfram, Reimar, Renate, and Eckart

The Russians are coming,
the Jews are being killed,
Vati is not well.

CHAPTER NINE

Origin, Purpose, and Destiny

After leaving the *Gymnasium*, I attended an all boys' high school. The separation of sexes in both the high schools and *Gymnasiums* was quite common in Germany at that time, and the only female in our school was the principal's secretary. I believe the absence of the opposite sex during that formative time of life prevents a lot of distractions and enables young people to focus on their academics. As a result, we received a good education. By the time we were sixteen and in our last year of high school, we were all able to read Shakespeare in English, as well as do trigonometry and basic calculus.

We also were spared another distraction that can damage the academic process: sports. No German high school or university had any type of competitive sports program, which is still true today. We did have a one-hour weekly gymnastic sports class, designed to teach us to have some control over our limbs and to advance good posture. Occasionally, the whole class would walk to the nearest public soccer field to play a game, which we enjoyed immensely. Apart from that, anyone who wanted to engage in any competitive sport joined one of the many local sports clubs. Because several of my classmates made a practice of ganging up on me for a fight during class breaks, I joined one of those clubs and took up judo. Before long no one bothered me anymore.

We also had no extra-curricular activities or parent-teacher associations or student groups in our schools. The purpose of high school was purely academic, with a small nod to physical fitness. We attended school six days a week, with Saturday being a half-day, and our summer recess lasted for two months. During the school year, students spent most evenings doing homework or interacting with their families.

Inevitably, during our studies, we came to the topic of modern German history. Although it was seven years after the war, we had not yet received new textbooks on German history, and the old books had been published by the Reich. Our professor, Herr Nicolai, made us go through our textbooks to blot out most anything that related to Nazi politics, and then we used those books until new ones were printed and distributed.

During my four years of high school, I sat in the same back left corner, where the benches were specifically designed for six-footers. Siegfried, who shared a bench with me, was the fastest 100-meter sprinter in all of Germany, and he was headed for the Olympics. It was always amusing when we went to the track. By the time Siegfried was at the 100-meter mark, I was just passing fifty meters. Then Siegfried started smoking, and his habit took a toll on his running ability. He soon lost out on track, and Günter, who shared the back benches with us, took Siegfried's place at the Olympics in Australia.

On one occasion, during a German history class, someone managed to obtain the answers to all the questions on an examination. To study German history, one must know the names of dozens of kings who fought each other, the names of their generals, the dates of these battles, and the outcomes. German history is so full of these sort of things that there is no time for historians to indulge themselves in the colors of the soldiers' garments or the number of buttons on their vests, as is the case in the short history of the United States. German history encompasses the memory of not just one or two wars on its soil, but of dozens of wars between dozens of kings. Every student in that class dreaded history exams, so when someone managed to procure the answers, they were passed from student to student underneath the desktops of the benches where we sat. Finally, Siegfried slipped that little piece of paper into my hand. When I touched the paper, there was a voice within me that clearly said, "No. Don't do it." Instantly, I shoved the paper back into Siegfried's hand and whispered to him, *"Nein, Ich will's nicht haben."* ["No, I don't want it"].

I listened to my heart, and I never regretted it. John the Apostle said of Jesus, *"That was the true light which lighteth every man that cometh into the world"* (John 1:9). Every person born into the world, whether in the jungles of Africa, the Andes of South America, the plains of the Ukraine, or the big cities of New York, Bombay, or Hong Kong, has a little light inside of him. This light is of Jesus and can also be described as the conscience by which we know right from wrong. No one is born an atheist; all are born with an innate knowledge of an eternal God and the difference between good and evil.

Even before I had read the Bible or knew anything about Christianity, I had this inner light, this conscience, which I tried to follow as much as I could. Each time we violate the law of conscience, our conscience becomes more desensitized, until finally we are able to do evil without any sense of wrongdoing. In the words of the Apostle Paul, our conscience becomes "seared," as with a hot iron (see 1 Timothy 4:2). This is why many people, having repeatedly violated their consciences, can lie without feeling guilty. The violation of the conscience always leads to a criminal mind, though that term is certainly not restricted to inmates living behind prison bars. There are people with criminal minds who live in beautiful homes, drive expensive cars, head large corporations, and feel perfectly comfortable lying, cheating, and stealing for the sake of profit. That is why I have never regretted saying "no" to that little piece of paper. I did not yet know God in a personal way, and I certainly did not know Jesus as my Lord and Savior, but I did know it was dangerous to oppose this guiding light within my conscience.

In my last year of high school, three years after hearing God's voice in the forest, my biology class studied evolution. I listened to this theory but could make no intellectual sense of it. As I looked about the class and thought about the millions of people in the world, I realized I had never seen even one of them who appeared 50, 40, 30, 10, 5, or even 2 percent ape. In order to accept evolution as a fact, I reasoned that countless species combining ape and man would have to exist simultaneously. Since that was not the case, I rejected the whole theory as a figment of man's wild imagination.

Years later, while attending the University of Wisconsin, my conclusion was bolstered by my genetics professor, who said that Darwinian evolution was a genetic impossibility. A physics professor then told us that Darwinian evolution was impossible by virtue of the law of increasing entropy, also known as the Second Law of Thermodynamics, which basically stipulates that all systems in the real world tend to go "downhill," as it were, toward disorganization and decreased complexity. It is similar to the natural disintegration that takes place with an untended garden. When I talked to my geology professor, he told me the Geological Column, much touted by evolutionists, only exists in school textbooks; it has not been found in the earth's actual geological strata.

Perhaps one of the strangest incidents I experienced regarding this particular matter was when I was a pre-medical student. A professor from medical school placed a drawing of Darwin's evolutionary tree on the blackboard. After the class was over, I approached the teacher and asked if he really believed in the theory of evolution. To my surprise, he answered, "No. Nobody in medical school believes in evolution outside the species." When I asked why he continued to teach it, he replied, "We have to teach something like this until something better comes along."

Of course, back in 1952, as a sixteen-year-old high school student in Hamburg, I did not have the knowledge of natural sciences that I have now. I simply had two things to guide me: logic and that guiding light within that warned me not to cheat on my exam. So, when our biology professor came to the end of the lecture on evolution and asked if there was anyone who would like to dispute this theory, I surprised everyone, including myself, when I stood up.

As the shyest boy in an all-boys' high school of 500 students, this was completely out of character for me, but my reaction was spontaneous. "*Ich muss Morgen dagegen sprechen*," ["I must speak against this tomorrow"] I declared. The class was electrified because it was the first time I had spoken out in the classroom. Indeed, I too was shocked, but I know now it was the power of God that raised me from my seat that day.

After hearing my completely unexpected declaration, the atheist professor said, "You have the whole science hour tomorrow."

When I got home, I asked *Mutti* if she had a Bible. She gave me her old Luther Bible, the one given to her at her confirmation when she was a young girl and that she had carried all the way through the flight from eastern Germany. I looked at the index and saw there were many books in this Bible, and I decided I needed to look at the most recent one to get information that would help me solve the Darwinian puzzle. That was the book of Revelation, and after just a few minutes of reading I was totally confused.

I laid the Bible down and said, "God, whoever You are, wherever You are, this is Your hour tomorrow. I don't know what to say. You are going to have to carry me through. I just plan to be embarrassed if You don't give me words to say." Then I went to bed and slept well. It was the first time I ever laid a matter in God's hands, the first time I ever trusted Him.

The next morning, I appeared in class and took my seat, still wondering what I would say. Shortly, the professor called me before the class. As I stood before them in my 6-foot 4-inch frame, I realized every eye was fixed upon me. Reimar Schultze, after four years of silence, was finally going to say something. You could have heard a pin drop. After what seemed like hours but probably was just seconds, these words came to my mind: *"Es kann nicht sein, es kann nicht sein, es muss einen Gott geben, es muss einen Gott geben!"* ["It cannot be; it cannot be. There must be a God. There must be a God!"] This is the first sermon I ever preached—short and to the point. I waited a little longer for the inner voice to speak to me again, but when nothing more came, I made a beeline for my seat in the corner of the room.

As I slid onto the bench, I was enveloped by the glory of God (though the word "glory" was not yet in my vocabulary), and God spoke to me: "I will give you the answers to the questions of origin, purpose, and destiny." That was the most thrilling moment of my life so far, more awesome even than when God spoke to me in the forest. I knew God had spoken to me clearly and precisely, and that He had promised to help me.

The timing was perfect. I was quickly approaching my graduation from high school, and I had been wondering what to do with my life. I had tentatively decided on becoming an officer in the Merchant Marine, primarily because it seemed a practical choice. It also seemed a challenging one, but I wasn't absolutely sure if it was the right thing for me to do. But now, with this recent promise from God spoken directly to my heart, I began to talk to Him, asking questions that I imagined only He could answer: Where did I come from? What am I here for? Where do I go when I die? What is the purpose of life? What if I end up with the wrong occupation or the wrong wife? What if I end up living in the wrong place, or follow the wrong ideas and principles? I didn't want to waste my life, and I knew that without these specific answers, I could easily do just that. And so, at the end of each school day, I hurried up the cobblestone road to our little apartment so I could read the Bible and pray to this as-yet unknown God.

After three months of this, without having received any blessing or understanding from the Bible, I went to a Lutheran minister and asked him what I must do to get to heaven. He answered, "You must do more good deeds than bad deeds, and heaven will be in your favor." I didn't like that answer because I wondered how I would know for certain if I had done more good deeds than bad. It seemed this minister had turned the matter of my salvation into a guessing game, and the guessing was up to me. I was disappointed and decided that perhaps this minister was not certain of his own eternal destiny and was therefore unable to help me with what I needed to know. I questioned how this man could be put in charge of thousands of dying souls when he could not clearly point out the way to everlasting life. Didn't dying sinners need more than a "wait and find out" answer?

I continued reading the Bible without receiving any understanding or blessing from it, and I continued to pray. Then, one day, I came upon Matthew 7:7: *"Ask, and it shall be given you; seek, and ye shall find; knock, and it shall be opened unto you."* This scripture stood out as if it had been written in the sky. I said, "God, if there's ever been a German who's asking, who's seeking, and who's knocking, it is I. If you are real, if Your Son, Jesus, is real, I will find what I am looking for. If I don't find what I am looking for, then all I experienced is not real; it is only a figment of my imagination, and the Bible is not true." Since Jesus said to seek and I would find, I fully expected Him to hold up His part of the deal. After all, I had nowhere else to turn for such answers.

As I continued my daily Bible reading, I came upon another verse that made sense to me, and of all places, I found it in the book of Revelation. I couldn't help but believe that Jesus was actually beginning to lead me in my search for truth, as I read the words of Revelation 3:20: *"Behold, I stand at the door, and knock: if any man hear my voice, and open the door, I will come in to him, and sup with him, and he with me."* I realized at that moment that Jesus Christ was standing at the door of my heart and He wanted to come into my life. Indeed, I wanted Him to come in, but I just didn't know yet how to open that door.

CHAPTER TEN

New Life in England

After six months of searching for God, I received an invitation to visit my Jewish grandfather in England for a couple of weeks. The day before I was to leave to return to Germany, where I would finish up my last semester of high school, I received a postcard with a picture of a castle and an invitation to attend a Bible conference in that castle. It was signed by evangelist Major Ian Thomas. I had never heard of the castle or the evangelist, and to this day I have no idea who gave my name to this ministry or how I was brought to the beginning of the greatest adventure of my life.

Since I did not really like school, and because I was searching for life everlasting, I wrote a postcard to my teacher, Herr Nicolai, and told him I was sorry to be late returning to school, but in compensation for being late I offered to give a speech in English upon my return. I signed it, Reimar Schultze, and sent it off.

Schools in Germany were extremely strict at that time, and students had to work hard and pass many examinations just to get into high school, let alone graduate. During those four years of high school, the students in the bottom third of the class academically usually dropped out. We had to be punctual, obedient to the teacher, and respectful of all authority. Arriving a day late for the beginning of my final semester of high school could have resulted in serious punishment for me, even expulsion from school altogether.

Therefore, when I wrote that note, I knew I was risking my future education. But I was on a quest to find God, and that was more important to me than anything else in the world.

As I arrived at that beautiful old castle in northern England, dozens of young people from all over Europe were already gathered in a large banquet hall, where tea was being served. It was an impressive room, with beautiful chandeliers and ornate stained glass windows that filtered in the sunlight. Looking out through one of the windows I saw meticulously mown, lush green meadows, and gardens with all sorts of lovely flowers. For a boy raised in a world of destruction, it seemed like a dream. There, in that lovely banquet hall, I felt the same presence of God that I had experienced in the forest in Germany. Immediately, I began to ask the young people in attendance to help me get saved. Two Germans tried but failed to make the plan of salvation clear to me. Then one of them said, "Why don't we send you to Major Ian Thomas? He happens to be in today."

So I ended up in the plush, comfortably snug little English office of Major Thomas, who showed me the way to God. He helped me understand that I was a sinner, with which I wholeheartedly agreed. Romans 3:23 says, *"For all have sinned, and come short of the glory of God."* He showed me that the consequence of sin is death, which is separation from God, for Romans 6:23 says that, *"the wages of sin is death."* But it continues, *"but the gift of God is eternal life through Jesus Christ our Lord."* Oh, yes, I knew that because of my sin I was separated from God, and I wanted to trade my spiritual death for spiritual life through Jesus. I wanted fellowship with Him.

Major Thomas told me that Jesus had died on the cross for me, taking the penalty of my sin upon Himself. He explained that by accepting Jesus' death as a punishment for my sins and accepting His life as my own, I could become a new creature in Him. He then took me to 1 John 1:9, which says, *"If we confess our sins, he is faithful and just to forgive us our sins, and to cleanse us from all unrighteousness."* Major Thomas then asked if I was willing to confess my sins, and explained that if I would, Jesus would forgive me and cleanse me through His precious blood. Upon hearing that, I was so amazed and overwhelmed that my spiritual eyes must have been as large as saucers.

Next, Major Thomas took me to Revelation 3:20, the same verse I had come upon in my own personal study. *"Behold, I stand at the door, and knock: if any man hear my voice, and open the door, I will come in to him, and will sup with him, and he with me."* He read the verse aloud and then asked me if I felt the Lord Jesus was knocking on the door of my heart. I said, "Yes, indeed. I know He is here, waiting to come into my life." Then he showed me Romans 10:9, which says, *"That if thou shalt confess with thy mouth the Lord Jesus, and shalt believe in thine heart that God hath raised him from the dead, thou shalt be saved."* The Major asked if I was willing to confess Jesus with my mouth, and I said I was. He then asked if the Bible said that he who confesses *will* be saved, or *might* be saved, and I replied that it says he *will* be saved, meaning that it would actually happen. And then he asked if I would repeat the following prayer after him, which I did.

"Dear Lord Jesus, please forgive me my sins. I'm so sorry that I have failed you. But, Lord Jesus, I now want to ask you to come into my heart to live within me, and I want to live for you. I receive you, Lord Jesus, into my heart now, and I thank you for coming in. Amen."

After I prayed that prayer, I felt the presence of the living God enter into my soul and body. I was born a new creature in Christ. Major Thomas looked at me and asked, "Has Jesus come in?" I replied with satisfaction, "He certainly has." That was the beginning of my Christian life. It made me a missionary, for everyone who has Christ in his life is a missionary, and everyone without Christ in his life is a mission field.

After I got off my knees in the Major's office, I was a different man. I was saved in the afternoon, and that evening I attended the first church service in which I truly felt the presence of the Lord. The young people were singing about the risen savior who was alive today. Oh, glory to His holy name! I knew—I *knew* that I knew—that Jesus was alive! I knew that He had risen from the dead. I knew that He was dwelling within me, and I in Him.

Because of the overflow of young people in the castle at the time, I was assigned to sleep above the horse stable in the hay. I will never forget the joy I felt as I climbed into that hayloft, clutching my suitcase in one hand and grabbing the ladder with the other. They could have assigned me a pigpen for the night, and I would have been content. With Jesus in our hearts, we can be content anywhere and in any circumstance. Indeed, this overcoming joy within my heart has never left me, nor has it changed or diminished in the last fifty-plus years.

When I awoke the next morning, however, I was supposed to give my testimony to the other young people in attendance. Being terribly shy, I decided instead to take an early train back to Germany. I have always regretted that I failed to witness for the Lord at that time. When we receive the Lord Jesus, we need to tell someone immediately, but I was too fearful to do so. I asked the Lord to forgive me, and I know He did; in fact, He gave me a chance to return to that same castle forty-five years later and to stand before 120 German young people to tell them what God began in my life on that very site so many years earlier. I also told them of the life of romance, thrills, and adventures I had experienced with my

Lord from that point forward.

Looking back on that experience, I realize now how inconsiderate I was to poor Major Thomas, who had graciously led me to the Lord and then had to get up early the next morning to take me back to the railway station because of my fear of speaking to crowds. His little car, however, just wouldn't start. The battery was dead, so he got out and cranked and cranked the engine until he was exhausted. Then, just when he was ready to give up all hope, the engine miraculously turned over and kicked in, and off we went. We traveled those narrow, winding roads of the rolling English countryside, driving on the left side of the road, hemmed in on both sides by stone walls that looked like they had been erected by the Romans over a thousand years before.

The journey back to Germany was a time of testing of my newfound faith. I was supposed to meet my grandfather Hans at the railroad station in Liverpool so he could give me money for food, but we missed each other. I went on to London, and as I arrived at Victoria Station, the main railroad station, I heard an announcement advising all travelers bound for the continent to spend the night in London because of a great storm in the English Channel. No one would be able to cross over, as all ferry travel to the continent was canceled.

I was stranded in a strange city, with only enough money to buy a cup of tea. As I sat down on a bench, I realized I had no choice but to trust God—and that, of course, is a very good place to be! Because of my extreme shyness and strong German accent, I was afraid to speak to anyone. The Germans had done much damage to the British during the war, especially to those in London, and I was considered by many Londoners to be "one of those people." And my looks certainly didn't help. I was tall and skinny, dressed in a jacket that was too tight for my shoulders, and pants that were too short and didn't match my jacket. In those days, as children grew and their clothes refused to grow with them and there was no money to replace those outgrown clothes, the children simply continued to wear them. Some were fortunate enough to inherit their older siblings' clothes, but the taller I grew, fewer hand-me-downs were available.

And so I sat, experiencing one of my first "waiting and trusting God" situations, when suddenly I saw a group of German young people coming through the railroad station. They all wore leather pants and little green hats with feathers, so I knew they were from some area of southern Germany. Without thinking, I jumped right into the middle of this group, standing out like a tall telephone pole, and began to move with them wherever they went. They were my safety, comfort, and protection. It was as if I had found a little island of my own country in the midst of a foreign land.

As they went through a checkpoint to catch the tube, or underground train, I went with them. We went from station to station under the streets of London. I did not know if we were going north, south, east, or west, but at least I had company. Eventually, the whole group exited and took the stairs up to a street somewhere in that great city.

My next memory is of standing in the hallway of the second floor of a white frame house somewhere in London. An old lady with white hair pointed to a little room and said, "This is your room." In that room was a bed and perhaps one or two other pieces of furniture. When I discovered there would be no charge for the room, I went in, lay down on the bed, and immediately fell asleep. The Scripture *Mutti* gave me at birth certainly came to bear here again: *For he shall give his angels charge over thee, to keep thee in all thy ways* (Psalm 91:11).

Sometime around dawn, I awoke and began to listen for a church clock to tell me the time, as I had no watch and did not want to miss the train to South Hampton, where I would board a ferry that would take me back to the continent. The problem was that I couldn't remember how I got from the underground station the previous day to that house, and I can't remember now how I got from the house back to Victoria Station. But somehow, the Lord Jesus Christ, in His great mercy, got me there on time.

I soon boarded the train, and from there I got onto a ferry that would take me across the English Channel to Holland. As we started out, I noticed it was still very stormy, and the boat listed heavily from left to right, back and forth. It was raining, and salt spray was blowing across the deck. Since I was a third-class passenger, I was not allowed to go inside, so I hung over the rail, feeling very, very seasick. With no money for food, I had not eaten for one and a half days. Many times, I tried to bring up food, but my stomach was empty. The greatest misery of seasickness is to have no way to relieve yourself. I've often thought that if my stomach had not been permanently attached, it might have ended up in the channel.

In the middle of all this misery, as I looked into the churning black waters and felt the cold spray from the waves, I met the devil head-on for the first time in my life. I had scarcely heard of the devil before, but I now recognized him immediately. Oh, yes, another new world—a dark, spiritual world—was opening up to me that day, and I realize now that if we aren't confronted by the devil very early in our Christian life, we may likely still be on the wrong side, and our conversion may not have been real. If we truly have been saved and then remain in Christ, we will be in frequent warfare against the powers of darkness (see Ephesians 6:12). There, in the midst of the roiling sea and my heaving stomach, the devil whispered to me, "How do you like your newfound faith?"

Without thinking, these words came out of my heart: "You old devil, even if I would go to hell, I would talk about Jesus until you spit me out of that place." It was there in the storm on the English Channel that I signed my marriage contract with God, for better or for worse, and I knew I would stay with my Jesus, no matter what.

Many people have said to me over the years, "Prove to me that there is a Christ. Prove to me that God loves me. Prove to me there is a devil."

"If you will just give up your rebellion," I tell them, "your sin, your criticism, your judgmental spirit, and ask the Lord to forgive you of your sins and to come into your life, He will give you all the proof you will ever need. But until you come to Jesus in humility, all the proofs that anyone could provide will never be enough for you."

That day, as I crossed the channel, I had all the proof I needed. I took out the reverse gear of my life, deciding never to backslide, never to quit attending church, never to stop reading the Bible, and never to miss praying in the morning. I decided to be true and faithful, and that going back was not an option. There was only one option for me, and that was to go forward. If I failed and faltered, I would ask the Lord to forgive me, and then I would continue moving forward. I am so glad I made that commitment as a teen. Now, more than fifty years later, by God's grace I can say that I have kept that commitment.

Have you removed the reverse gear from your life? If not, will you do it today? I promise you will never regret it, especially when you stand before the judgment seat of Christ. For then you will hear these wor ds of the Lord, *"Well done, good and faithful servant; ...enter thou into the joy of thy lord"* (Matthew 25:23).

After finally arriving back on the continent, I disembarked and then boarded the train that would take me to Hamburg.

Trains in Europe have compartments, and it is a very nice way to travel. The only other person in my compartment was a well-dressed, professional-looking Swedish gentleman. He soon took out an orange, and right away my gastric juices began to run. My mouth puckered, even as I told myself that if he asked me if I wanted some of his orange, I would say no the first time, out of politeness, but I would say yes the second time, because I was very, very hungry. It had now been two days since I had eaten, and I was also dehydrated. Of course, humans can endure a lot more than that, but growing young people can really tell when they miss a few meals.

Well, indeed, the Swede asked me if I would like some of his orange, and I said no, just as I'd planned. Unfortunately, he never asked again. By the time I got home to our little place in Bergedorf, I was so weak that it took both of my hands and all of my strength to turn the large key in the keyhole of our apartment. I immediately went to sleep, and as I recall, I did not awaken for about sixteen hours.

Once home, I did not want to fail in witnessing again, as I had in England, so I told my mother the next day, "*Mutti*, I have found the Lord Jesus Christ. I have received Him in my heart." But *Mutti* said nothing. She just wanted me to continue helping her wash the dishes, and so I did.

At that time, I was enrolled in the *Christlichen Pfadfinder*, the Christian Boy Scout movement of Germany. At the next meeting I told my superior, a pillar in the Lutheran church with a doctor's degree in pedagogy, "Doctor, I want you to know that I received the Lord Jesus Christ during my visit to England. Jesus is in my heart."

This doctor, whom I had considered a man of God, glared at me, as if fire were coming out of his eyes. His forehead turned red, and he said, "'Blasphemy! Blasphemy!'"

I had now received two responses to my testimony that Christ had come into my life. My mother said nothing, and this supposed believer called me a blasphemer. By the grace of God, I was neither offended nor shocked. I knew *Mutti* was very private about her faith, and I recognized this dear gentleman who called me a blasphemer came from a theological position that believed a holy God would never enter into a sinful man. He was not aware that Christianity is supernatural, that it is only by supernatural means that our hearts can be cleansed by the blood of Jesus, and that Christ can dwell in us and we in Him. Perhaps the man did not know that the phrase "in Christ" is used seventy-four times in the writings of the Apostle Paul, meaning that true Christians are *in* Christ and He is *in* us. Jesus said in John 15:5, *"I am the vine, ye are the branches: He that abideth in me and I in him, the same bringeth forth much fruit: for without me ye can do nothing."*

Certainly this church leader did not know that the blood of Jesus can cleanse us from all sin and keep us from all evil. Many people who go to church really do not know their Bibles, and it takes the precious Holy Spirit to illuminate God's Word to us. However, the Holy Spirit will not do so until we seek God with humility, brokenness, and a penitent heart. The Pharisees did not have such hearts; therefore, they never really understood the Scriptures, and they killed their long-awaited Messiah.

Following those two incidents, I thought nothing more of the whole matter until a few weeks later, when I was called to attend a council meeting of all the scout leaders of our city. There were perhaps fifteen to twenty "gray heads" sitting at the table, and here I was, a young fellow of sixteen. They talked for a while, and then the gentleman across from me said, "I want to see your scouting license." I gave it to him, and he said, "You'll never see it again." At that moment, I was excommunicated from the Christian Boy Scout movement of Germany because I confessed that Jesus Christ had come into my life.

This time I was not prepared for what occurred. I rode my bicycle back through the rubble to my apartment and went into a deep state of grief and shock that lasted several weeks, actually resulting in my hair graying a little, even at that young age. But the Lord did comfort me. Isn't it wonderful that the Lord allows us to share in His grief and sorrow over the hearts of men? Indeed we know that if we suffer with Him, we shall also reign with Him (see 2 Timothy 2:12).

After a week or two, I met a Christian who said he had started an underground Christian Boy Scout troop, and he asked if I would like to join him. I said I would, so we got together and worked with a few young people. Going underground meant we would be operating illegally, without a license, and if found we could be arrested.

We met in secret in a home and named this new group "Dietrich Bonhoeffer," after a courageous Lutheran pastor who took a stand against Adolf Hitler during World War II. Because of this stand, which included helping to compile plans for assassinating the *Führer*, Bonhoeffer eventually was hung by the Nazis. But while he was in prison, he wrote a number of letters and books, the most famous being *The Cost of Discipleship*, a book that has been used by God to strengthen and encourage many believers.

There are countless blessings in being a follower of Jesus, but there is also great cost. In fact, it will cost us everything to be His disciples. Therefore, Elvina M. Hall said, "Jesus paid it all, all to Him I owe." My experience with the Christian Boy Scouts was my first lesson in the cost of discipleship.

Jesus had to die on a cross to save us. We have to die on our cross to follow Him. Jesus said, *"If any man will come after me, let him deny himself, and take up his cross daily, and follow me"* (Luke 9:23).

It was evident that the Lord was with me despite the

set-backs, and soon I would meet a saint of God who would introduce me to the true family of God, the Church Universal, the invisible body of believers that spans the continents and the centuries. Meanwhile, I prayed daily and read my Bible faithfully, waiting for the Lord to show me what to do and where to go next.

CHAPTER ELEVEN
Faith Tested

After graduating from high school, I became a machinist's apprentice and worked in that program for about three years until our family emigrated to the United States. At the time, an apprentice's salary was about five cents per hour, just enough to buy the train tickets I needed to get to work and back, with a trifle left over.

When I started working at the factory, I was one of about eleven trainees, all of us sixteen years old. German teenage youth rebuilt Germany after World War II because many of their fathers had died in the war, and others had not returned from the Russian prison camps. At first, we were all assigned a workbench with a vise, as well as the following tools: a hacksaw, three files—rough, medium, and fine—various sheets of sandpaper, an emery cloth, a square, and a caliper. We were then told we had to create a perfect cube, square on every side, out of a thick iron rod. We all began to work at the same time, and it wasn't long before we had blisters on our hands, as the cubes got smaller and smaller in our effort to square them up on all six sides. During the process, several of the young apprentices became angry, feeling they were wasting their time on such a pointless assignment when they should be learning to run the machines, particularly the large turret lathe that sat in plain sight in the middle of the work area. As frustration mounted, some of them began shooting rubber bands at each other. One or two quit the job, while others worked haphazardly and halfheartedly on the cube project.

After about six weeks of this monotonous routine, the master craftsman called us all together and said, "Give me your cubes." Of course, by now they were rather small, and none of us had obtained the perfection we thought was expected of us. Each time we checked the cube against the square, we found at least one place where some light showed through between the square and the surface.

We fully expected the master craftsman to examine each cube and grade us accordingly. Instead, he collected our cubes and threw them into the scrap pile without even looking at them. "The test is over," he said. "How well you did with the cube is not the important thing. We were looking for character. We observed and watched every one of you every day to see how you worked—if you worked with diligence, with care, putting your heart into your work. We wanted to know what kind of material we had inside of you before we proceeded with the apprenticeship program. Also, we decided that the person with the best character would become the leader of the rest. That person is Mr. Schultze."

I'm glad *Mutti* had prepared me for this test, for it was surely her training that enabled me to do my best at a seemingly pointless job. What a reminder that was to me that we are never alone. Even when we think no one is watching, God's eyes are going to and fro across the earth, looking for someone who is faithful and can be entrusted with the treasures of His glorious kingdom. Had *Mutti* not scolded me so severely when I turned back in that rainstorm years earlier, I very well might not have passed this test. But as a result of *Mutti's* chastisement, I learned to do my best with whatever came my way, no matter how small the assignment. That lesson has paid off well on the blessing side.

Many parents fail to discipline their children adequately, choosing instead to spoil them. If they do discipline them, it is infrequent, inconsistent, or done in anger rather than love. The book of Proverbs, written by King Solomon, considered the wisest mortal man of the Bible, has these admonitions for parents: *"Foolishness is bound in the heart of a child; but the rod of correction shall drive it far from him"* (22:15); *"The rod and reproof give wisdom: but a child left to himself bringeth his mother to shame"* (29:15).

During the first year of my apprenticeship program I was without a church, as the church I had attended when I was with the scouts did not want me because of my testimony, and I assumed, rightly or wrongly, that the other churches would feel the same. Then one day, I answered the doorbell and came face to face with a young man who was nearly my height, with blond hair and blue eyes, who said, "I've just come from Copenhagen, and I heard that you are a Christian. I'd like to invite you to my church."

I never learned who in Copenhagen knew about me or my Christianity, because while we were in the camp up there and even while we were passing through Copenhagen, we had absolutely no contact with any Danish people, except for the time *Mutti* met a Danish pastor, and that had been seven years earlier. In any case, the young man's name was Helmut, and he invited me to come to his church. He said he would stop by to pick me up every Sunday morning. "I will take the train to your place, and then we will walk together to the railroad station. We will ride one train, transfer to another, then walk to the church, which is right behind the University of Hamburg."

And that is exactly what he did for me, every Sunday morning, Sunday evening, and Wednesday evening for about a year. Helmut never failed to stop by to pick me up. I believe every new convert needs someone like Helmut, a faithful encourager like Barnabas, a believer in and follower of Jesus, who took the new convert Saul of Tarsus (later known as the Apostle Paul) under his care: he looked after him, nourished him, encouraged him, and instructed him until Paul became a mighty man of God.

Oh, if every new convert could have just one person to look after him for one year, praying for him daily, picking him up (where appropriate) for church, and taking him back home on Sunday mornings, Sunday evenings, and for the midweek service. I easily could have found my own way to that church after the first time, but Helmut insisted he would do that for me, and I'm so glad he did.

How many converts has the church lost for lack of a Barnabas? We have great joy when new people come to church, and we give them special attention; but within a few weeks, that attention fades away, and the converts get tangled up in some bush by the wayside. We either don't see them again, or they begin to develop bad habits, like skipping a service here and there, and they fail to become true disciples of the Lord Jesus Christ. New converts are so weak, especially if they have been spoiled in the early years of their lives. They need to be yoked with strong Christians for a while to learn how to pull through the hard places. Have you ever made a new convert your weekly responsibility for a whole year? If not, pray about doing so.

The church I attended with Helmut was a fellowship of between 200-300 believers, who met in a rented hotel room behind the university. During the services, four or five men sat on the platform; in the two years I attended, I never figured out which one was the pastor—perhaps some, or all of them. The services averaged between two to three hours in length, and consisted of one or more of those men sharing precious truths, remaining seated while they spoke. The services also included laymen's accounts of personal experiences with God, as well as corporate singing and prayers offered by several members of the congregation.

It was obvious the Holy Spirit was leading these services, because nobody was in a hurry to go home, and I never saw anyone glance at a watch. I remember thinking this must have been the way it was when Jesus was teaching in Galilee. When our Lord spoke, hours rolled by, and sometimes days. For example, Jesus had people with him for three days before He fed them miraculously with loaves and fishes.

In the average church today, many worshipers consider a one-hour service too long. They get fidgety and want to go home because the Holy Spirit is not leading and their souls are not being fed. The services are generally monotonous and predictable, with no surprises. When the Holy Spirit leads, every moment becomes a pleasant anticipation. In fact, I never saw a church bulletin with a printed program until I came to America.

In Hamburg, after the Sunday morning service ended around noon, I was invited to the home of one of the elders. Normally, there were eight to ten people at the dinner table, and while we ate, we talked about Jesus, His wonderful works, His great love and precious mercy. It was as if the church service had not ended but had simply been adjourned from the sanctuary to the elder's home. By mid-afternoon, I went back to my apartment, rested a little, and then Helmut picked me up for the evening service. That is the way I learned to keep the Sabbath Day holy. Sunday was entirely devoted to God. I spent the entire day resting and feeding on heavenly manna. Truly when God said, "keep the Sabbath day holy," he did mean the entire day, not just part of the morning.

The evening service was nearly as full as the morning service, though a bit shorter and nothing like services in America, where nearly half the congregation stays home.

Our midweek services were also well attended, but shorter because people had worked all day.

I hadn't attended the church long before I got involved in the young people's group. At the time, there was a certain area of our city where the government had cleared away the rubble and set up barracks for youth who had lost their parents. These were orphans who had no place to go, and whose behavior had become problematic. Social workers tried to help them with their grief and anger and bitterness, but they got nowhere. Finally, the city government asked our young people if we would be willing to go into this camp of despair to see what we could do. They offered us a thousand marks, a considerable amount of money at that time, and our youth leader began to prepare us for ministering to these children who had suffered so greatly.

When the youth leader announced the first preparatory meeting, about fifteen to twenty of us responded. Then he announced another meeting the next week, then another one the following week, and so on for several weeks. Fewer people came each week, until attendance had dwindled to a handful. Many were willing to go at first, but they were not willing to be engaged in a long period of preparation to enter this dire mission field. At last, there were only two young people left. One was a seminary student from a Baptist Theological school, and the other was me, an apprentice in a factory. With the leader, who also was a seminary student, there were three of us. That's when the leader said, "Now I believe we are ready to go into the barracks."

We had one barrack for meetings, where we set up games and chairs and tables for times of fellowship and for preaching the Word. After a day's work at the factory, I rode my bicycle forty-five minutes on Monday, Tuesday, Thursday, and Friday nights to get to the barrack, then came home late, running my bike lights as I rode through the city.

Wednesday and Sunday nights I was in church; Saturday was my only night at home.

On the average, we may have been in the barrack working with the youth from two to three hours each night. In the corner of a large room, a section was set aside, separated by curtains hung on wires. In that corner was an iron bed. The leaders told me that while they worked with the young people, playing games, sharing, befriending them, and then holding a meeting so they could present the gospel to them, they wanted me to go into that curtained-off area to pray. It was there that I really learned to pray—to pray hard, and to pray by faith. I prayed between one and two and a half hours at a time, on a concrete floor with my arms resting on the bed, interceding for lives to be changed.

When I began those prayer vigils, I had no idea how important it was to learn the discipline of prayer. But a few months after I came to the United States, one of the leaders wrote to tell me a great revival had broken out among the young people, and many of them had been saved. I believe, by the grace of God, that my prayers made some small contribution to this mighty work of God.

This was the first time in my Christian life that I actually recognized prayer being answered, though it didn't happen without much patience and persevering. A consistent prayer life is one of the marks of the victorious Christian. The Apostle Paul said in 1 Thessalonians, *"Pray without ceasing"* (5:17), and Jesus said *"that men ought always to pray, and not to faint"* (Luke 18:1). Men *ought always to pray.* What men? Did Jesus mean that *some* men should always pray...or did He mean *all* men, *all* believers?

Jesus said men should *always* pray and not faint. In other words, when the human spirit feels faint and wants to quit, we need to keep praying. When the feeling of faintness comes again, we may need to pray some more. The Bible teaches that prayer is life, and life is prayer. If we don't pray, we lose our connection with God. If we don't pray, we do not receive the spiritual virtues and strength that are essential for following Jesus each day, moment by moment. If we don't pray, we will not get the things God planned for us to receive, even before the foundation of the world.

This is why James said, *"ye have not because ye ask not"* (4:2). Had I not prayed for God to remove the bombings from my nightly dreams, I might have continued to be bombed until the end of my life. Had I not prayed with others for young people to be saved in Hamburg, they might not have been saved. If I do not pray each morning that God will help me with my work and help me to be at the right place at the right time with the right words, it will not happen. There are many definitions of prayer, but in this context, the best one may be that prayer is asking God to do things He otherwise might not do. Prayer, one man of God said, is ten times more important than anything else we can do.

Another thing I learned to do during this time was to witness. When I first worked at the factory and was learning to run the machines, I sang the great hymns of the church. I sang from the depths of my heart and with great energy, and in return I received strength to keep the faith. The machines were too noisy for others to hear the words, but they certainly knew what I was singing about and to whom. During the course of our apprenticeship, we worked six days a week, for a total of forty-eight hours. I was the only Christian in that factory of about 100 men, so I had quite a mission field.

As part of our apprenticeship program we spent one day each week in trade school, where we learned blueprints, metallurgy, economics, and other subjects. One day my professor said to me in the middle of class, "Herr Schultze, you are the only Christian in this classroom. Would you be willing to tell us about your Christianity next week?" I had never said a word in that class. No one ever did; we simply listened to the professor. But somehow he knew I was a Christian—the only one in the class.

The following week, I gave my first religious talk since finding the Lord Jesus. I went to the blackboard and drew a large circle on it and said, "This circle represents your life. If Jesus Christ is in this circle, He is in your life, and you are a Christian. If He's outside of the circle of your life, then you are not a Christian."

Then, using Revelation 3:20 as my reference, I told them what they needed to do to receive the Lord Jesus into their hearts. I told them if they would do what the scripture said and invite Jesus into their hearts, they would know that Jesus Christ is alive and has risen from the dead. I said that would be the empirical evidence by which they would know that Christ was in their hearts. After I made my brief presentation, the professor said, "I need to ponder these things for a while."

While I was still working in the factory, Major Ian Thomas came to visit Hamburg to minister to youth in a number of churches. One night he stayed with our family, and the following day I heard him speak the most remarkable words imaginable. We were driving down the *Autobahn* (highway) in heavy fog, able to see nothing more than the center line of the highway in front of us. Suddenly he told me that the Lord wanted us to go to a certain village the next day. I immediately gasped in my soul. The Lord was telling Ian what to do? God was speaking to a mortal man, who was sitting next to me? Fantastic! Oh, I thought, if God would speak to me just once, it would be one of the most wonderful things that could happen! Little did I imagine that through the coming years the Lord would speak to me, not once but thousands of times, to direct my ways.

I had been born again, I was learning to pray and witness,

and now my next great lessons on my journey of faith were to be learned in America.

CHAPTER TWELVE

The Cigar Box

While I was working as a machinist's apprentice in Hamburg and trying to win young people to Jesus in the evenings, something wonderful happened in a sleepy little Midwestern town on the other side of the Atlantic Ocean. Jean Skaife, a young, newly married, slender brunette, who lived in Wisconsin, was asked by her pastor to do something she didn't particularly want to do. Following is Jean's account of the results of her acceptance of her pastor's request and of how a cigar box connected her with the Schultze family, so many miles away.

*****

My story goes back to the mid-1940s, when I was a young woman in my twenties, and I was asked by my pastor if I would teach a Sunday school class for nine-year-old boys. At the time, I had never taught Sunday school. In fact, Sunday school was not one of the high points of my life. And yet the minister had said, "We have a need." Then he handed me the teacher's manual. I took it, wondering what I was going to say to all those kids, but I agreed to give it a try. I soon found myself telling them stories from the Bible about the Jewish people and their history.

Then one day, in the back of the manual, I saw an article about the people in Hamburg, Germany, refugees who had returned from exile to the Jerusalem Church in Hamburg and needed any help we could give them. They needed little things, like pins, needles, combs, and soap—things the church could hand out to these refugees as they came home.

I decided to tell this story to the kids, as I thought they might be interested, and we could make a project out of it. So I told them this was a modern-day story of the Jewish people, not the ancient history I had been telling them. I don't think they realized the war was just over and the people were in great need. But we talked about it, and I asked them what they were going to do.

We soon had a project going, and the class gathered things together to make a small package that would fit into a cigar box. They brought pins, combs, pencils, and other small items, wrapped them in the package, and sent off the cigar box to the man at the Jerusalem Church who had written the ad asking for help.

A few months went by with no word. Of course, packages weren't sent by air in those days, so it took quite a while for our cigar box to arrive in Hamburg. Eventually, a letter came from a woman at the Jerusalem Church. Her name was Sister Caroline Eisner, and it was her job to reach out to the returning refugees. She wrote, "I have a family that I think I'd like to give the little cigar box to." The family's last name was Schultze.

The kids were so excited to get that reply, and we soon struck up a correspondence with Sister Eisner and the Schultze family. The oldest son, Eckart, did most of the writing. He sent beautiful handmade Christmas cards and notes, which I kept and which have become more and more precious to me over the years.

Soon I moved from my small town to Waukesha, Wisconsin, and told the story of the cigar box to my neighbor. I was rather excited about having made the connection with the family in Germany, and also about how pleased the Sunday school kids were regarding their correspondence with the Schultzes.

Then, one day in 1949, my neighbor told me her Presbyterian minister, Rev. Young, was going to Germany on a tour of various churches. I don't know what possessed me to think that I, a stranger, could go to this big church, walk into the pastor's office, and hand him a name and address in Hamburg, but that's exactly what I did. I know now how difficult it is to look up people in foreign countries, but at the time it never occurred to me how great a favor I was asking. In fact, even as Rev. Young put the address in his pocket, he told me he doubted anything would come of it.

Well, that jacket just "happened" to go to Europe with him. The tour began in Norway, Sweden, and Denmark, but when the group got to Hamburg, the bus broke down. No one in the group had any contact with any churches there at the time, but then Rev. Young remembered the address in his pocket.

He soon located Sister Caroline Eisner and found she was only a few blocks away from where the tour group was staying. In fact, through my correspondence, she had known about Rev. Young's coming to Europe, and she was quite pleased to hear from him. She came to speak to the tour group, and they were so impressed with the work she was doing that they collected all the extra things they had with them—soap, candy, and other practical items—and gave them to Sister Caroline for the Schultze family.

Soon after Rev. Young returned to Waukesha, my neighbor rushed over one Sunday morning to convince me to go to church with her because the pastor was going to talk about his trip and how I was connected with it. I agreed to go, and was fascinated as I sat and listened to Rev. Young give his three-point sermon about the three memorable people he had met on his European tour. One of those three people was Sister Caroline, with her spirit of service to God's family. Included in that portion of his sermon was the story about my Sunday school class and the Schultze family. I was moved to tears as I listened to him recount his meeting with Sister Caroline and then tell the story about the cigar box that had united people on opposite sides of the ocean.

After church, Rev. Young stopped me at the door and told me he had a gift for me from Sister Caroline. It was a little bookmark, a metal cutout of the Jerusalem Church, with a velvet ribbon attached to it. Rev. Young then told me if I ever got a chance to go to Europe, I really should meet Sister Caroline.

As my husband and I returned home that day, I distinctly remember saying, "I'm going to go to Europe and meet Sister Caroline." I had no idea how that would happen because we certainly didn't have that kind of money. But I began to work at the Waukesha Lime and Stone Quarry office, and by 1950, I had accumulated the needed funds, and so I set sail across the Atlantic, headed for Hamburg.

It was from that ship's deck that I first beheld the ravages of war, still severe after four years. I had arrived in a city that was completely torn apart, with entire blocks leveled. The Jerusalem Church also had been bombed, but they were doing a great job of repairing it. There was a hospital connected with the church; Sister Caroline put me up in one of the hospital rooms, and then took me around to view her work and ministry firsthand. One day, we went to the orphanage and took the children on a picnic. Another day, when we were returning from the docks, she said we had to stop and pick up a little cake because she had invited the Schultze family to tea.

What an experience! I was so excited to have the opportunity to finally meet this family. I don't know how much they remember of that day, but I remember Renate, with her long blonde pigtails, accompanied by two of her three brothers, Reimar and Wolfram. The children didn't say much, leaving their mother to do most of the talking. Toward the end of our visit, she asked me if I would find someone to take in her oldest son, Eckart, who was sixteen at the time and had chosen not to accompany the rest of the family when they came to meet me. She told me she had relatives in Argentina, but she really wanted her children to go to America. I didn't think it could be done, but I told her I'd try.

When I got home, I went to see Rev. Young and told him how thrilled I had been to meet Sister Caroline and the Schultze family, and how close I had become to Sister Caroline. Rev. Young asked me to speak to his college class about my trip, and then, a few days later, he called and offered me a job as his church secretary.

After I had worked there for a while, I told the church Session (governing board) that I knew of a young man in Germany who needed a sponsor to come to America, assuring them he had a trade and spoke English. Rev. Young was very much in favor of it, but the Session declined, explaining they had experienced some disappointments working with refugees in the past and didn't want to have any more to do with them.

I was so angry that I went home in tears. I talked with my husband, Charlie, about it, and he suggested that we, as a family, could sponsor Eckart. A number of church people thought we were crazy to take on so much because we would be responsible for Eckart until he was twenty-five. But we moved ahead, and the next thing I knew, I was in Milwaukee signing papers for the oldest Schultze brother to come and live with us. When he arrived in 1953, I was expecting a baby, so in a very short period of time I became the "mother" to both a nineteen-year-old "son" and a baby.

Eckart was very resourceful, even managing to get himself from the train station to our house in the country. He quickly explained that the reason he had not come to meet me in Hamburg was that, as a sixteen-year-old, he thought he had better things to do than have tea with someone he didn't even know.

Eckart stayed with us for awhile, and then moved to the YMCA in Milwaukee to be near his machinist job. Within a year, he sent for his sister Renate and then the two of them got a Lutheran church in Milwaukee to sponsor the rest of the family. Within a matter of a few years, every one of the Schultzes received a university degree, even the mother, who quickly procured a job teaching French and German in Milwaukee.

I am so pleased that I have lived long enough to see the outcome of the story. I agreed to take care of that Sunday school class when I had no idea how I was going to do it, but I am so thankful that I did. I praise and thank the Lord for having brought me to this point in my life and giving me the honor of relating this story. Except for the Lord, I would not be here to tell it.

*****

Isn't that an amazing story? There I was, employed in a factory in Hamburg, and God was working things out to bring my family and me to this country. None of this was our doing; it was the Lord's work. Perhaps the Lord has something marvelous in preparation for you right now, whether near to you or thousands of miles away, and He will bring you to it in His perfect timing, for He has promised in His Word that *"The steps of a good man are ordered by the LORD"* (Psalm 37:23).

CHAPTER THIRTEEN
Coming to America

I will never forget the cake and tea we shared with Jean Skaife in that little apartment in Hamburg so many years ago. We children were very unsophisticated and shy and thought little would come of that brief visit with the nice lady from America, but we were wrong. What began in the late 1940s as a step of obedience by a young woman agreeing to teach a Sunday school class of nine-year-olds ultimately impacted more lives than anyone involved could ever have imagined. So many Christians, when asked to serve in their church and meet a need, refuse. They say, "I am not interested"; "I don't have the time"; "I don't have the gifts." What do they miss when they refuse to meet a need, and what does the world miss when the dear people of God decline to make a sacrifice? Jean responded to her pastor's request by saying, "Sunday school teaching is not my interest, but yes, I'll do it to meet a need." Jean felt inexperienced and unqualified to take on this particular task, just as we all do when asked to meet certain needs that don't fall into our areas of expertise, but God used her willingness in a mighty way.

Jean Skaife had no idea that forty-five years after she took on a job for the sole purpose of meeting a need in her church, one of the many results would be that millions would hear the gospel preached in China, India, Japan, Europe, and

Indonesia. She did not know that Bible studies, born out of the lessons of one of those bashful Schultze boys in Hamburg, would one day be taught in Siberia, Moscow, Latvia, Africa, and the Far East, where people would find Christ and be established in their faith. And all these wonderful things that God has called and allowed me to do are just the beginning. Many others will go forth as a result of these teachings, which are, in large part, a result of one woman's obedience to fill a need.

As mentioned previously, soon after Jean's watershed visit to Hamburg, our family came to the United States in three stages: first, Eckart; one year later, Renate; *Mutti*, Wolfram, and I the following year. We arrived as "displaced persons," meaning we had been forced to relocate during the war, and we were politically and medically processed. My mother, Wolfram, and I came over on a DC 6, a four-engine, propeller-driven aircraft, operated by the Flying Tiger Freightliner. I was nineteen, and none of us had ever been to an airport, let alone ridden on a plane. As we boarded this huge, gray monster, the day was overcast and my emotions were in turmoil, bouncing back and forth between fear and hope. I was leaving my dear Christian friends with whom I had worshipped and prayed so often. Would I find such people in the new country? Everything familiar was being left behind, and yet, the thought of America, the great land of opportunity, intrigued and inspired me.

This was the fourth time we had been forced to abandon all our belongings, except what we could carry on our backs and the little bit of luggage we were allowed to bring along (though *Mutti* did manage to find a way to ship her treadle sewing machine). Since we had no money to take with us on our trip to a new country, *Mutti* insisted we put on as much clothing as possible so we wouldn't have to purchase any when we arrived. So, even though it was July and the temperature was warm, I donned an undershirt, a shirt, a sweater, a jacket, and finally a winter coat. The plane was not pressurized, so we could not fly much higher than 12,000 feet above sea level, and it was equipped with uncomfortable military seats. On top of that, directly across from me sat an old lady, perhaps in her eighties, thin, pale, white with fear, and airsick. It would be quite a trip!

As we flew out of Hamburg and made our way westward, one of the four engines of the aircraft failed, and we had to land in Paris and wait several hours for repairs. Our next stop was for refueling in the Azores Islands. Because of the weather conditions, sometimes the plane had to fly above the normally assigned, comfortable altitude for unpressurized aircraft, and did it ever hurt our ears! Yet, we were all happy, and the excitement built with every mile that brought us closer to the "land of the free."

Finally, we landed at Idyllwild International Airport, now Kennedy International. It was July 19, 1955, the hottest day of that entire year in the east and central United States. The humidity seemed unbearable, and oh, how we sweated with all our extra layers of clothing! Finally, after several hours of making our way through Customs, we boarded a train to go to Milwaukee, where we would live for the next several years.

First Impressions

My first impression of America was that the people were very casual compared to the Germans. They were also very friendly and open, keeping little to themselves. It was quite common in Germany, when riding the crowded trains, not to hear a single person talk for five, ten, or even twenty minutes. In America it seemed like everyone talked to everyone else nearly all the time. People in our new homeland were comfortable being free because they had always been free.

But by 1955, even ten years after the war, Germans were still close-mouthed from fear of speaking openly; they were also traumatized by the terrible war experiences and the humility of defeat. It was very rare, therefore, to see a smile on anyone's face in the land we had left behind.

So many changes assaulted my senses in this new land. One of the first things I noticed was that the cities were not especially clean. In Hamburg, all the glass panes in the railroad station dome had been shattered and were now missing, allowing rain and snow to pour down on everyone. For years after the war, trains traveled between endless piles of rubble where passengers' loved ones had met their death, continually reminding the survivors of their losses. But by the time I left Germany, the rubble on the streets had been cleared away, and the streets and sidewalks were kept clear and clean. No shopkeeper or homeowner ever allowed trash to remain in front of his building, as everyone owned and knew how to use a broom. But in America, people threw their trash everywhere.

Another thing that struck me was the abundance of automobiles—and they were all so big! But what disturbed me the most, cutting me to my very heart, was the clothing style of the women.

Let me insert an explanation here. Jesus said in the Sermon on the Mount that if a man looks at a woman to lust after her, he has already committed adultery in his heart. Men have to be careful not to take a second look, but why on earth would a Christian woman dress in such a way to entice men to take that second look? Why do American women believe the world's shabby definition of beauty that focuses only on the outward appearance?

So many have fallen for the devilish lie that in order to be attractive, they must be "sexy." As a result they are enslaved to ungodly standards and encourage men to sin. God cannot be pleased with this.

Godly women will dress to please Jesus, not to entice men. Let me challenge you, dear lady, to develop your inner beauty and loveliness. And meanwhile, find new ways to be fashionable and modest at the same time.

When I arrived in the United States, I had never seen a woman wearing shorts. German women were still wearing skirts, and longer ones at that. I thought it strange and unbecoming to see even middle-aged and older women so uncovered. And cheerleaders at ball games with their skimpy skirts were quite a shock.

Americans simply have no idea what it does to people from foreign lands who come here and see the immodesty in our schools and colleges, on our streets and our television screens. In most countries of the world, women will not even wear tight garments that accent the curves of their bodies. In other words, women dress in such a way so as not to lead men into temptations. Again, godly women will dress to please Jesus, not to entice men to lust after them. It is important that all of us, especially women, remember that Jesus' wedding feast is our goal, and it is before Him that we must all stand to give an account on the last day.

In the same way we consider the Arab world to be Islamic, so the Arabs consider Americans to be Christian. By observation, they associate Christianity with nakedness, not realizing that Jesus has nothing to do with such exposure.

The lyrics to "Keep Thyself Pure," one of my favorite songs, expresses my feelings on the matter:

Keep thyself pure! Thrice blessed He
Whose heart from taint of sin is free.
His feet shall stand where saints have trod,
He with rapt eyes shall see his God.
Oh Holy Spirit, keep us pure.
Grant us Thy strength when sins allure.
Our bodies are Thy temple, Lord;
Be Thou in tho't and act adored. Amen.[1]

Upon our arrival in the United States, my ears were assaulted by many new expressions, and I soon learned that in order to understand what was being said, I would have to grasp the meaning of those expressions. For example, in my native land I never heard anyone say, "Take it easy." Taking it easy was for those who were too sick or too old to do anything else; young people were to be ambitious, industrious, and hard working. To "take it easy" in Germany was to lose one's job and self respect—it was like a sin, and was associated with laziness and indifference.

Another expression I had to get used to was "I'm so glad to see you." In Germany, at least at that time, nobody ever said they were glad to see someone unless they already knew that person well. When someone in America first spoke those words to me, I was tempted to ask, "What makes you say you are so glad to see me? You don't know a thing about me. If you would really find out about me, you may find that my convictions run entirely contrary to yours." However, I soon learned this was just an expression of politeness and wasn't supposed to mean anything beyond that.

There is something about living in the American culture that causes us to say things we don't really mean. Shortly after I arrived in Kokomo, Indiana, a middle-aged lady said to me, "I'd like to see you sometime, Pastor." I immediately took out a piece of paper and said, "I can see you next Tuesday afternoon at 2 P.M." The look on her face registered her shock. She hadn't really meant what she said, but I took her at her word and put down a day and an hour to visit with her. When she came to meet with me on Tuesday afternoon, she was discouraged and perplexed, but when she left, she radiated so much joy about Jesus that for weeks after, her fellow worker on the assembly line remarked about the divine smile upon her face. During our meeting, this dear lady had had a new experience with the Lord, and she was glad I had taken her at her word and set an appointment on the spot.

Almost all cultures have aspects that are good, as well as aspects that are not good and need to be changed. How do we know whether certain cultural behaviors or expressions are good or not? We know by the Word of God that good culture comes out of the Judeo-Christian ethic. For example, the Judeo-Christian ethic tells us that when we say something, we ought to mean it. We are to say what we mean and mean what we say. Did Jesus ever say something He did not mean? Or where in the Old Testament do you find God the Father saying something He did not mean? What would it be like to have a god whose word was not 100 percent reliable? If that were the case, we could not stand on a single promise in the Bible; the Scriptures would be worthless. Therefore, aren't we Christians worthless if our words are not reliable?

And yet we are guilty of that very thing. We sing "Holy, Holy, Holy" in our churches, despite having no intention of being holy. We sing "I Surrender All," while holding on to what we have and grasping for more. We sing "Jesus Is All the World to Me," while we can't even come up with a tithe on a regular basis. We sing "Sweet Hour of Prayer," while most of us have never spent thirty minutes in prayer. We sing "I Love to Tell the Story," while in reality we are too ashamed to speak of Jesus at work, at school, or in the office. We sing "Oh, For a Thousand Tongues to Sing My Great Redeemer's Praise," while we have more complaints coming out of our mouths than praises to God. Too many of us are like actors on a stage; we have a difficult time being real. If we are genuine Christians, then we say what we mean and we mean what we say.

Despite these negatives, America is one of the greatest countries in the world; it is inconceivable to think of a world without the U.S.A. Every time there is a flood, a hurricane, an earthquake, a tornado, or any kind of natural disaster

anywhere in the world, America is there to help. Many
nations drag their feet when it comes to offering assistance,
and some refuse to give at all, but not so with America. I
believe what is written on the Statue of Liberty is of divine
origin:

"Give me your tired, your poor,
Your huddled masses yearning to breathe free,
The wretched refuse of your teeming shore.
Send these, the homeless, tempest-tossed to me,
I lift my lamp beside the golden door!"[2]

Americans cherish their freedom. Indeed, America was
founded by men who came seeking freedom. This country's
drive and desire that all men in the world be free runs deep
in America's blood. Throughout the years, the United States
has sacrificed thousands of young lives on the battlefields of
the world to make this dream of freedom possible for other
nations.

America believes in forgiveness and reconciliation.
America knows how to forget the pain and disappointment
of the past and get on with life. America is forward-looking,
innovative, and adventuresome, and it has a unique drive to
do everything with a lot of fanfare and gusto. America is also
impatient and wants everything done fast. We drive fast, we
eat fast, we work fast, and we think way too fast.

I'm thoroughly convinced the U.S. has a divine mandate
to be a leader of the world. America is the only country
that has consistently and strongly stood by God's covenant
people, the people of Israel. America was the first country to
recognize Israel in 1948, and, although at times it has pressed
Israel too hard, most often it has been there to defend that
tiny nation. This pleases God, for God said to Abraham in
Genesis 12:3, "*And I will bless them that bless thee, and curse
him that curseth thee: and in thee shall all families of the*

earth be blessed." Because America has stood with the sons
of Abraham, God has stood with America. As a result, even
the newest immigrants can sing:
"America! America!
God shed His grace on thee,
And crown thy good with brotherhood
from sea to shining sea!"[3]

Becoming All Things to All Men

I came to this country of freedom after having seen and
experienced much hunger, poverty, and destruction, so it
was difficult at first to believe that anyone could be a sincere
Christian and drive a big automobile. Also, during my first
years here, I had a hard time believing a person could be a
serious follower of Jesus if he did not eat everything on his
plate, simply because I knew there were millions of people in
the world who were starving. It is easy to see how much our
childhood experiences, our culture, and other influences mold
our thinking and establish our value systems. And though
these values may be noble, they do not necessarily reflect the
true "spirit of Christ," which I now know can fit in as easily
with the poorest of the poor as with the richest of the rich.

Many communists see Jesus as a poor radical
revolutionary. People from other cultures and ideologies see
Him as a capitalist, teaching a prosperity theology. So many
dedicated, wonderful Christians from India, Africa, and other
underdeveloped countries can be harsh and condemning of
our American way. They say if we would share more with
them and live more like them, many souls could be saved.
They have fallen into the trap of equating spirituality with
living in near poverty. Such an attitude does not correspond
with the teaching or life of the Lord Jesus Christ. The fact is
that the poor have nothing to give to the poor. Hence, only
rarely has God called a man to poverty.

The Lord is calling all of us Christians to frugality, as that is the proper use of goods to God's glory. Yet, this call to frugality must never come near to trumpeting the glories of poverty. Rather, everything in the Christian realm must be related to love, and the Apostle Paul said that we can give all our money to feed the poor, yet if we do not have love, we are nothing. We can therefore be just as spiritual when we are rich as when we are poor. Some of the most spiritual men in the Bible were rich. Others who had little were just as spiritual. But because all of them had God, all of them were great givers. All of them knew that the more we give, the more we receive. There is a divine mystery in all this that defies reason. If you give 10% of your money or substance to the Lord, your remaining 90% will go further than if you had kept 100%. Jesus said, *"Give, and it shall be given unto you"* (Luke 6:38). When you stop giving you start dying.

It was actually my older brother, Eckart, who awakened me to my distorted views on big Chevrolet automobiles and throwing uneaten food in the garbage can. Eckart had already been in this country two years and had adjusted, but *Mutti*, Renate, Wolfram, and I had just arrived and were still working our way through the culture shock. *Mutti's* meals were always simple, frugal, and relatively healthy. But on one particular Sunday, Eckart put a little too much on his plate. In other words, as the saying goes, his eyes were too big for his stomach. So when he was full, he refused to eat any more. This, in *Mutti's* careful eyes, was nearly a mortal sin. She went on and on, chastising Eckart for wasting food while millions were going hungry. Eckart took it for a while, until finally he had enough. He exploded into *Mutti's* face— which is a bit like a private standing up to a general—and said, "I've had enough of this. I'd rather throw this waste into the garbage can than to have it hang around my hips." *Mutti* was shocked by his outburst, but she never attacked him on the subject again. Renate, Wolfram, and I agreed heartily with Eckart, though silently, and made a great cultural adjustment on the spot.

I must admit, though, that I still sense an uncomfortable nagging when I see a piece of bread on the pavement, especially when someone steps on it, almost as if they were stepping on me. I know it is just a case of matter stepping on matter, atom upon atom—so my mind tells me—but I still remember what it's like to be hungry and how grateful I would have been at the time for that piece of bread on the pavement.

It is natural, when we visit another country, to suffer some kind of culture shock. However, if we live in that country and refuse to make the necessary adjustments, we will continue to be foreigners in that new land; we may as well go back to where we came from. Our family learned to love our new country as much as we loved the old one, and we became willing to defend America, just as we were willing to defend Germany. Immigrants must adapt and learn the new language, no matter how difficult. But as Christians, we must not adopt the sinful ways, traditions, or practices of our new country. Our first obligation is always to Jesus, and we must keep ourselves pure in His sight.

While I began my life in this country as a somewhat isolated, weird radical, with the heavy burden of my cultural upbringing on my back, I slowly began to shed that burden piece by piece, and to connect more and more with the people around me. I became less stressed, more relaxed and focused. I stopped majoring in minor truths and minoring in major truths, learning instead to become all things to all men. Slowly, more love and understanding began to flow between my fellow men and myself.

If we do God's will, we are in His kingdom. And His will for us, although the same for everyone in certain areas, is different for each of us in other areas. God has a peculiar calling upon each of us, and that includes everything from our walk with Him to the kind of house we live in and the type of transportation we use. We must let God be God— without exception. By letting God be God, Abraham became rich materially. By letting God be God, Paul became poor materially. But both lived by faith. Both found God sufficient for all their needs. Both were content with what they had, and both will be found at the throne of the triune God forever.

God can meet the needs of a man of faith as easily in Africa and India as in the United States of America, whether in a storm, a fiery furnace, or a lion's den. He will be there for all His children everywhere in the world, in all kinds of circumstances. He is not one God in India, another in Africa, and another in Canada. Yet we in America, who have so much more than our brothers and sisters in underdeveloped countries, must be willing to share our blessings as Paul admonishes us to do in I Timothy 6:17-18, *"Charge them that are rich in this world, that they be not highminded; nor trust in uncertain riches, but in the living God, who giveth us richly all things to enjoy; That they do good, that they be rich in good works, ready to distribute, willing to communicate."* On the other hand, the poor must learn to exercise faith in God and not become beggars to the rich.

A great man of faith, George Müller of England, made a commitment at the beginning of his orphanage ministry never to ask anyone for a penny. He wanted to have what God had for him and not be limited to what man could or would give. He put his whole ministry entirely into the hands of his Heavenly Father. Eventually, he housed and fed over 2,000 orphans without asking a penny of anyone or sending out a letter expressing a need. His ministry was a ministry of faith, without hinting.

On one occasion, hundreds of orphans were seated in the

mess hall, ready to eat breakfast. Everything was there except the milk. Müller prayed something like this: "God, You have never failed me; I know You will not fail me now." At that instant, a horse-drawn milk cart lost a wheel in front of the orphanage door. The driver rushed into the orphanage and asked Mr. Müller if he could take some milk to lighten the load so the cart could be jacked up and the wheel replaced. Mr. Müller gladly complied.

We must learn to stop asking men to meet our needs and start asking God. If we don't get what we ask for, it is either because God doesn't want us to have it, or because we need to keep praying and believing. When we ask man for something, we get what man can or will give, and there will be little if any blessing in it. By asking man, we are telling both man and God that we have no faith. But by putting our needs into God's hands, our faith will come alive.

The Apostle Paul, to be effective for Christ, continually adjusted to the various cultures he encountered. He used these brilliant words to give us the secret of his success in reaching people: *"To the weak became I as weak, that I might gain the weak: I am made all things to all men, that I might by all means save some"* (1 Corinthians 9:22).

And so I adapted to life in my new country, becoming all things to all men, that some would be saved. I connected within reason, eating what Americans ate, sleeping where they slept, and driving what they drove. America is simply not a country where you ride on a water buffalo down Main Street in rush hour traffic. It is not a place to build bamboo shacks on lots in the suburbs. In fact, you can't even get a license for that. This is not the place where you can have a church service in an open field all year long. When it rains or snows and begins to get cold, you need a building with a furnace and insulation.

This is America, and the Schultze family became a part

of it when we moved here. Within a year, I bought a big 1951 Buick Roadmaster, which seemed to have more chrome on the front bumper than anyone could carry in a bucket. The car was five years old, a really lovely automobile. I paid $125 for it, and my bad feelings about Christians driving big cars went out the exhaust pipe. I began to realize it was more important for me to keep my eyes on Jesus and to keep every moment sacred for Him than to worry about what kind of car I, or anyone else, was driving.

All of this was a good learning experience and a major attitude adjustment for me. With that adjustment made, we can now look at some of the specific experiences I had in my new country.

CHAPTER FOURTEEN
First Job, First Church

I arrived in Milwaukee, Wisconsin, on July 19, 1955. The next day, I started a job at Allis-Chalmers, a heavy equipment factory. I tried to explain that I was a machinist with work experience, but because I spoke British English with a German accent, I couldn't make that clear, so I was hired as a chip wheeler rather than a machinist. My job was to go from machine to machine with a long hook and a wheelbarrow, pull out the metal chips, and then take them to the dump.

I was being tested again, but I have come to believe that Christians are tested by God nearly all the time. Thanks to my previous experiences and *Mutti's* training, I performed my duties faithfully, removing the chips to the best of my ability. Several months later, I asked for a transfer, once again attempting to explain that I was an experienced machinist. This time, they put me into a department where they gave me an air-powered drill and a grinder, and asked me to drill out all the little pits, the defective air holes, in the big turbine. I was no longer removing chips, but I wasn't working as a machinist either. Indeed, I felt more like a dentist, drilling out cavities.

After a few more weeks, the union decided to go on strike, something I knew little about. Hitler had abolished the unions, and after the war Germans were too busy trying to rebuild a destroyed country than to organize unions that demanded rights or better working conditions. No one in post-WWII Germany was in a striking mood; we had a common goal, which was to build and work together. The idea of striking against an employer who had graciously hired me, a newcomer to this country, and paid me more than five cents an hour amazed me. I also remembered the scripture that says, "...*be content with your wages*" (Luke 3:14). I was content, so I told my fellow workers, "I'm not going on strike. I'm glad I have a job!"

The union people said I would have to join the strike, but I refused. The shop emptied out until I was the only man working in a factory of about 3,000 employees. Then three large, muscular men threatened me, saying, "You have to leave the factory. This is a closed shop, and when it is time to go on strike, we all go...or none of us go." That is when I understood that there was a law involved, so I left my workbench, never to return to that closed-shop employer.

I immediately got another job in a small machine shop, this time being hired in as a machinist. This shop employed about a half-dozen men, and some of the first things I saw when I walked in were the glossy colored pictures of naked women hanging on the wall. These pictures were about five or six feet tall and about two feet wide, so there was no way to avoid them. Now I had another problem. I was in a new country, and I knew I needed to adapt to that country's customs, but this was something I could not adapt to or accept. So, after all the men had left work on my first day, I took those pictures down, tore them up, and threw them in the trash. What a response I received from the men the next day! One of them actually attacked me physically. But, thank God, in the ensuing process, neither the attacker nor the defender was hurt, and the pictures stayed down.

I later discovered that for many people in America, when

church ends on Sunday morning, their supposed allegiance or duty to God and His ways ends as well. I was amazed to discover that many who attend church often live as those who don't attend. It may be that some of those men in the machine shop were church members; if so, it didn't dampen their interest in those provocative pictures. I was willing to adapt to a new culture, but I had drawn the line at accepting the culture's sinful elements. I still marvel today that I was not fired, for even my boss could hardly say a sentence without an obscene word. Surely, the hand of the Lord was upon me when I took that stand.

I might very well deal with the problem differently today, simply because I am more mature and experienced, but I surely would deal with it, one way or the other. The Apostle Paul said to his new young convert Timothy, *"Let no man despise thy youth; but be thou an example of the believers, in word, in conversation, in charity, in spirit, in faith, in purity"* (1 Timothy 4:12). I never realized, until I reached my forties and fifties, the powerful effect young people have on adults when they courageously and zealously take a stand for Jesus. I took a similar stand for Jesus in my sophomore year at the University of Wisconsin. While attending organic chemistry lectures I had a professor who was quite free in the use of obscene language. After a few classes I visited him in his office and asked him if that was proper for him to use those kind of words. He immediately apologized and said that he should know better since he once was a Quaker (people who profess a high standard of holiness). He never used a bad word after that encounter. If all Christian young people would speak up for Jesus in our high schools and colleges, what a difference that would make! When the anointing is upon young people, spiritually dried-up adults are strongly convicted and the devils tremble.

God works differently through young people than through

older ones, and He works uniquely with each individual. There is a hint in the book of Acts that in the last great revival—the one that will "out-Pentecost Pentecost"—young people will be in the forefront. *"And it shall come to pass in the last days, saith God, I will pour out of my Spirit upon all flesh: and your sons and your daughters shall prophesy, and your young men shall see visions, and your old men shall dream dreams"* (2:17). The older ones will dream, but the younger ones will prophesy and act. If young people will take a bold stand for righteousness, conviction will fall on those around them.

Young or old, we all must realize that if we want to live for God, we have to separate ourselves from the things of this world. The Apostle John said, *"Love not the world, neither the things that are in the world...For all that is in the world, the lust of the flesh, and the lust of the eyes, and the pride of life, is not of the Father, but is of the world...but he that doeth the will of God abideth for ever"* (1 John 2:15–17).

The first principle of Biblical theology is the principle of separation. In the book of Genesis, the book of beginnings, it is recorded that God's first act was to create light, and then He separated the light from the darkness. His next act was to separate the land from the water. Continuing through the Scriptures, we see that the founding of the nation of Israel also began with a separation: God separated Abraham from his kindred, from his family, and from his country in order to make him entirely His. Even the first chapter of the book of Psalms, the greatest devotional literature in the world, begins with the principle of separation: *"Blessed is the man that walketh not in the counsel of the ungodly, nor standeth in the way of sinners, nor sitteth in the seat of the scornful"* (1:1). God will do nothing of eternal value in or through us until we have separated ourselves from every unclean thing, both in thought and in action.

Not long after I tore down the pictures in the machine shop, I had another unforgettable "first." It happened as I attended my first church service in this beautiful country. It was a large church, with 600 to 700 in attendance. As I came into the vestibule, I was handed a sheet of paper, which I now know was the bulletin, but at that time I had never seen such a thing. Then several men shook my hand and told me they were glad to see me. Of course, I did not yet know they were just being polite and offering an expression meant to make me feel welcome. It sounded to me as if they had been waiting for me all along and were planning to do something special for me.

I was puzzled but sat in one of the pews and began to look over the paper I had received. On it was printed a list of things we were going to do in the service. Indeed, to my great surprise, we did exactly what was written there: the service began with an opening prayer (the invocation); then came the opening hymn, the announcements, the offering, special singing, and another congregational song; after that the pastor gave the sermon, the congregation sang the closing song, and then the pastor pronounced the benediction. We stood when there was an asterisk beside an item on the list; otherwise, we sat. And we finished on the hour, right to the minute.

This type of worship, I learned later, was followed, with little variation, in nearly every church building throughout the country. Because of the predictability of the service, people often became sleepy or fidgety before it was over. With my background, I found this type of service quite surprising and more than slightly boring. I was used to services that lasted two or three hours and left parishioners wanting more; here, within fifteen to twenty minutes, I found myself glancing around for the nearest exit. I did not feel any anointing or any presence of the Lord. However, since several men had said they were so glad to see me, I stayed in my pew after the service ended, waiting for them. But, lo and behold, no one came; they all were headed out the door. It left me wondering why they had said they were glad to see me.

When I returned to the evening service, I decided at least half the people had fallen sick since the morning service. But as I looked around the half-empty sanctuary and meditated on the situation, I realized there had to be another cause. I later learned the large portion of people who had attended the morning service but did not return in the evening were not sick at all—they simply did not have enough interest in church to come back. It was even worse at the midweek service. This time, nearly half of those who were there on Sunday night were absent. I soon discovered most church members were more interested in going to ballgames or watching television than in worshiping the Lord Jesus.

When I looked for prayer, I discovered there was no earnest prayer meeting in that church. The only consistent prayer time I found was a few brief moments during the midweek service, allocated for the sick and otherwise afflicted of the congregation.

Since then, I have also discovered the most common method of promoting church growth in this country has become the lowering of standards. The lower the standard, the more people will enter the universities, the military, and the churches. As a result, church growth is not always a good sign; it may just reflect the tragic fact that pastors have given up trying to maintain the high standard of the Holy Scriptures. (Of course, there are exceptions to this, but all too often it is the sad truth.)

After one of the services, I was invited to the home of two ladies who were about ten years my senior. When I arrived at their apartment, I expected we would follow the pattern I knew from Hamburg, which was to continue in Christian fellowship. Instead, one of the ladies turned on the television to watch the Lawrence Welk show. This particular show, if you are old enough to remember, consisted mostly of a band playing lively music, individuals or groups singing, and people dancing. To me, it was a very worldly show. I could hardly believe that these two ladies, who had just been in the house of God, would now turn their attention to a totally different world.

At that moment, I felt totally cut off from any genuine spiritual fellowship. I was looking for true Christians, but it seemed I could not find them. Desperately, I went to a few churches, looking for some sincere followers of the Lord who did not want "just a little bit of God," but all of Him.

One day I noticed a newspaper advertisement that said something similar to, "We invite you to our revival service with such-and-such an evangelist from August 15 through 20." At first, I was elated because I had heard a little about revivals in the past. But when I saw that the revival would begin and end on certain days, I was confused. How could that be? How could they know that revival would start on a specific day, and why would the Holy Spirit want to stop it on another specific day?

But, out of curiosity, I decided to go. There I saw what was considered a standard "revival" in this country. Someone hires a preacher, who comes from many miles away, delivers an evangelistic message for a few days, and is paid a set amount of money. Perhaps a few people come to the altar, and occasionally someone gets saved, but after a few weeks, things settle down to the way they were before. I considered a revival to be when an entire community or church was turned right-side up for God and remained that way for a while. What I observed at my first American "revival" was nothing like that.

After that experience, I went into a state of depression,

even though things were going well at work. I had such a longing for fellowship in the Holy Spirit with other committed Christians that I wanted to go back to Hamburg. Every day after that disappointing revival experience, I lay on my face and cried out, "Lord, let me go back home!" This went on for almost two years, until the Lord suddenly got me on my feet, never to lie on the carpet in self-pity again, but to love and adapt and go to work for Him.

It was then that the Lord began to teach me to take people from where they were to where God wanted them to be—and of course, that is also what He was doing with me.

CHAPTER FIFTEEN

Give Me Death, or...

After working in factories for a year, I had saved enough money to enroll at the University of Wisconsin in Milwaukee. The idea of borrowing money for education, graduating with a financial burden, and carrying that burden into a young family never entered into the mind of any of the Schultzes. We were all going to work our way through college—blood, sweat, and tears—whatever it took. *Mutti* was strong on education. She pounded it into us that without an education, we would not go anywhere, and she saw to it that we followed her orders. That is the German way, of course, to follow the *Führer*—even if it is your mother—or your good days may come to a miserable end.

I think God was on my mother's side in this matter, and so we children had no choice but to comply. The Apostle Paul wrote, *"Children, obey your parents in the Lord: for this is right"* (Ephesians 6:1). Further, *Mutti* had earned her right to keep pushing us on and on, ever higher. She had sacrificed a lot just to keep us going through all the hard war and post-war years, and we knew she had done it for us.

Because of this, the five of us enrolled at the university. *Mutti*, in her fifties, even took some courses; later, after all of us children got our degrees, *Mutti* enrolled to get her Master's degree in Education so she could teach French and German in the public school system. Eckart and Wolfram enrolled in engineering school, Renate in library science, and I in pre-med. In addition, we all worked to help pay the rent.

I did run into one problem as I tried to get enrolled. The registrar asked for my high school diploma, but I had forgotten to bring it from Germany. When we left Hamburg, we took only the essentials; at the time, it seemed more important to pack my toothbrush than to spend time looking for a piece of paper. The registrar, however, appeared to doubt I ever had a diploma. She then asked how much education I had. I told her I had completed five years of elementary school and four years of high school, a total of nine years, which was three years less than my American counterparts. The problem was that I had spent one year during my elementary years playing chess in a detention camp instead of attending classes. Also, high school in Germany starts at age twelve and ends at sixteen. The registrar, of course, didn't really care about all that. "Here you are," she said, "a foreigner with a foreign language. You can't produce a high school diploma, and on top of that you're minus three years of what you need to start college here. What makes you think you can make it?" I don't remember what I said in response, but I do remember what I thought. I believed I could make it because *Mutti* said I could.

After a little more discussion, she said she would give me an entrance examination, which proved to be a terrible experience. The exam was full of words I had never seen before. As a result, I read the questions but couldn't understand the meaning. I had been educated in Germany, which had not prepared me for an examination geared toward someone who had been educated in America. I tried for about half an hour and then gave up. Consequently, I flunked the test. My hopes for a university education looked dim. But then God intervened. At the end of the test session, I could hardly believe my ears when the registrar said, "You failed the test, but I will put you on one year's probation." And so I enrolled as a pre-med student. This was just one more example of how, when you follow the Lord the best you can, He opens doors that previously were bolted, chained, or even welded shut.

Relieved at being enrolled, my ambition kicked into overdrive—or maybe I was just out of my mind. Whatever the reason, I took seventeen credit hours. And because I needed more money, I took a four-hour night job as a lab technician at the Ambrosia Chocolate Company. Can you imagine a machinist turning into a lab technician in a chocolate factory overnight? It can only happen in America, the land of opportunity. In Germany it would require at least four years in college to get the title of lab technician.

Soon after I began attending classes, I was elected president of InterVarsity Christian Fellowship, a Christian student organization that seeks to encourage Christian college students to live for Jesus while on campus; it also helps students win others to Christ. As president, I started a couple of Bible studies on campus. One day, while witnessing to a student in the cafeteria, I was surprised when he said to me, "You are trying to convert me, aren't you?"

I responded in the strong German way, looking right into his eyes with an, "Of course I am." Then he asked if I was a better person because I was a Christian. I responded by simply repeating the line I had heard Sunday after Sunday from the pulpit, which was that Christians are not better, they are just forgiven. The student then told me if Christianity wouldn't make him a better person, he didn't want any part of it. And he turned and walked away.

I realized at that moment that the student was right, and I felt as if I had been betrayed by those who had told me otherwise. If Christianity doesn't make us better people, what is the point? If Christianity doesn't make us better, we have an impotent Jesus. Many questions began to pile up in my mind, like sharp arrows piercing my soul.

I reasoned that if Jesus is our life, and if His Spirit enters into our hearts at conversion, then either we should be better people as a result, or we have a dead Christ living within us. I knew Jesus was not dead; I knew He was not weak; I also knew His Spirit had entered my heart, so I had to be a better person than I was before. I then asked myself if someone could truly abide in Christ without his whole life showing the evidence that he has been and is still with Jesus. Impossible, I decided.

I then began to examine this doctrine of "saved sinners." Where does that expression come from? It is not in the Bible. Indeed, they are two contradicting terms, referred to as an oxymoron. It is like saying "clean filth." Filth is not clean, and that which is clean is not filthy; it is either one or the other. Can we be saved and be in sin at the same time? Can an evil heart bring forth good, or can a good heart bring forth evil? If we are not saved from sin and its power over us, what are we saved from? Why would we call Jesus a Savior?

These sharp arrows continued to lodge in my heart, as I pondered these issues. I realized something was very wrong with some of the doctrines I had been taught, and I thought, *I cannot go on with my Christianity; it doesn't work. There are some things that are very wrong with it. Where is the right doctrine? Where is the overflowing joy in my life and in the hearts of those of the congregation where I worship? Why am I such a spiritual skeleton after three years of Christianity? How is it that after church many people are so easily drawn to the television set?* I realized I had to start doing my own thinking, rather than going by what I had heard from others. I needed to hear from God.

As I went home that day, I felt as if I wanted to die. I could not live any longer unless I had a new revelation of Jesus. I couldn't seem to find it in the church, so I decided I needed to get it directly from the throne of God. I even considered quitting college just so I could spend more time getting to know God, but there was the "*Mutti* factor." Actually, it was now the "*Oma* factor." We had begun to call *Mutti* "*Oma*" (grandmother), because Eckart was now married and had his first child. We had all come to enjoy calling *Mutti* "*Oma*," as it seemed a more affectionate expression. But call her *Mutti* or *Oma*, she would never let me quit college for what she would have considered religious reasons. She wanted me to get my degree and "make something" of my life. I know many parents feel the same way, often glorifying education above spiritual things, such as knowing God, serving God, walking with God, and even character development.

At the time it was impossible for me to set aside more time for God with seventeen credit hours, my involvement with InterVarsity Christian Fellowship, and four hours of work at night. Death seemed sweeter to me than going on without true victorious Christian living as I knew it had been experienced by those men and women of God I read about in the Scriptures. Yet, I saw that if God would, in His mercy, grant me a painless disease that would lay me aside without the distraction of suffering, I would have the time I needed to get to know Him. So I asked God to either take my life or give me a painless disease. This may seem a brash petition, but I was twenty years old, and twenty-year-olds can come up with some daring thoughts they might not entertain later in life. At that particular time, however, my great yearning desire to have a full and complete walk with God caused a continual fervent petition to pour forth from my heart.

Thank God, He answered my prayer! The next morning, as I was brushing my teeth, I saw blood on my toothbrush. Glory, glory, glory! I realized I had a painless disease—tuberculosis. I recognized it immediately because my father had died of a combination of that disease and malnutrition. Miraculously, the next day a mobile X-ray unit from the TB sanatorium arrived on the college campus, and I was the second student to be X-rayed. Indeed, within a few days, the public health nurse rang my doorbell, and I was off to a TB sanatorium, where I spent sixteen wonderful months with a painless disease, free to focus my thoughts and heart upon the Lord. Isn't Jesus wonderful? He gave me the desire of my heart, as He will do for anyone who sincerely and fervently seeks Him for His glory.

Though some might wonder if the possibility of death caused fear in my heart during that time, I can honestly say it never even crossed my mind. All my thoughts were focused on God. As long as I had Him, death was irrelevant. God was everything; death was nothing. I saw in this disease an act of God's mercy, giving me time to draw closer to Him so He could draw closer to me (see James 4:8).

What is the use of being a doctor or a lawyer or a businessman or an engineer if we are not walking with God? We are born into the world to walk with God, and after this life, to meet God and live with Him forever. Enoch walked with God, and he was taken up from the earth without dying. Was he a vinedresser, a shepherd, a builder, or a blacksmith? What was his occupation? The Bible does not say because it does not matter. The only thing the Bible writes about Enoch was that he lived, he walked with God, and God took him (see Genesis 5:24).

In the final analysis, we need to look at everything from a historical perspective—not years from now looking backwards, but looking back through the eyes of eternity. This does not mean God is indifferent about our vocational choices—absolutely not. God is not indifferent about anything. He has a purpose for everything in our lives. After all, life should be a composite of billions of sacred moments lived out in His holy presence. But our vocational choices, even if the right ones, pale in comparison to our need to *do justly*, to *love mercy*, and to *walk humbly* with our God each day (see Micah 6:8).

I had tuberculosis because I wanted what Micah 6:8 taught. And so, I took my Bible and my pajamas because that was all I needed for my time in the sanatorium. *Oma*, of course, was not as happy as I was about the whole process. In fact, she hit bottom during that time. She thought I would be the third family member to die—first *Vati*, then Elke and now me. When I entered the sanatorium in 1956, many people still died of tuberculosis. But a promising new drug came on the scene at about that same time and soon made its way into our health institutions.

At the sanatorium, I was assigned a bed in a sunroom with about seven other men, who represented an interesting combination of personalities and ages. Having experienced communal living in the detention camp, I had no problem with that aspect of my situation. I was twenty years old, the youngest in that room, while the oldest was in his sixties. Immediately, I felt comfortable with what I considered my new family. My first thought was that God had placed me there as a missionary, with the potential of six conversions. Actually, it turned out the number of potential converts was only five because one of these men was a young Pentecostal preacher. But as young and inexperienced as I was at evangelism, the burden for the lost never left me. I knew I was sharing a room with five men who were not ready to meet God and were totally oblivious to the judgment to come. I had a responsibility to show them the light, and I felt responsible for their eternal destiny.

To this day, I do not understand why Christians dread being confined to nursing homes or hospitals or other such institutions, particularly at the end of their lives. It is a privilege because God is giving us the opportunity to lead people to Jesus. We are locked in with these people twenty-four hours a day, and we have all the time in the world to give ourselves to this mission of speaking to them about the condition of their souls.

So many Christians have not led or pointed even one soul to Jesus in their entire lifetime. What a joy it would be to arrive in heaven and hear someone say, "Thank you for bringing me to the Lord! Had it not been for you, I wouldn't be here!" It should be the heart's desire of every Christian to have that experience some day. When we, as ambassadors for Christ, find ourselves thrown into a situation with unbelievers, the physical setting is completely irrelevant. We have been given the opportunity to tell others of God's great love for them, and that is much more important than whether we have a private bathroom or use a communal bath down the hallway. It does not even matter whether we are mobile or confined to our room, nor if we eat bread or soup or a three-course meal. When it comes to the issues of life and death, all these other things are trivial. With Christ we are rich, and we should want to share His riches with others.

That is the way things were for me in the sanatorium. I got to know the young Pentecostal preacher, and since both of us had memorized a lot of scripture verses, when the lights went out at night, we began to call them out, one after another, sometimes for hours. As we did, five unconverted men lay there in the dark, with no choice but to listen. Of course, that preacher and I were young and perhaps may have seemed a bit pushy to more mature Christians, but again, as Paul told his disciple Timothy, *"Let no man despise thy youth."* God used that time in the sanatorium as a period of "iron sharpening iron" (see Proverbs 27:17), as the two of us young fellows strengthened each other in the faith.

Soon after I entered the sanatorium, my younger brother,

Wolfram, was also diagnosed with tuberculosis and ended up in the bed next to me. In a matter of days, the scripture quoting between the Pentecostal preacher and me got into Wolfram's heart, and he received the Lord Jesus and immediately began preaching from bedside to bedside.

Oh, how glad I was for that young Pentecostal preacher! After a year of going to several churches and youth groups and serving as president of IVCF, I had finally met a witnessing Christian, the first since leaving Hamburg. In every church I went to in Milwaukee, the Word was preached, and people even carried their Bibles to church, as well as on buses and streetcars. But when it came to someone whose Christianity showed on his face and who used the Word of God for the purpose of witnessing, I found almost no one. Many Christians seem to consider their faith a tradition to be followed with stoic regularity, rather than something to be lived twenty-four hours a day.

During my time in the sanatorium, some of my college friends, particularly those from my campus Bible studies, began to visit "poor, sick Reimar Schultze." They came to pray for me, and they looked so discouraged that I was sick. They did not realize that I had prayed to get sick and that I was not interested in getting well until I knew God in a greater way. I did not want to get out of that place until I could say, yes, Christians are better than non-Christians. I wanted to be able to say with certainty that Christians are not only a forgiven people, but also a transformed people—transformed by the power of God, victorious over sin, and hating and rejecting sin with a passion.

One day Kim B. came to see me. Kim had been attending one of my campus Bible studies, and we were both shy and backward. After a ten-minute visit of nearly complete and very awkward silence, I said to him as he stood at my bedside, "Kim, I believe you need to go home and give your heart to

Jesus." He left without answering a word, went home, knelt down by his bed, and gave his heart to Jesus.

The minister from the church I had been attending also came to visit me a couple of times. He had a Doctor of Divinity degree and was a wonderful pastor. Every one of his nearly 1,000 members received a personally signed birthday card from him each year, which told me something about his heart. But when I asked him questions about things I had recently read in the Bible, he could not or would not answer. My questions were followed by a long silence, and I knew he did not share my passion for more of God.

During my quest, I frequented the little stained glass-windowed chapel in the basement of the sanatorium. I was there for one to three hours before breakfast, worshipping and crying out to God to cleanse me from unpleasing attitudes, desires, and reactions. After several weeks of praying and reading from the Bible, I met Rev. C. T. Hollingsworth, who was also a patient. Rev. Hollingsworth was a Scottish holiness preacher in his sixties or seventies, six feet tall and as broad-shouldered as a barn door. He stood erect and reminded me of Moses, with his straight silver hair and a twinkle in his blue eyes, and he often visited the other patients to talk with them about the Lord.

When he arrived at the foot of my bed, he fixed his eyes on me and began to quote scriptures on holiness. At the end of each quotation, he hit his cane on the tile floor. I responded with scripture after scripture, emphasizing the grace of God—the things I had been taught in my church. After a number of visits with that kind of exchange, I capitulated and said, "I need to be holy. I need to be sanctified. We all need to be holy."

Yes, we need to hear about the grace of God, but also about His holiness. The Apostle Paul said in Hebrews 12:14, *"Follow peace with all men, and holiness, without which no man shall see the Lord."* Jesus said, *"Blessed are the pure in heart: for they shall see God"* (Matthew 5:8). And Paul wrote to the Christians, the born-again people in Thessalonica, *"For this is the will of God, even your sanctification"* (1 Thessalonians 4:3).

Being pure, being holy, and being wholly sanctified are all one and the same. Sanctification has two steps: first, there is being set apart for God; second, there is filling up that which is set aside for God. I shall share more about this later.

The point is that God lifted a veil from my spiritual eyes. After I met Rev. Hollingsworth, I knew that conversion was just the beginning of a great journey, and the Scottish preacher set me on a hopeful pursuit of heart holiness that would bring me into heart intimacy with my Savior, which was my dream. I wanted the Holy Spirit to live in my body the same way in which He lived in the body of the Lord Jesus 2,000 years ago.

I asked Rev. Hollingsworth how I could be cleansed from the sinful Adamic nature still residing in my heart, and how I could be entirely sanctified, fit for the Master's use. Rev. Hollingsworth responded, "I don't want anyone to think I am indoctrinating you. You will find the answer in the book of Romans, chapters 6—8." From that day forward, I paid special attention to those three chapters while I met with the Lord in the basement, asking Him to illuminate them to me. Some days I spent a whole day on just one or two verses.

While in the sanatorium, I also took correspondence courses from the University on American History and Spanish so I could at least keep up a little on my studies. A few times each week, to relax my mind, I spent several hours in a basement workshop, working with wood for the first time as I built a table for my unknown future wife. We need balance in every area of our lives because, even spiritually, we can push ourselves so hard that we go beyond the point of victory, beyond the point of receiving what God has for us. This can lead to fanaticism, legalism, mental disorders, and utter uselessness to God and His church. Working on a table for the wife I had yet to meet helped me keep the various areas of my life in balance.

Concerning my physical condition, the new medication for treating tuberculosis seemed to significantly lower the mortality rate. I received this medication, but after about six months, X-rays showed no improvement in my health. I had an abnormal strain of TB bacilli that was resistant to this medication. They injected my strain of bacilli into a guinea pig and then tried another medication on the pig, but it died. Shortly after, the Chief of Staff and some interns stood around my bedside and told me there was no hope and I was going to die. I was utterly amazed at their words. I wondered what made them think my life was in their hands, when I knew it was in the hands of God, as it had always been. It was in the hands of God when we faced the Nazis, when the bombs rained down from the sky, when the Soviets invaded our town, and when our ship was fired upon by artillery. I knew life and death were in the hands of God, and I was ready for either.

After more time passed, the doctors took new X-rays. For the first time, they now said my infection was localized in such specific areas they were able to do surgery and cut it out. Consequently, I had surgery on one lung and then the other, just a few weeks apart. Dr. Viggo Olsen, my surgeon, was once an atheist, but an objective atheist rather than a prejudiced one. He was therefore willing to study evidences for the Christian faith. He read some of the great Christian apologists and soon became a Christian and went to Pakistan as a medical missionary. I believe when a person with a sincere and honest heart meets the person of Jesus, he will be drawn to Him.

While this doctor prepared me for my lung surgery, I asked if he would also operate on my legs. Standing between the bunk beds for much of those three days and nights while on the Red Cross train during our escape had set me up for the early development of varicose veins, and I had suffered constant pain in my legs since I was seventeen. So, while in the sanatorium, I also had a vein stripping on both legs, a procedure that has been repeated three times since, at ten-year intervals.

The sanatorium was not only helpful for my physical healing, but it also served as a place of deliverance from doctrines that imprisoned me. That time served as a powerful reminder of the calling for my life. When I was praying in the basement chapel those many days in the sanatorium, the Lord said to me, "I'm not calling you to be a physician of the body, but a physician of the soul." The dark cloud that hung over me when I entered the sanatorium sixteen months earlier had lifted. When I left that place, I certainly was not finished with my pursuit of holiness or sanctification, but at least I knew which general direction to head in the ensuing years. It was time to go back to college, finish my bachelor's degree in pre-med, and then go from there to seminary to become a teacher of the glorious gospel of Christ.

The Schultze family and grandparents
Hans and Frieda Benningson,
England, 1948.

CHAPTER SIXTEEN

Why Don't You Start Obeying God?

I was penniless throughout most of my college days. I received a scholarship for books but had to raise the rest of the money myself. For the most part, my breakfast consisted of uncooked oats with milk and sugar, and cold pork and beans out of a can for lunch and supper. I spent some of my summers working in a factory as a machinist, and I also worked for the Library of Congress at the University. Every book published in communist East Germany at that time went through my hands. I had to scan each one and write a summary for the library reference cards. In my last year of college I also "babysat" a radio transmitter for the Federal Communications Commission.

In Madison, during my junior and senior years, I rented a little room on the second floor of a home owned by a sweet old widow lady. There were three students on that second floor, and we all shared the same bathroom. When I moved into my room, I again began to experience a desperate desire to see a soul saved. I had not been able to lead anyone to Christ for a while, and I had come to the point where bringing a soul to Christ was more important than grades or books. After all, since I was no longer headed for medicine, my grade point average did not matter that much anymore.

I had three pieces of furniture in that room: a little old

desk, one chair, and a bed. Each day, I knelt down at my bedside and asked the Lord to give me a soul. I didn't know how to witness, since no one had ever taught me, so I did the only thing I knew how to do: I called out scripture verses to the two students who passed by my room. It had worked in the sanatorium, so I decided to try it again. I almost always kept my door open, and each time one of the students passed by, I shot a scripture verse out the door at him.

My main burden was for Joe, the president of his Methodist youth group back home. He was a chain smoker and showed no evidence of Christianity. Most Christian college students leave their religion at home because few have more than a thimbleful of it anyway, having attended church or youth groups simply to please their parents.

Many parents worry about their children losing their faith in college, and well they should. Most parents don't witness at work, make no effort to win souls or attend prayer meetings, and spend more time watching TV than reading the Bible. As the parents live, so do the children. If parents are lukewarm in their faith, so are the children in almost every case. Children lose their faith when they leave home not because they chose the wrong college, but because they went to college without possessing a faith worth dying for. If parents are firebrands for Jesus, most of their children will be likewise. Instead of losing their children in college, their children will finish college having led other souls to Jesus. We need not fear secular colleges; we need to fear a backslidden condition within us and our children before they leave home. If we backslide in our hearts, the world will more likely change us than we will change the world.

And so, every time Joe walked by my room, he got a Bible verse, whether he wanted it or not. It might have been from Genesis, Exodus, Leviticus, Matthew or Mark, Romans or Revelation. Joe never responded—at least, he never stopped to talk to me—but I kept it up. After about six months, he came by on one of those rare times when my door was closed. He knocked, and when I invited him in, he said, "Reimar, I want to get saved." I was so happy! Joe and I knelt down next to my one chair, and then Joe repeated the sinner's prayer after me. When we were done, he said, "Reimar, I don't feel any different." That was hard on me because when I prayed the sinner's prayer in 1952, I immediately felt the presence of the Holy Spirit enter my heart. But Jesus helped me respond to Joe, just as He always helps me in every area of my life.

"Joe," I said, "you asked Jesus to come into your heart by faith, and salvation is by faith. So if you keep believing, in time you will have the witness of the Holy Spirit." I knew God honors the faith of those who persevere, for Jeremiah 29:13 says, *"And ye shall seek me, and find me, when ye shall search for me with all your heart."*

I was confident in my assurances to Joe, because God surely keeps His promises. Christianity is not primarily a religion of feeling, but of faith, and there is such a thing as the witness of the Holy Spirit, which becomes a gift to every true child of God. Romans 8:16 tells us, *"The Spirit itself beareth witness with our spirit, that we are the children of God."* I knew God would bring that to pass in Joe's life.

A few weeks later, Joe stood at the door of my room, smiling from ear to ear, as he said, "I have the witness of the Holy Spirit that I am a child of God." He had quit smoking, and became a witness for Jesus and a strong pillar in a Pentecostal church. He was going all the way! Twenty-five years later I called him, and he was still going strong for the Lord. It is worth noting here that sometimes the witness of the Holy Spirit is delayed until the fruits of repentance are evident. God does not forgive where there is no repentance.

As for myself, I continued to pursue a deeper relationship with God. While attending InterVarsity meetings at the

Madison campus, I met a graduate student named Dallas Willard. Dallas was a Baptist minister, who felt God's call to teach philosophy on a secular campus, so he was working on his Ph.D. When he saw I was struggling, he invited me to his apartment where he lived with his wife, and we soon began meeting together about once a week in "bull sessions," as students used to call them. Most of the time, Dallas probed me in various areas of knowledge. No field of learning was beyond our examination. Dallas broadened my understanding, and time and again pushed me beyond the limits of my mental and spiritual beliefs. It was a great time.

Finally, seeing my difficulty, my struggle for my soul, Dallas said, "Reimar, have you ever considered obeying God? Why don't you just start obeying God?"

I was stunned. After eight years of being a Christian and being in church every week, nobody had ever talked to me about obeying God. I said, "I never thought of it."

Dallas then challenged me by saying, "Why don't you start doing it?"

"I will," I vowed, and I meant it.

The book of Jeremiah tells us the first thing God wanted Israel to do after leaving Egypt was to obey Him: "...*Thus saith the LORD God of Israel; Cursed be the man that obeyeth not the words of this covenant, Which I commanded your fathers in the day that I brought them forth out of the land of Egypt, from the iron furnace, saying, Obey my voice, and do them, according to all which I command you: so shall ye be my people, and I will be your God*" (11:3-4). When they obeyed God, He brought them into a marvelous place. "*That I may perform the oath which I have sworn unto your fathers, to give them a land flowing with milk and honey, as it is this day. Then answered I, and said, So be it, O LORD*" (11:5). Obedience is every bit as important as faith, for without obedience, there will be no flow of milk and honey in our lives.

Now I had two unresolved items of business on my religious agenda. One was this matter of sanctification, and the other was obeying God. Suddenly I got the revelation that if I obeyed God, I would end up being sanctified. Jesus does not fill anyone with the Holy Spirit unless he is obedient. We see this in Acts 5:32: *"And we are his witnesses of these things; and so is also the Holy Ghost, whom God hath given to them that obey him."*

I knew I could obey, for *Mutti—Oma—*had taught me to do so. She never had to say anything twice, for we were taught to obey at the first request. This type of obedience training needs to be accomplished in the first year of a child's life, and certainly no later than the first eighteen months. If it is not done successfully by that age, accomplishing it after becomes increasingly difficult. Susanna Wesley was one of the most successful mothers who ever lived, and here is what she had to say on the matter:

"When turned a year (and some before), they were taught to fear the rod and cry softly; by which means they escaped the abundance of correction they might otherwise have had...

"In order to form the minds of children, the first thing to be done is to conquer the will and bring them to an obedient temper.

"I insist upon conquering the will of children betimes, because this is the only strong and rational foundation of a religious education; without which both precept and example will be ineffectual...I cannot dismiss this subject. As self-will is the root of all sin and misery, so whatever cherishes this in children insures thereafter wretchedness and irreligion. Whatever checks and mortifies it (self-will) promotes their future happiness and piety."[1]

Mrs. Wesley's words carry great weight because she

gave the world the Wesley brothers, John and Charles, and
God used those two Wesley men to save eighteenth-century
England from moral decadence, as well as economic and
social disaster.

As I grow older, I see more clearly with every year that
I had the most wonderful childhood because my mother
insisted on total obedience. She prepared me to obey God in
both pleasant and unpleasant circumstances. I cannot think
of a greater contribution a mother can give to her children.
If a child has material things and comforts without having
learned obedience, it would be better for him never to have
been born.

When Dallas Willard asked me, "Why don't you just start
obeying God?", I added obedience to my faith, and I began to
see the importance of obedience throughout the Scriptures,
beginning with Adam and going all the way into the book of
the Revelation. Jesus Himself said, *"If ye love me, keep my
commandments"* (John 14:15). Christianity is nothing more
or less than doing the will of God. Our Lord warned us in
Matthew 7:21, *"Not every one that saith unto me, Lord, Lord,
shall enter into the kingdom of heaven; but he that doeth the
will of my Father which is in heaven."* I discovered that I
needed to obey Jesus just as He obeyed God.

Rightly did John H. Sammis say in his gospel song:

> Trust and obey for there is no other way,
> To be happy in Jesus but to trust and obey.[2]

If we want to be happy, to be blessed by God, we must
obey Him. Indeed, the whole history of Israel is full of this
truth. Whether God blessed or punished His covenant people
was entirely dependent on their obedience. It is no different
with us, the people of the New Testament covenant today.
Disobedience in God's children is God's greatest headache.
It is no wonder that in 1974 God called me to start a "Call

to Obedience" monthly letter and eventually a "Call to Obedience" radio program that now reaches millions of people to help them get into all that they were born to receive. As disobedience took man out of fellowship with God, obedience is an essential element to bring him back into fellowship with his Maker.

The Schultze family receiving Christmas gifts
at the Jerusalem Church, Hamburg.

Jerusalem Sisters ministering
to Jewish refugees.

CHAPTER SEVENTEEN
This Is Your Wife

During my last two years of college, I realized I was incapable of choosing the right wife. I did not know what was ahead for me, and so I did not know what I needed in a wife. I also realized that the American practice of dating was an ungodly and unwise procedure. It is impossible to know how many hearts have been broken and how many have lost their virginity by playing this dangerous dating game. As I prayed about this, Jesus spoke to my heart: "I will tell you when you see the wife I have chosen for you."

During Christmas break in my senior year, I attended a Bible Conference in the Colorado Rockies sponsored by InterVarsity Christian Fellowship. On the first day, while walking on a gravel road in the forest, I saw a black-haired young lady coming toward me. I did not know her name or where she came from, but Jesus said, "This is your wife." When God speaks, there is no need for a vote. Our part is simply to trust and obey. From that moment on, I watched that young lady whenever she was not watching me. I learned her name was Marcia, but I did not approach her. I treated her the same as I treated all the other young ladies at that conference. I believe I had only one conversation with her during the whole week in Colorado, and that lasted about thirty seconds.

When I returned to college, I decided to give myself

over to a prolonged period of prayer, in order to have the Holy Spirit confirm the witness I had received in Colorado. Each morning, while in my regular prayer time, I laid the issue before the Lord. Each morning for sixty days, the Lord continued to confirm what He had revealed to me in the Rockies: "This is your wife."

From what I have seen, most marriages are out of divine order, the result of decisions of the flesh: sexual attraction, common interests or goals, and chance meetings. These decisions made in the flesh, though they seem right and wonderful at the beginning, carry the seeds of discord, discouragement, and strife, which often lead to stressed marriages and divorce.

It should not be so for Christians. Here are some points we can use to discern that our choice is of the Holy Spirit and not of the flesh:

1) Our choices must not violate the Word of God. Paul said, *"Be ye not unequally yoked together with unbelievers..."* (2 Corinthians 6:14). It is against God's will for a believer to marry an unbeliever.

2) We must come to a point of total neutrality in our choices, which is not easy. We are weak in the flesh and readily prejudiced toward a person who has all the qualities we think we would like in a spouse. But we must consider that such beautiful persons may actually belong to someone else and not to us. We must be careful not to get intimate with a member of the opposite sex, for if we do, it is easy to "fall in love" and we will quickly lose our spiritual discernment. Remember, love blinds, meaning once we have fallen in love, our spiritual and mental faculties become severely impaired! We must wait upon the Lord until we can say with all our heart, "Lord, Thy will be done and not mine." We must crucify our prejudices, our

preferences, and our leanings because they are likely to tilt our choices in the wrong direction.

3) When we come to the point of total neutrality, the Lord can witness to us about His choice. If we have pure hearts and the witness is continuous over a period of time, it is likely to be of the Lord. This is why I waited and prayed for sixty days, to be sure the witness was continuous. God is not the Author of confusion. If the witness is off and on and off again, then the Lord is not in it. The Lord does not confuse His children, but the devil will use confusion every chance he gets.

4) Whenever possible, if you know those who have faithfully walked with God for a long time, you may also check with them on this matter. Of course, you should not marry until your future spouse is also clear about the issue.

When we first met in Colorado, Marcia was in nursing school in Chicago. After my two months of prayer and God's confirmation, I obtained her address from a friend and wrote to her. Shortly thereafter, we met in Chicago. The moment she stepped off the elevator, I thought, *This is it! She is beautiful; she is special.* Marcia was twenty-four and had never dated. She lived a godly life, was faithful in prayer and Bible study, and was a woman of purity. Isn't the gift of virginity one of the best things to give to your spouse?

I had not known that when Marcia first saw me she also had taken an interest in me, but she went back to Chicago with the thought that this was too good to be true. By the time she received my letter, she had given up on me, but marriages are "made in heaven," if we let God have His way. And so we met at last.

I had no automobile, so I took the train to Chicago. Marcia had a car, and she let me drive. As soon as she sat down in the passenger seat, the Holy Spirit's presence filled the car with peace, comfort, and confirmation. I knew I was "home" with this woman.

I had come to Chicago early in the morning, so we had breakfast together, then went to the Moody Church for the Sunday morning service. Honestly, I can't remember anything much of the sermon, but I remember the joy of sitting next to my new treasure. After the church service, I drove my new sweetheart to the lakeshore, pulled into a parking lot, and gave her a biblical exposition of Romans 6—8. Later in the afternoon, we went to the Chicago Museum of Science and Industry. That was our first day together.

Although I had a clear revelation of marrying Marcia the first time I saw her, she needed a little more time before she was absolutely sure, even though she wanted to be with me continually after that first date. But she needed time, and I needed patience. Young men and women have to be careful not to push the other party into a premature marriage relationship. We need to be gentle, longsuffering, and trusting, and not get into the flesh or we will lose what God has planned and provided for us.

Finally, the time came for me to introduce Marcia to *Oma*. I knew, of course, that sooner or later I had to make that bold move, and so I did. After that meeting, Marcia became exceptionally affectionate with me. I could tell she was now ready for me to say the "big words," but it was only years later that she confided to me about what had cemented her decision to marry me. She explained, "When I saw how you treated your mother with kindness, love, and respect, I knew that is the way you would treat me. It gave me the final assurance from God about our marriage."

Generally, we can say that the way a daughter responds to her father is the way she will respond to her husband, and the way a young man responds to his mother is the way he will respond to his wife. Young man, do not fool yourself into thinking that if a young lady is disrespectful to her father she will be any other way with you. And young lady, don't let yourself be fooled into thinking if your boyfriend does not respect his mother and treat her as a gentleman should he will treat you any differently. What I am telling you here, young people, is worth more than all the money in your bank.

I do not remember how I proposed to Marcia, but I clearly recall how I asked her father for permission to marry his daughter. On a sweltering hot Midwestern summer day, I dressed for this solemn, sacred occasion in a sports coat, a decent pair of pants, a white shirt, and a tie. I would have worn a suit, but I did not own one until I was thirty, so the sports coat had to do. I drove the five-hour journey from Madison to Indiana in an old car without air conditioning, first on the Interstate, then the state highway, then the county roads, and finally the gravel roads through the nearly ripe cornfields of Allen County, Indiana. I was now hot and sweaty, and as I traveled through the seven-foot high cornfields, the dust filtered into my vehicle and attached itself to my damp clothes.

As I turned in to my prospective father-in-law's farmyard, I expected him to be dressed as I was, including a tie. After all, this was not only a great event for me, but also for him. He was giving away his only daughter and best farmhand, onion peeler, watermelon picker, corn husker, truck driver, and hunting and fishing companion. I was wrong. I had forgotten this is America, home of the brave and land of the free—and the casually dressed. Argyl, then about 280 pounds and six feet tall, met me as he walked out of the house, wearing only a pair of green khaki pants. He had little hair on his head but more on his chest than any man I had ever seen, and, yes, he was barefooted. I, of course, stood there like a 6'4" beanpole, dressed to the hilt and covered with dust. What a pair we were, meeting for the first time and dressed as oppositely as any two men could be.

We sat down on the curb of his driveway and, noting right away that he was not a man of many words, I quickly asked if I could marry his daughter. His answer was a handshake and the words, "You bet." That was it, and in a matter of an hour or so I had my first experience of sitting on an International tractor, pulling a four-bottom plow.

Argyl grew all sorts of vegetables on his farm, including corn. In Germany, corn was fed only to pigs and cattle, but there I sat, staring at a big plate in the center of the kitchen table, stacked high with corn on the cob. It was one of the last things I wanted to eat. But as I watched, they all picked up the hot buttered cobs and began to chew the corn right off of them. Realizing this feat had to be accomplished without the assistance of a knife or fork, I too picked up an ear of corn, and in no time I had butter on my nose, cheeks, chin, and fingers. I wanted to run to the restroom to wash my face, but since nobody else did, I endured the smearing. And so, I ate my way through the corn to get my wife. Looking back more than forty-five years later, I must say it was worth the chewing.

Then, on the night of January 19, 1962, Marcia and I left Madison to drive to her parents' home in Indiana to get married, not having the slightest idea of the battle we would face during the next eighteen hours.

We drove my father-in-law's big, heavy Chevrolet station wagon, loaded with our few belongings and a half dozen or so boxes of empty canning jars. When the Lord told me to marry Marcia, He did not tell me I would be marrying a girl who liked to grow and can her own vegetables. Years later, when four children had been added to our family, I once counted 1,000 full canning jars in the basement. In addition, the Lord did not tell me that for years we would travel to revival meetings with the trunk of our car bulging with one suitcase, two sewing machines, fabric, and eventually a computer and cameras.

Do you remember Jesus' parable of the kingdom of God being like a treasure hid in a field? He said, *"Again, the kingdom of heaven is like unto treasure hid in a field; the which when a man hath found, he hideth, and for joy thereof goeth and selleth all that he hath, and buyeth that field"* (Matthew 13:44). We learn in the parable that the man was interested only in the treasure, but in order for him to get it, he had to buy the whole field. That's how it is when God provides us with a spouse. Just as we gain an entire field to obtain the treasure, so we gain relatives and family traditions when we obtain a spouse. At times, we may discover things in that field that we would prefer not to have inherited.

Marcia was driving as we headed for our wedding in Indiana. *Oma* was in the passenger seat up front, and I was lying down on the backseat. Behind my seat were all those empty canning jars. We were on the Tri-State Toll Road that bypasses Chicago, and the highway was covered with ice. In the darkness, a semi-tractor piggy-backing another semi-tractor pulled in front of us to make an illegal U-turn. Marcia hit the brakes, but to no avail. Our car slid into the back tires of that tractor at about fifty miles an hour.

I fell off the backseat onto the floor, and some of the jars fell down on top of me. *Oma's* head hit the windshield and shattered the glass, while Marcia was thrown forward, with her chest pressed against the steering wheel. With our wedding scheduled for the next day at noon, we all ended up in the hospital emergency room, waiting to be examined. Thankfully, X-rays showed *Oma's* head had not sustained any serious injury. By the grace of God, we were all released to go our way, but the Chevy was totaled.

I soon found a telephone booth and began to make calls

to car rental agencys. As I stood there in that phone booth, I fought one of the greatest spiritual battles of my life. "Break off this marriage," I heard a voice say. "God is not in it. This is your last call."

It seemed as dark inside me as it was outside the phone booth. I prayed. I cried out to God. I pleaded for mercy. And that was exactly what God wanted. When the lights go out, God wants us to pray. When a hill gets too steep, God wants us to pray. When we feel walled in, God wants us to pray. I am glad I have read my Bible, for that is where I learned that when we get into hard places, we can always find a way out through prayer.

And so, after I prayed for a while, the light went back on in my soul. "Jesus," I said, "You told me for sixty days that this is my wife. You are not the Author of confusion. The voice that says to break off this marriage is of the devil." And that settled it for me. Had I not already prayed those sixty days for confirmation, I do not know if I would have pressed through with the wedding in that great hour of spiritual warfare, but I do know that when we get a revelation from God, we will face the devil on the road to the fulfillment of that revelation.

We finally located a rental car and continued our journey toward God's will. As we drove farther south and then east into Indiana, the freezing rain became heavy snow. The visibility was terrible, and it took us until breakfast time to arrive at my in-laws' home. None of us had gotten any sleep. Instead, I got a haircut, and a few hours later, Marcia and I became husband and wife, with ten people present to witness the occasion.

We did not have any money for a honeymoon, so we spent one night in a cheap motel that resembled one of the Mexican migrant huts located on farms around northern Indiana. Instead of a wall separating the bedroom from the bathroom area, there was a curtain, and the springs in the bed were so worn it was easier to get into bed than out. But at that point we were thankful just to be together at last.

Now the time for adjustment had come. Since I did not get any pre-marital counseling and neither of us had read any books on marriage, we had some surprises in store. Never had I imagined the great difference between men and women. We see a glimpse of it before we are married, but reality sets in when we begin to live together every day. Since, for the most part, I had been raised without a father; I had never observed how a husband and wife interacted with one another. Still, I should have known a lot more, since I learned in college about the sex chromosomes. A man is XY, and a woman is XX. Every single cell, from the ones in the toenail to the ones in the hair on the head, has either an XX or XY chromosome, depending upon whether a person is male or female. That is what makes men and women so completely different.

I also should have known that women are vastly different from men in every area, not only in looks, but also in how they view things, how they think and reason, and what interests them. I did not understand why a woman would say she wants to go to the store to buy one thing and then come out thirty minutes later with ten things; or why she would want to drive across town to save five cents on a gallon of milk when it costs more in gasoline to get her there. I did not understand why a woman would want to stop at garage sales or rummage sales on the way to some important appointment, saying, "Honey, it will only take a minute or two." I had to learn how long a woman's minutes were and to juggle this whole thing into my schedule the next time we went somewhere.

I did not know then that little things are so important to women, or that they need a constant flow of love and affection all day long. I have since learned it means more to a woman to experience a constant stream of kindness and thoughtfulness from her husband than to get a new refrigerator or couch or dining room set. A man cannot buy himself into a woman's heart by giving her things. Love cannot be purchased or maintained by gifts. A woman craves fellowship with her husband—kindness, sweetness, thoughtfulness, tenderness, dependability, and communication. If she receives that kind of love, she gets energized beyond a man's fondest dreams, and she becomes dynamic and almost inexhaustible in her efforts to help and please her husband.

And so, at the beginning of our marriage, I discovered I had two choices: I could be irritated by these differences, or I could learn to enjoy them and realize that God made women this way because He wanted to. I came to understand there was just no point in trying to change my wife's cells from XX to XY, because if I succeeded, she would be just like me, and that is not what I wanted either. I could enjoy this feminine creature "as is" or spend the rest of my life thinking it should be otherwise. Oh, what rest and joy husbands and wives will receive once they learn to enjoy their differences and use them to add strength to their marriage!

Now, rather than being annoyed at garage sales or denying my wife such pleasures, I use those opportunities to witness for Jesus. And rather than growing impatient in a parking lot while five minutes turns into twenty and one purchase turns into five, I use that time to pray. There are so many needs to pray about, and the car is a perfect prayer closet, a sort of little sanctuary. As a result, I have learned to be thankful that my wife got five items instead of one, for had she gotten only one, I would soon have missed the other four at breakfast, lunch, or dinner.

Of course, women also must adjust to men's ways. Often men have situations at work or difficulties in relationships, and they just need time to themselves to think things through. When women observe their husbands in those contemplative times, they often think they are being non-communicative, or they imagine their husbands are upset with them. Women need to understand that though they open up and talk to each other about nearly everything, men tend to keep things inside. Men work things out within themselves, and they seldom talk to other men about their feelings and their inner thoughts. Neither do men want to be bothered during this thinking-through process. If men need help in this process they will ask for it, but they don't want it forced upon them. Wives should not push their husbands nor pressure them to open up, for that only makes things worse. Women need to let their husbands be men at such times, and then trust that God will work everything out as it should be.

Women also need to understand that men need respect, honor, and, of course, sex. If they do not get fulfillment from their wives, they will be tempted to get it elsewhere. This is a wicked world, and husbands and wives need to hold tightly to Jesus and to each other in order to resist temptation.

A man alone is so much more helpless than a woman. He needs her for a thousand things, but especially to cheer him on in his daily battle in his vocation and avocation. When I first married I knew very little about carpentry, yet I decided to build my wife a sewing machine cabinet. It was a carpenter's nightmare and I was ashamed to show it to anyone, but my wife cheered me on so that I actually had the courage to complete the project, and in the process my carpentry improved. Years later, Marcia and I had fun smashing it to smithereens, after which I built her a new one I was not ashamed of.

In many ways a wife "makes or breaks" a man. She has the power to make her husband a success or a failure, so the power of a woman who sticks to her calling to help and support her husband is incalculable!

Generally speaking, successful marriages in parents breed successful marriages in children. Children learn what love is by seeing their father love their mother. Children will recognize unconditional love as their father relates to their mother, never scolding, teasing, or speaking harsh words to her, but always loving and forgiving her. As children learn this unconditional love, they will get the proper perception of the unconditional love of God toward them. They will understand they have a loving, caring, and forgiving God who never fails, and who is willing and able to carry them through the hard places of life, even as their father has done for their mother through many storms and struggles.

Just as children learn from their father about the nature of God's love, they also learn from their mother how to respect and submit to God's authority. If their mother talks back to their father, when these children are grown they will likely talk back to God. They will argue with, accuse, and blame Him in times of crisis or difficulty, saying, "God, where were You when this calamity happened?"

Husbands and wives need to pray together regularly. They need to conduct daily family devotions, with the father gathering his family together to read the Scriptures and pray. This can be done at breakfast time, at dinner, or in the evening before bed.

Because the Lord has been merciful toward Marcia and me, teaching us to keep Him in the center of all things throughout our many years of marriage, we can now claim these words from the Holy Scriptures as having come true: *"Praise ye the Lord. Blessed is the man that feareth the LORD, that delighteth greatly in his commandments. His seed shall be mighty upon earth: the generation of the upright shall be blessed"* (Psalm 112:1-2).

CHAPTER EIGHTEEN
What Is a VD Investigator?

After we were married, Marcia and I rented a beautiful, isolated little cottage in a wooded area, about thirty feet from a lake near Madison, Wisconsin. This lovely place had lots of large windows and seemed like a little paradise after the confined living quarters both of us had as students. The setting was also ideal for my last college course in Limnology, which is the study of lakes. Our class would go out onto a lake and study its oxygen content, its flow at various depths, and its marine life.

Toward the end of that semester, Marcia and I began to pray about God's direction for the next segment of our lives. Marcia was pregnant with our first child at the time, and since the Lord had told me He wanted me to be a physician of the soul, the logical thing would be to enter a seminary. We visited a theological school not far from us and met with the academic dean. While we were eating lunch, I asked the dean what the school believed. "Sir," he responded, "we are not attempting to be so presumptuous as to claim to have any answers. We are still trying to learn to ask the right questions."

When he said that, I knew in my heart I was at the wrong place. I thought, *If after 2,000 years of Christianity, we still don't have the answers and are still trying to find out how to ask the right questions, then we are in terrible shape.*

Joseph Stalin, the Soviet dictator of WWII who murdered 43,000,000 of his own people, attended seminary. I wonder if his professors had no answers for his questioning mind. How much damage has been done when questions of inquisitive young minds have not been answered—damage to them, their children, and the world?

We went back home and continued to pray, but I received no witness to apply to another theological school. Whenever there was a question of what to do, I turned to the Word of God. I knew the Bible said if a man does not work, he should not eat (see 2 Thessalonians 3:10). It was obvious I needed a paycheck—soon. In the last few weeks of college, representatives of industries and branches of the service came to the university campus to hire students. My younger brother was hired by Boeing Aircraft Company to work on the super-sonic airplane, which was later scrapped. My older brother was hired by a hydraulic company, and my sister got a job as a secretary. But I was still without work.

One day, as I walked through the university halls, I saw a notice outside one of the classrooms: "Hiring for CDC" (then the Communicable Disease Center of the United States Public Health Service, now the Centers for Disease Control and Prevention, Health and Human Services). There was an opening in the interview schedule right then, so I stepped into the classroom and was interviewed by an officer of that agency. He kept talking to me about something called "VD" for about a half an hour, but I had no idea what he meant. All I knew was I needed a job because my wife was pregnant, we were in desperate need of money, and I was willing to take any employment within reason.

After I went home, I asked my wife, who is a nurse, "What is VD?" When she explained that it stands for venereal disease, I understood the job I had interviewed for was a venereal disease investigator. I knew what venereal disease was, but I had never heard the abbreviation.

About two weeks later I received a call from the CDC telling me I was hired and had the choice of working in Chicago or Detroit. I chose Detroit. No other job had opened up for me, and I believe the Lord provided this employment, as it was not yet time to pursue my theological training. I thought, *If God still needs me in the ministry, He certainly will let me know some day.* From then on, I put the whole matter of the ministry into His hands and out of my mind, sensing I was not yet equipped for that work.

Marcia and I found a small apartment in Detroit, and I went to work immediately. On my first elevator ride at the Social Hygiene Clinic, my Christianity was tested. As another new recruit and I rode up to the third floor with our boss, who was chewing a cold cigar, he said, "Now you know, fellows, you will have to work on Sundays once in a while. When you get on a hot trail, you can't just break it off on Saturday and expect to be able to get back to it on Monday. You have to get on with it right away and stay with it."

Immediately, out of my heart and mouth jumped the words, "Sir, I do not work on Sundays. I worship on Sundays."

The boss responded, "Then you cannot work here."

I said, "Fine! I will just leave."

After we passed the second floor, he said, "Let's just wait a little. Let's just try it."

In that moment, without being prepared, I was confronted with a great and far-reaching decision: Would I, as a young husband and prospective father, begin to sacrifice my Sundays for work, or would I keep the Lord's Day holy and be willing to suffer the consequences? The earthly consequences of not working on Sundays could have been unemployment, underemployment, or ridicule. The eternal consequences would be sacrificing the blessings of God. What would I face on Judgment Day if I decided to ignore the principle of obeying God in all circumstances? Most of the seven young men hired with me were church members, but I was the only "nonconformist," in that I decided in the first hours of my new job that Jesus would be first, my family would be second, and my job would be last. I would rather sleep on the streets than violate the law of God. Furthermore, to live without God is the most dangerous thing we can possibly do.

It is practically impossible to raise a strong Christian family without keeping the Lord's Day holy. If we compromise in one area, before long we will compromise in another. Right there, on that first day of work, I drew a line of no compromise, declaring that Sundays belonged to God, no matter the cost. Of course, there is a biblical exception allowing lay people to work in life-saving occupations like hospital, fire, and law enforcement.

Consider the pain many mothers experience as they sit in their church sanctuaries with their little ones while their husbands are at work. How much do mothers suffer when their husbands are not next to them in the most important family activity of the week, which is worship and prayer? How hard is it to raise the children to be all for God when the father is a compromiser? I would rather be a janitor with a low salary and serve the Lord by raising godly children than have a huge palace with lovely cars, while having sold out to the pressures of the world.

And so, I went to work, trusting Jesus to keep me faithful. Moses, Joseph, and Daniel were also non-conformists for God's sake, and they made it to the top. I knew God could also do that for me if it pleased Him.

My job consisted of interviewing people who had venereal disease, especially syphilis and gonorrhea, and finding out the names of all those they had sex with in the previous six months. I was then to find those individuals in their neighborhoods, somewhere in the big city of Detroit, and draw blood from them, which I would turn in to the clinic's laboratory for evaluation. If the blood test was positive, I would go back out and bring the people in for treatment.

Another of my responsibilities was to visit forty physicians a month and help bring their knowledge of venereal disease up to date. Many physicians, especially the specialists, had forgotten the symptoms of the various kinds of venereal disease, since they were not treating those diseases in their everyday practice.

It was not always easy to find the persons suspected of being infected. While most of my colleagues worked on Sundays to pursue a case, I was with my family in the house of the Lord. After six months, my boss said to me, "I want you to know that you are the only person in the history of CDC in Venereal Disease Control who's ever had a hundred-percent success rate." By the grace of God, I had an elder Brother named Jesus, Who helped me find every suspect, even though I often had no more than a first name and a skimpy description and general vicinity in which the person resided.

Oh, what a difference it makes when we take Jesus to work with us! Later on, when Marcia and I had four teenagers in our home, I never allowed them to work on Sundays, except in nursing homes or hospitals. Yet my children always had jobs, and each Sunday, our family worshipped together.

Every time I was under pressure to compromise in work situations, I stood strong, except for one time I regret to this very day. Just a few weeks before I was to enter Asbury Theological Seminary (by then we had two daughters), I was in great need of finances. I took a job as a semi-truck driver, even though I had never been inside a cab of a semi-truck. As I said before: this is America, and anything is possible!

My father-in-law supervised the license bureau, and he had discovered there was an opening for this position, so I took my chauffeur's license test and passed. I still remember, as I went into the office of the big truck yard in Harlan, Indiana, that the secretary said, "Here are the papers and the key for the truck. Have a good trip." She didn't ask if I had ever driven a semi or how much experience I had. She simply sent me out the door to the double-decker, eighteen-wheeler I was to take to New Mexico, 1,200 miles from Harlan.

For the first time in my life, I climbed into a tractor-trailer, and I prayed, "Jesus, help me!" I turned on the ignition, played with the gears to see which one would pull the best, and drove the rig out of the compound. Then, as soon as I could, I found a place to pull the truck off the road and studied the whole thing more carefully.

On the trip, for some reason, I did not have Sunday on my mind. I was just going to drive down there, deliver the load, and come back. But one day of the journey, as I drove through a little town, I saw people pouring out of their homes, beautifully dressed and carrying their Bibles. That's when it hit me: "This is Sunday!" I was wearing blue jeans and an old flannel shirt, and driving this big old truck. I was so ashamed of myself. As far as I can remember, that is the only day in my life that I ever worked on Sunday. I'm thankful Jesus has forgiven me, but it has left a little scar in my spiritual history that I will never be able to remove in this life. But, thank God, someday it will be removed when I see Jesus face to face. Isn't that marvelous? yes, yes, yes...

Shortly before the year's end in Detroit, Marcia called me at the office and told me she was ready for me to take her to the hospital to deliver our first child. As most fathers would, I drove home faster than normal. The snow was beginning to fall, making driving a little more challenging. It was obvious Marcia was going to deliver that day. She had experienced a lot of difficulty in carrying this little one, nearly suffering miscarriage several times throughout the pregnancy. She was only in her seventh month, and her labor pains were strong and close together.

Marcia was admitted to a Catholic hospital. I was not allowed to be in the labor room or even on the same floor where the delivery would take place. I had to wait in the lobby on the first floor until the doctor came down to tell me about the birth of our child.

Not only was that an eventful day for Marcia and me, but for the whole world as well. While I was waiting, in the very hour our daughter was born, I heard President Kennedy announce on the radio that the United States Navy would intercept Russian ships carrying missiles to Cuba. We were on the edge of World War III, which could possibly have been a nuclear war.

About that time, the doctor came down and said, "Mr. Schultze, don't get excited. You have a baby girl, but her lungs are not fully inflated, and she only has a fifty-percent chance of living. We will not know for seventy-two hours whether she will live or die."

Within my heart, I immediately began to cry out to Jesus, *Oh, Lord, how can I comfort my wife? What can I tell her?*

I entered Marcia's room and saw her lying there peacefully. The baby, whom we would name Esther, was in an isolette in one of the intensive care units. As I approached my sweetheart, she saw my anxious face and said, "Honey, we have already given this child to the Lord. She belongs to Jesus, and He can do with her as He pleases."

Oh, glory to God! Isn't Jesus wonderful? Here I came to comfort my wife, and she had already been comforted by the greatest of all Comforters. And so, she comforted me. Indeed, we had prayed all those months, "Jesus, this is your child. We will raise her for you." Esther was three pounds and fourteen ounces, and in those days and in her condition, it would take a miracle to keep her alive. But after about forty-eight hours,

her lungs began to open, and she was transferred from the
isolette to an incubator. She remained in the hospital four
weeks until she was placed in her mother's arms for the first
time. (Only a mother can understand what it feels like not
to be able to touch her newborn for a month.) This precious
daughter, our firstborn child, is now a pastor's wife and has
two wonderful children who also love the Lord. On top of
ministering to the church people and those in the community,
Esther heads up a Christian school. Needless to say, God
had plans for Esther's life, and He intervened to ensure they
would be fulfilled.

Soon after Esther was born, I ended my first year at
the CDC. My boss called me into his office and offered me
his position, since he was being promoted, but I was not
interested. I was looking for another opening, and at that
particular time, the United States Government passed the
Vaccination Assistance Act because the level of immunization
protection in our country had become dangerously low and we
were also suffering from the polio epidemics. The vaccine for
that crippling disease had just been developed and approved
in 1962, and Congress had allocated funds to put one man
into every state to set up mass immunization clinics.

The position in Alaska was still open, so I applied and got
the job. Within a few weeks, we were living in that beautiful
state. It was there my wife gave birth to our second daughter,
Karin, now a pastor's wife as well, whose influence of godliness
is affecting many precious hearts. Both our daughters were
married by the witness of the Holy Spirit. Their marriages,
as well as that of their parents, were made in heaven. Both
had kept themselves pure, as had their husbands. I am glad I
signed up for nonconformity. Purity is the best way—without
it Christianity is despairingly worthless. Of course, Jesus
extends grace to those who have strayed into sinful behaviors
and later repented, but oh, the joy and rest of being spared
those consequences!

Marcia and I loved Alaska. We rented a small log cabin near the end of the road going out of town, which was really going nowhere. Juneau, the capital city, has no roads going into it. It is located in the Gastenau Channel, with mountains and ice fields rising up all around it. The only access is by water or air.

The log cabin where we lived was located in a thick pine forest, with the trees so close together that very little light filtered through. It was common knowledge in that area that almost every year someone—mostly visiting hunters or tourists unfamiliar with the area, which was populated by black bears—disappeared in those forests, never to be found. The whole ground was covered with a heavy carpet of moss, blanketing the thousands of rotting old trees and rocks on the ground.

Once or twice a week a black bear would visit our backyard to look for mice in the decaying tree trunks. When he got too close to our back deck, we just slammed the door on him. We could never let our two-year-old daughter play outdoors alone.

Although it can be dangerous, Alaska is beautiful. Once we drove to an open place on the edge of the water and a couple of whales rose nearly straight up about twenty feet into the air, only about a half-mile from the road where we were parked. It was such a magnificent sight we could have sung:

> *O give thanks unto the Lord; for he is good:*
> *For his mercy endureth for ever.*
> *To him who alone doeth great wonders:*
> *For his mercy endureth for ever.* (Psalm 136:1,4)

One day, Marcia and one of our neighbors went out to sea in a little boat and came back with a nineteen-pound salmon she had caught. My dear wife was grinning from ear to ear and had an unusual gleam in her eyes. Her daddy was very proud when she told him about it, as he was a trapper and a fisherman, and Marcia was his only daughter.

I was on a two-year government contract in Alaska, and after about one year of setting up clinics and overseeing mass immunizations, I was being prepared to become the regional director in San Francisco. Then the Lord said to me, "Prepare for the ministry—now!" After all I had been through in the previous two years, my time had now come to go to seminary.

So many times, we get ahead of the Lord. This is especially serious for young men and women who enter the ministry. They receive a call, and immediately they want to go to the mission field or step into the pulpit. Sometimes a "call" means to go out at once, but more often it means to *prepare* to go out.

God has a calling for each of us, but many times we need years and years of preparation. We need to go through numerous experiences, tests, and moldings before we can be trusted to enter the mission God has destined us to fulfill. Too many rush into the ministry without having gone through God's apprenticeship program.

When Jesus said, "Go to seminary," I was only one year and three months into my two-year government contract. I was obligated for another nine months, and was therefore in a very difficult situation. I wondered why Jesus couldn't wait just nine more months and then send me after I had finished the government contract. I was at a real point of conflict. If I went by reason, I would simply say, "Lord, if I quit now, I will break the contract. I'll be a bad witness to all the people I have witnessed to on this job." That is what reason said, but revelation said, "Quit now and trust Me." Reason has its proper place, but when revelation comes, reason must take the backseat every time.

I was in this battle between reason and revelation for a little while, but I was determined to follow the revelation of the Lord and trust Him for the rest. I felt like I was dying; I felt a little like Abraham who, against reason, obeyed God and traveled to Mount Moriah to offer up his promised son as a sacrifice to God, except that it appeared to me that my sacrifice was my integrity and my testimony.

Determined to follow God, I boarded an airplane and flew to San Francisco to meet with my boss at the regional office, praying all the way. This thing about leaving a bad witness at the Juneau and regional offices after everyone had learned about my Christianity weighed heavily upon me, but God had to be obeyed. My credentials had to be laid on the altar of sacrifice, even if it meant I would look like an irresponsible fool.

Slowly and hesitantly, I entered the office of the regional director, sat down in front of his desk, and explained the circumstances. "I know I am under a two-year contract, and it was my full intention to honor it, but God is calling me to the ministry."

My boss, a short, stocky man, puffed blue smoke from his big cigar, paused briefly, then gave another puff. Finally, he said, "If God calls you, you'd better go."

Although I kept my composure on the outside, I was shouting on the inside. My credibility, rather than having been lost, had gained in weight. Perhaps this man had never heard of someone forsaking his job to follow Jesus. He did not appear to have darkened the church door much; it is questionable if he went to church at all, except perhaps for funerals or weddings. Yet, somehow he had enough sense to know what Christianity was supposed to be. He seemed to understand that when Jesus calls, He must be obeyed instantly. Maybe my boss had seen too many Christian churchgoers compromising, going by reason, trying to look civilized, responsible, not making waves, not getting radical. Possibly he knew people who tried to play both sides of the equation—the world and the church—unaware that this never adds up to anything of value in God's eyes. Perhaps, for the first time, he saw somebody willing to take up the cross and follow Jesus. For whatever reason, he said, "If God calls you, you'd better go."

I was released from the government job, but my boss also told me, "Since you are leaving before the appointed time, the government will not move you and your family back to the lower contiguous states. You will have to pay your own moving expenses." I told him I understood, and went on my way.

I had less support and sympathy from some of my relatives and acquaintances. *Oma*, especially, was unhappy that I would give up a well-paying job on my climb to the top in order to stoop down to a ministerial position with most likely a lower salary to support my wife and two children. She knew many ministers' salaries were below the poverty line, and it was quite common for ministers' wives to work in order to supplement the family income. She also may have known that many ministers have to move about every three years because the church votes them out, putting great hardship upon their wives and children.

I flew back to Juneau, shared the good news with my sweetheart, and asked, "Where shall I go to seminary?" The last seminary didn't seem to have any answers, so I got a catalog from the library with a listing of all the theological seminaries in the United States. I prayed, "Jesus, I am going to pray for guidance. All these seminaries are listed in alphabetical order. I'm going to start with A and work my way through the alphabet. As I take my pen and bring it down the pages, I want you to stop me when I come to the right one." I never made it out of the A section. When I came to

Asbury, the Lord said, "This is the seminary for you—Asbury Theological Seminary." It was in Wilmore, Kentucky, and I was in Juneau, Alaska, 2,400 miles away—as the crow flies.

I think I may have heard a little about this seminary at one time or another, and I perceived it to be some little primitive place in the Appalachian Mountains. But the Lord had spoken, and I was ready to go. I sent a letter of application to the seminary and then began getting things ready for a move.

At the same time I had to get things organized at my workplace. I had one public health nurse, two RNs, one educator, one communication specialist, some secretaries, and some clerical workers on staff, and I needed to prepare them for a smooth transition to their next boss.

At home, Marcia and I began to sell almost everything we had, at whatever price we could get. I then put my wife and daughters on an airplane from Juneau to Indiana, where they stayed with Marcia's parents until I was ready to start classes at seminary.

After they left, I bought a little four-by-eight-foot homemade open trailer and hitched it to my Dodge Dart coupe. Although the Dodge Dart was a small car, it managed to pull the trailer quite well. I filled the trailer full of what furniture we had left and stacked boxes up to the roof on the inside of the car. I had so many boxes in the front seat next to me that I had to keep my right arm up on top of a box while I drove. In this fashion, I went all the way from Juneau to northern Indiana, a trip of 3,200 miles.

I did not have time to wait for an answer from Asbury Theological Seminary as to whether they wanted to have me or not. School would start in three weeks, and it would take about one week of driving to get to Indiana. I thought to myself, *Regardless of whether they want me or not, God told me to go there, and I am going.*

As there were no roads going out of the Alaskan state capital of Juneau, I drove my car and trailer onto a ferry and took a beautiful 350-mile long boat ride down to Prince Rupert, British Columbia. The next leg of the journey was about 100 miles of gravel road through the forests. I drove the winding road high above the Frasier River on my left. Snow was falling, and suddenly a huge animal, as large as a horse, loomed before me. As I came closer, I saw it was a bull moose. Oh, what a glorious surprise the Lord gave to me as I traveled alone through the wilderness of Canada!

A little farther on, I felt a sudden jerk and discovered that the tongue of my trailer had broken loose from my automobile. I was now dragging this trailer by the safety chain on the gravel. As I always did when I was in trouble, I prayed. I had no idea how many miles I would have to drive to get to a welding shop, but I said, "Jesus, help me!" In just a few minutes, blue flickering light shone through the snowstorm—a welder at work at a gas station! It seemed like Jesus was whispering in my ear, "I am with you; I will never leave you nor forsake you." The welder took care of the problem right away, and for some reason the trailer pulled better than it did before.

The Scriptures say that if God watches over the little sparrows, how much more does He watch over us? Yes, when I was a baby, *Oma* wrote my name next to the underlined verse of Psalm 91:11: *"For he shall give his angels charge over thee, to keep thee in all thy ways."* That prophecy was not only fulfilled in the ashes of Hamburg and during the years in the detention camp, but in a forest of British Columbia. I know this verse will follow me to my death.

When I arrived at my in-laws' home, I had only two weeks to make some money in order to go to seminary. By this time, I had received word from Asbury that they had accepted me for enrollment. Now who would hire a young man for a job for only a week or two? I went to an employment agency called Manpower, which looks for temporary jobs for anyone willing to work. Of course, Manpower pays minimum wage for most of the work they have to offer, but that was fine with me. I was willing to work for $1 an hour if need be. I knew that if we are faithful in little things, God will give us much more. It is of great concern to me that so many college students, upon graduating, won't work for minimum wage. Many will not take a cleaning job. They think they deserve more and better. But they don't understand the scriptural principle that if we are willing to begin at the bottom, God will see that we have everything we need, and eventually we will move up. I believed that if I did my best, Jesus would do the rest, and I have found that to be true throughout my life.

My first assignment through Manpower was to lift fifty-pound bags of flour. All night long, I took the bags off a conveyer belt and put them into a boxcar headed for New York City. From there, the bags were shipped to Thailand to feed the hungry. If I ever left a place of work with a sore back, that was surely the case the next morning. Thank the Lord, the following day, I received another job: I was to sweep out a huge warehouse with a large broom. It took me all night to complete the job, and oh, was it dusty! It wasn't long until I tied my handkerchief around my face so I wouldn't breathe any more dust than necessary. God had told me to go to seminary, and I was doing the best I could to raise the money for it.

At this point God did His miracle, and the truck-driving job I mentioned earlier opened up for me. Doesn't the Bible tell us that if we are faithful in the little things, God will put us over ten cities (see Luke 19:17)? It is when a man is given little assignments that his inner and true character is revealed. When I returned home from delivering my load to New Mexico, I received a huge paycheck, enough to defray the beginning of the seminary costs and acquire the housing we needed.

Asbury Seminary is one of the few remaining holiness institutions in our country. It was founded around 1900 on the teachings of the great English evangelist John Wesley, which flourished in the eighteenth century. Many scholars attribute the salvation and revival of England to the preaching of John Wesley.

An Anglican minister, John first decided to go to America to convert the Indians, but after he had preached there for some time—very unsuccessfully, I might add—he realized he himself was not converted. Discouraged, he returned to England. On the way, his ship ran into a terrible storm. Everyone was terrified of death, except a group of Moravian Christians, who remained calm throughout the ordeal. It was obvious to John they had peace with God, and he did not. The event made a great impression on him.

Not long after his arrival in England, John attended a Bible study where the leader read the preface of Martin Luther's commentary on the book of Romans. John remarked that his "heart was strangely warmed," and later interpreted this event as the time the Holy Spirit entered into his life and he was converted. Since this happened at a place called Aldersgate, it has been referred to ever since as Wesley's Aldersgate experience.

By about 1900, according to many godly people in the Methodist movement, Wesley's doctrine of holiness was beginning to be lost in that church. To preserve this precious doctrinal teaching and to bring the Methodist Church back to the purity of its birth, Asbury Theological Seminary was founded.

In the winter of 1963, I entered this seminary at twenty-seven years of age, a father of two little girls and the husband of a very precious wife. I had no idea what lay ahead, but I knew God was directing me.

CHAPTER NINETEEN
Preparation for Ministry

During my time at Asbury, Marcia worked the afternoon shift as a nurse in a local hospital in order to put me through seminary. We made this arrangement so our girls would always be with one parent or the other. Of course, I had the easier part. I only had to feed the children supper and, most of the time, change the babies' diapers only once before bedtime. What a wonderful joy those little girls were to us! They were so excited about Jesus and so hungry to learn about God, as they still are today.

Some of my finest memories of Asbury were my personal acquaintances with three seminary professors: Dr. Kenneth Kinghorn, Dr. Robert Coleman, and Dr. Thomas Carruth. Dr. Kinghorn knew church history and how to teach it so everyone enjoyed his courses. Because I wanted to make the Great Reformation of the sixteenth century the subject for my Master's thesis, I was delighted to have Kinghorn as my principle professor in that area. What a difference a professor can make in the halls of learning. Some are famous for scholarship, but they cannot teach. Some can teach, but they are not exceptionally brilliant. Kinghorn was both brilliant and a good teacher.

Another great enjoyment to me was Dr. Robert Coleman, professor of Evangelism. I found Dr. Coleman really was trying to obey the Holy Spirit in the midst of the institutional system. Indeed, it was not uncommon, while he taught one of his classes on evangelism, for some student to be convicted, go to his knees beside his desk, and cry out, "Jesus, please save me!" The word got around that if someone arrived at seminary unsaved, there was a great possibility of his being converted in Dr. Coleman's class.

Dr. Coleman was also greatly effective and unique in his approach when he went on home visits. He was known never to cross the threshold of any home without first kneeling at the door in prayer. He also was known for carrying his Bible wherever he went. When he preached, this slender, six-foot-tall professor had such fire upon him that his straight black hair would fly from side to side. It was quite a sight to behold.

Willing to give us some of his personal time, Dr. Coleman announced to his class that if anyone wanted to join him for prayer once a week at 6 A.M. in his office, he would be happy to have us. Two other students and I joined him each Tuesday morning. What a wonderful memory I now have of hearing that dedicated servant's agonized cry for revival. I had never heard anyone in any church agonize in prayer, as if the whole world's future depended on it. I knew Moses and Abraham prayed that way, as do all the great saints. James also encouraged us to pray in this way: *"The effectual fervent prayer of a righteous man availeth much"* (James 5:16).

My third fond memory of my time at Asbury was of Dr. Thomas Carruth, the greatest orator I ever knew. When I first saw him, standing straight and tall, I thought he, like Rev. Hollingsworth (in the sanatorium), looked like Moses. Dr. Carruth and I were newcomers to the seminary, and he had become aware of the fact that, at that time, there were no seminaries in the United States with courses on prayer. He went to the Eli Lilly Foundation and told their board of directors that these preacher boys were coming out of our seminaries without being men of prayer. He then asked if they were willing to do something about it. Eli Lilly responded by agreeing to underwrite the Department of Prayer and Spiritual Life at Asbury Theological Seminary. To the best of my knowledge, Dr. Carruth became the first professor ever to be installed by any seminary to lead that position.

Dr. Carruth started his first class of the semester quite differently than other professors. In his southern drawl, he said, "Is there any one of you boys in class who doesn't want to worry about your grades while you are studying about communing with God? Well, if so, I want you to raise your hand now, and I will just give you an A, and you will be all done with your grade." Only three or four hands of about twenty went up, my hand being one of them. Then he said, "You fellows just come down to my office after class, and I will put your grade in my book." Most of the students thought it was too good to be true to receive an A before the class even started, so they didn't take Dr. Carruth up on his offer. But Dr. Carruth was not as much interested in academics as he was in seeing students' hearts become one with God.

While there will always be those who doubt and question every good opportunity, there will also be those with the spirit of the Queen of Sheba who, when she heard about the wealth and wisdom of King Solomon, did not say, "It's too good to be true; therefore I shall not go see him," but rather, "It's too good to be false. I had better get on my way to see this great man of God." We must be so careful not to allow a cynical spirit to come upon us when we see men and women of God fail. The failure of finite human beings does not reflect upon an infinite God who never fails. And because of God's faithfulness to work out His purpose in us, we must not give up on each other either. To do so is to chance missing something truly wonderful. We must read our Bible from beginning to end to discover that God has always had true servants who have not defiled themselves.

Dr. Carruth was one of those servants. So after class, I went to his office and said, "I would like to have my A." He opened his grade book, asked for my name, and marked my grade for the semester: **A**. Both of us were smiling. I'm sure this approach would not have been appropriate for other courses where the mastery of the subject could be clearly measured, but how do you measure man's communion with God and put a grade on it? Perhaps, unknown to him, this professor put his finger on the very thing seminary students need more than scholarship: communion with God. Isn't that what you wish for your pastor, to have communion with God more than perfect sermons? Don't you want his whole life to be an illustration of walking with God, even as the prophets of old were?

Not only did Dr. Carruth have a vision for the great need for fellowship with God, but he also saw the need for living examples of that communion. I wish the entire world could have listened when he spoke about God and when he prayed. It was as if God Himself were speaking through lips of clay. Dr. Carruth spoke and lived by the revelation of the Holy Spirit, and I too wanted to be such a man. I immediately put academics second and communion with God first. Beware of the man who does not!

There were two other professors at Asbury who seemed to bring a greater vision of the kingdom of God to my seminary days: Dr. Rose and Dr. William Arnett. Both preached sanctification and the need for us to be a holy people, and their classes and messages re-ignited my desire to be all God wanted me to be.

Asbury had a small prayer chapel next to the main sanctuary, a place for students to come and meet with God. I was saddened that in the two and a half years I was there, I found only about four or five out of the 300 or so students regularly frequenting this place of prayer. As a whole, when young men enter seminary prayerless, they leave the same way. They may get a license to preach from man, but not necessarily from God. And when they get into their pastorates, the business of the church often crowds out the little bit of praying they were trying to do. Statistics today tell us the average pastor prays only about four minutes a day. How can a pastor who spends no more than four minutes a day in God's presence presume to lead his flock in the ways of the Lord?

I graduated from Asbury in 1967, but I excused myself from the graduation ceremony because I felt it would add nothing further to my education. However, in retrospect, perhaps I should have been there, simply out of respect for my elders. While my fellow students, dressed in their beautiful robes, marched down the aisle to get their diplomas, I sat on a tractor pulling that four-bottom plow, getting a field ready to plant for my father-in-law. And perhaps I got started to plant a whole lot more than corn that day.

Graciously, Asbury sent my Master of Divinity diploma to me a year later, and I was officially numbered among the clergy. But though I had a deep yearning for God and a head full of doctrine, church history, and Bible knowledge, I was still very much unprepared to pastor a congregation and to walk as Jesus walked. I joined the 90 percent of ministers who found their seminary education woefully inadequate for the work of the pastoral ministry. I had received a Master of Divinity degree, but I left that wonderful institution neither feeling like a master nor possessing much divinity. I felt I was still at the bottom, looking upward for much more help.

Sister Caroline Eisner

She connected the Schultzes
with the American lady.

CHAPTER TWENTY
My First Pastoral Experience

During my second year at seminary, I was encouraged to take what is known as a "student charge," meaning I would be assigned to preach at a nearby church each Sunday, giving me some practical preaching experience. My church assignment was located in the Kentucky hills, about an hour and a half drive northeast of the seminary.

This was quite a new adventure for Marcia and me and our two little girls. Leaving the seminary campus, we took county roads, the Interstate, more county roads, and finally a narrow gravel road that wound higher and higher up the spine of a mountain until we came to the crest of the hill. Here we found a small white frame church building sitting directly across the road from a gigantic black tobacco barn. We were in tobacco country, and depending on the direction of the wind, our church services were saturated with the tobacco's rich aroma. Kentucky is known for horse racing but also for tobacco and the black barns where the leaves are dried. At the time, I claimed to be a holiness preacher (in the making), and needless to say, tobacco and holiness are worlds apart.

As we approached the church the first time, we noticed most of the congregation was outside, enjoying the intermission between Sunday school and the worship service. We got out of our car, and immediately one of the lay leaders came to me and, with a lit cigarette dangling from his lips, said, "Hello, I'm the Sunday school superintendent. I want you to know right away, don't ever touch our Sunday school, and don't ever touch anything in the church. The only thing we want you to do is preach." That was my introduction to that church, the first words I, as a pastor, ever heard from a layman. But I was glad to receive those instructions, because preaching was all I wanted to do anyway.

How that little Methodist congregation put up with me for one year is a marvel. Yet they were experienced with student ministers and had learned to adjust to each of them. On top of that, with the exception of two men, everyone in the church was involved in the tobacco-growing business. After church each Sunday, we were invited by one of six families to a great dining experience. Normally, the dinner table was loaded with chicken and at least one other type of meat, potatoes, beans, and various other food items. Though there was practically no financial compensation for our services and ministry at the church, the people made up for it by providing us with the best meal we had all week, a welcome relief from our usual inexpensive repast of hot dogs and potato salad. In spite of all the tobacco around, we loved the people at that little church, and they loved us.

Although I don't remember making any spiritual impact on that congregation, I am thankful for the practice in preaching. Probably my most significant contribution to that already small church was that I reduced their membership. It is not that the attendance dropped that year, but as I reviewed the membership list, I found the names of people who had been dead for years and others who had moved away long ago. I therefore did the most natural and logical thing: I removed those "non-attendees," dead or alive, from the list, much to the dismay of the District Superintendent. Other pastors before me had neglected the list for years, so when I removed the names, it made the Superintendent's annual report about that church to the Bishop look rather discouraging.

In the last few months of seminary, I had been in prayer as to where God wanted us to go. We were not affiliated with a denomination; we only wanted the leading of the Holy Spirit, for to miss that is to miss all. I told the Lord I was willing to go anywhere: to the Baptists, Methodists, Pentecostals, or Disciples of Christ, wherever He chose. When we walk with God, our choices—the choices of the flesh—always come head to head with God's choice. Whenever we come to this point of conflict, if we choose by the flesh, we crucify Christ. But if we choose in the Spirit, we crucify the flesh, our self-life. The secret of living is in dying (see John 12:24). By the grace of God I was ready for God's choice, whatever that happened to be.

George Washington Carver, the great black American scientist, once said that we cannot expect a revelation from God until we have come to a point of total neutrality. That is, until we have come to the point where we have no prejudices or personal choices toward any one thing but the will of God. I knew all along that my primary calling was not to be a pastor. Somehow, deep within, I felt I was called to be a teacher, but then, not exactly that either. I knew there was something else, something broader God was calling me to beyond teaching, which I am still waiting to see fulfilled. At that time, I thought I would go on to get my doctor's degree in Church history and teach in that area. I was encouraged to apply at Emory University in Georgia, but the witness of the Holy Spirit was not in that choice. It was a choice of the flesh.

Just before finishing my studies, I learned of a certain denomination I felt was closest to the teachings of the Bible, so I submitted an application to the denomination's leaders.

Then I went to one of their ministers' meetings and sat in the presence of several very seasoned, elderly ministers who were considering my application. After they asked me a few questions, they became rather upset with my answers. They wanted me to come up with some statement of loyalty to their particular programs and institutions. I believe one of the causes for so much division and spiritual barrenness in our churches, is that too often people are converted to denominations rather than to Jesus himself. When I told these brothers that my loyalties had to be first to the Lord Himself, the meeting was over. I returned to the seminary, rejected in my first effort to join a religious organization or movement.

A few weeks later, a pastor in that particular organization invited me to their church headquarters to meet with one of the top leaders of that group. When I gave this brother the same answers I gave the men in Kentucky, he got up from his chair, walked over to me, and said, "This is what this denomination is all about." He then asked where I wanted to pastor. It was in my heart to go to the Northwest, so when he asked if I would consider Canada, I quickly agreed, as I considered that part of the Northwest.

The man then pulled out three files of three churches in the province of Alberta and asked if I had a preference. There was a small church in a small town, a larger city congregation, and a college church, which was associated with the denomination's Bible College. As I prayed, the Lord directed me to take the city church.

Most lay people have no idea what goes into the making of a minister, nor do they know much about the process of placing a pastor with a church. I think it is important for those who fill the pews to know the struggles, the battles, and the problems related to a minister's life. Each pastor's story is different, of course, but this is my autobiography, and after forty years of pastoring, I can assure you my story is not much different from many others in the ministry.

Having received God's direction, we rented a large U-Haul trailer, hooked it up to our car, and stuffed it to the hilt with whatever would fit. After cramming the rest of our belongings into the car, we started on the five-day, 2,100-mile journey from Wilmore, Kentucky, to Edmonton, Alberta, Canada. We seldom exceeded forty-five mph because at any higher speed, the trailer began to whiplash. Still, we enjoyed the trip immensely, tenting along the way in state parks or KOA camps. Esther was four years old, and Karin was two. Before our trip came to an end, our girls were already in love with camping.

And so it was in 1967, at thirty-one years of age, that I finally started my fulltime ministry with my first church in Canada. I immediately learned that no occupation is as difficult and beset with as many trials, battles, and joys as the work of the ministry. But once a minister is fully in his calling and he maintains a strong prayer life, he will feel God's grace abounding and overflowing in all his needs.

Upon our arrival in Edmonton, the congregation gave us a wonderful welcome, and we quickly settled into the parsonage about three doors from the church building. At the time, the congregation consisted of about seventy people in the Sunday morning service, and to this day I can say this was the most organized church we ever pastored in my forty years of ministry. It was a very active church, with plenty of committees and boards, Sunday school, Boy Scouts and Girl Scouts, and a Bible program for the children. Basically, they had very good lay leadership, and the church ran smoothly. The salary at the time of our start was $75 a week, which was fairly reasonable for the time. With my background of living with little, my wife's frugality, and our family's few wants other than the Father's will, we were able to manage quite well with that amount.

There are two principles we laid down early in our marriage that have greatly impacted our family, our ministry, and the spiritual lives of our children and grandchildren. One principle is that mothers belong in the home to raise the children, and the other is that the Lord's Day is to be kept holy, as I have already shown.

We had decided quite early in our marriage that Marcia would not go to work while we had children, and preferably not after they were grown. We both agreed once a woman becomes a mother, her first and fulltime calling is in the home, raising the children for the Lord. There is no higher calling for any woman. Of course, there was that little stint of two and a half years when my wife worked to put me through seminary, but that was an exception and completely within God's will, and in that time we seldom allowed our children to be without one or the other of us.

One of the reasons America has gone into a moral tailspin since the 1940s is that during WWII, mothers abandoned motherhood. They went to work and fell in love with their own incomes and professions, and the children were turned over to babysitters, daycare centers, and nurseries. The training of children, especially the development of character, suffered a great blow. Strong character-building makes a strong nation. The absence of character always impoverishes both the individual and the nation.

Excellent grades and a string of degrees do not buy anyone a place in heaven. But character, molded by the Lord Jesus Christ, gives children a front seat at the throne of God. We must continually think about life beyond this one. There is a little phrase in the Bible that says, *"Prepare to meet thy God"* (Amos 4:12). We must always keep this admonition before ourselves and our children. Indeed, it is better for a child not to be born than to have his own way, fulfill his own desires, and end up on the pathway that leads to eternal destruction and separation from heaven.

Solomon, the wisest mortal man who ever lived, said, *"Train up a child in the way he should go: and when he is old, he will not depart from it"* (Proverbs 22:6). This process of training cannot be accomplished with children spending hours with babysitters or in daycare centers or nurseries. It cannot be done effectively by mothers who come home with their energy sapped, having given their best at work, with few resources left to put into mothering at the end of the day. Occasionally, God in His mercy will do a miracle under these circumstances, but these miracles are the exception and not the rule.

For us, every Friday night was family night. Children need their mothers, but they also need to bond and interact with their fathers. Every Friday after lunch I kept my schedule clear so our family could do things together, whether it was going camping, playing games, bicycling, visiting the zoo, etc. We didn't have enough money until years later to go get ice cream or eat at McDonald's, but since we never did that to start with, our children were not even aware such places existed. Marcia always had something nice and special for us to eat, and we had such fun times together. We kept this up from shortly after our children were born until they were grown and left the house.

When my oldest daughter was thirty-five, she told me, "Daddy, the most memorable experiences I had were when I heard you praying and agonizing in the office, and when we went camping in the Rocky Mountains." We even camped when our children were in diapers—and that was before disposables!

We had so many delightful and unforgettable experiences together, particularly when we were camping with another family. At one time, sitting in a circle around the campfire at sunset, we took turns praying. During that prayer time, I opened my eyes and realized a skunk had joined the prayer circle only a few feet from my sleeping Black Labrador, Duke. I assure you my prayers took on a different tone at that moment, but just as we said, "Amen," the skunk moved towards the trees, the dog awoke and got a whiff of the interloper, and off he went in hot pursuit. Of course, our dog got sprayed and quickly headed for the stream, where he managed to get himself fairly well cleaned up, but not enough to earn his normal space in the tent that night. But Duke was helpful at campsites, particularly when it came to warding off occasional bear visits. During another campsite adventure, Duke met his first porcupine. It took two of us to hold him down and one to pull the barbs out of his tongue, eyelids, and nose.

We have many other fond memories, such as the time the girls and I crossed a swift-running, ice-cold mountain stream. I balanced a long staff in my hands, with one girl clinging to each end. The girls were in the rushing stream up to their chests, and I was in up to my hips. We had to secure our footing each step of the way between rough, slippery rocks lodged on the bottom of the stream. It was scary, wild, and wonderful. The kids never forgot things like that. Years later, our adopted son Chester made his own unforgettable memory when he slid down a steep hill covered with tiny little cactuses.

Preachers' kids lose their way so many times because they are neglected by their pastor-fathers, who are "busy doing good." The children get leftover, burned-out pieces of love and energy. The father says he's busy with "the Lord's work," but doesn't the Lord's work include our own children? Didn't Jesus say, "[Allow] *the little children to come unto me,... for of such is the kingdom of God"* (Mark 10:14)? Our children did not get all the clothing and gadgets their peers had, but they got lots of love, excitement, and adventures. Someone once said, "If Christianity does not begin at home, it does not begin at all." When a pastor loses his wife and children, he loses his credibility. Paul says that "deacons must rule their children and home well" (1 Timothy 3:12). It is no sin for a pastor to spend adequate time with his family; rather, it is a sin not to.

Of course, there are always emergencies, and the pastor's family must learn to understand and accept that. I had my first such emergency in Edmonton when the phone rang at 1:30 in the morning. A man called from the downtown bus station to say he had just gotten out of prison but had no money to take a bus to Whitehorse, about 1,000 miles northwest of our location. He said he had gone through the Yellow Pages and called thirty-two parsonages, and no pastor was willing to get out of bed to help him. I put on my clothes and drove to the bus station to pick him up, then headed northwest through the cold "no man's land" in the middle of the night. While playing nervously with an empty Coke bottle, my passenger told me he had served a long prison term for murder. I listened, praying and trusting Jesus as the man talked, and then began to share the gospel of Jesus with him. I told him about Jesus' wonderful love and forgiveness, and how it could be his if he would repent of his sin and ask the Lord to come into his life. Shortly after, he joined me in a prayer to receive Jesus into his heart.

By about four in the morning, I realized I had to turn around or I would not have enough gas to get back home. I stopped at the next village and pounded on the parsonage door of the Episcopal Church and woke up the priest. Sleepily he came to the door, and I told him this man was now his. The priest called the deputy sheriff, who had an empty bed in the local jail, so they put him up there for the night. Knowing he was in good hands and I had done all I could, I drove into the sunrise to return to my family, feeling good because I knew this was what it was all about to be a pastor.

My second emergency was when a divorcee named Wilma called me at the church one afternoon. This was an era when there was seldom more than one divorcee in the whole church, and Wilma was deeply depressed. "Pastor," she said, "I have set my house on fire. I'm going to burn myself up." I immediately hung up the phone and called the fire department. When they arrived, they found Wilma in the smoke, but she was all right. A few months later, Wilma had an experience with the Lord in which she was filled with the Holy Spirit and became one of the most dynamic Christians I have ever known. I still remember the day in late fall when I baptized her in an ice-cold, fast-running, turbulent river. For a moment we both thought we were going to be swept away, but it was another one of those experiences when it felt good to be a pastor.

While pastors need to balance helping people in dire situations and spending time alone with their families, the family of a good pastor soon finds out they all must make sacrifices, especially in emergencies. Pastors are like doctors—on call twenty-four hours a day, seven days a week, and working most of the weeknights. In a good pastoral family, all members act together to do whatever it takes to shepherd the flock.

If a pastor does not lay down sound biblical principles in the beginning of his ministry, sooner or later he may become a failure in the work of the Lord. At the time of this writing, statistics show that only one out of every 100 seminary graduates retires as a pastor, and the average minister leaves his pastorate in his seventh year to do something else. The main reasons for quitting are discouragement and financial.

Keeping the Sabbath day holy, keeping the mother at home, and having family time are vital principles that help keep ministerial families strong. Of course, for the pastor to keep the Sabbath day holy means taking an entire day off during the week, because for him Sunday is the hardest day of work. God said there were to be six days of work and one day of rest from that work. That principle is stated in the Ten Commandments and has equal standing with all the other nine. In other words, it must be taken as seriously as "Do not commit adultery" or "Do not kill."

Just as a layman will not be blessed if he works on the day of worship, neither will the pastor if he does not rest one day during the week. The sad reality is that many pastors cannot get a full day off during the week unless they leave town. People get sick, die, and experience crisis situations any day of the week. I even have people call me from other cities with critical problems that need immediate solutions, and it makes no difference what day it is. I have had calls from my staff on my days off, needing help to make serious business decisions. Consequently, I schedule both Mondays and Fridays as my days off so I can be assured of getting the equivalent of one real day of rest. I can tell you now, after forty years of ministry, that I often receive the most significant revelations from the Lord on my days off.

One of the most necessary ingredients for a successful pastorate is divine love. It is the most powerful transformer of human hearts. During one of my pastorates, a young preacher named Leon, along with his wife and three little girls, came to visit our church. Leon had been in my youth group during my second pastorate, and I had not seen him since his teenage years. He told me he had gone through three pastorates in the last eighteen months. Obviously that brought a lot of pain, frustration, and upheaval to him and his family. I prayed about his problem, and Jesus said, "Have him preach the evening service for you." As Leon was preaching, I noticed the spirit of frustration, anxiety, and anger underlying his otherwise positive sermon. After the service the Lord said, "Get him a new suit, tie, and shirt." I asked a couple of businessmen in my church to take care of that for me.

Six years later I talked to Leon again and asked how many churches he had pastored since our last contact. He said he was still in the same Methodist church, and they lived in a perpetual spirit of love and revival. It seems when we put that new suit, shirt, and tie on Leon, we clothed him in God's love. The anger, resentment, frustration, and anxiety left his wounded spirit, and he became a vessel fit for the Master's use.

If only congregations could grasp the great truth that the more love they put into their pastor, the more help he will be to them. Sometimes it takes only a little thing to turn him into a new man.

In terms of the pastoral ministry, I discovered it seems best if a minister can restrict himself primarily to the preaching of the Word and to prayer, and leave the rest of the work of the ministry to the congregation. (In most cases, it is the congregation that stays and the pastor who leaves in a few years anyhow, though it may be different if the pastor starts a work himself and serves a congregation for a long period of time.) It was truly of the Holy Spirit when the first ministers decided to *give ourselves continually to prayer, and to the ministry of the word"* (Acts 6:4). Let the deacons take care of the rest. The modern concept that a minister is to be an administrator or a coach does not line up with sound biblical doctrine.

We all need to be committed to prayer, both pastors and laity. Praying pastors eventually beget praying congregations. Prayerless pastors encourage prayerlessness in the parishioners, and when there is prayerlessness in a congregation, frivolity, foolishness, jesting, and joking abound.

Indeed the lay people in my congregation in Canada did everything and just let me preach and pray. As a young minister, I liked the arrangement. I went to the people with the understanding that I had little knowledge of how to administer church programs. I knew I needed to learn from them as they were learning from me. This congregation loved me and followed me as much as they knew how. With great joy, they told others about their wonderful man of God, which brought more people into the sanctuary; within one to two years, the congregation had doubled in size. But in the second year the leaders began to question me, and in the third year they opposed me, which was also Jesus' experience. His first year of public ministry was a year of popularity; the second was a year of questioning; in the third year, they killed him.

In the third year at the church in Edmonton, I was encouraged by the Superintendent of my denomination to have an American evangelist come up to hold revival services for one week. In those days the average evangelical church held one week of revival service and one week of missions conference each year.

Rev. Robert Morgan was one of the meekest, most soft-spoken little evangelists I had ever seen. He hardly ever raised his voice; his sermons were practical and no longer than twenty minutes; and the Lord directed him marvelously. He knew nothing about what was going on in our congregation, nor did I have any perception of the magnitude of the dissatisfaction toward me in the church leadership. Perhaps the worst I ever heard of the problem was when one of the board members approached my wife and said, "We certainly appreciate you, but we just can't stand your husband."

I am not saying this to make any church leader look bad. As a matter of fact, from their perspective, they had every reason to be concerned. Their sincerity to serve the church was no less than mine. I loved those men and respected them dearly, and do to this day. They were some of the finest men the institutional church could produce. But I want to give a realistic perception of what it is to be a pastor, from a pastor's perspective. I want to make it clear how easily problems and misunderstandings arise between a minister and his flock, and to help us all prayerfully guard against such division.

At the time I was also taking some courses in theology at the University of Alberta. One day, as I was walking from one building to the next to change classes, I bumped into my wife, who was holding our one-and-a-half year old, newly adopted son in her arms. Marcia was noticeably upset about something, and she exclaimed, "They are going to oust us tonight!" That meant the church had planned a congregational meeting without informing me in order to vote us out of the church, and that is exactly what they did. I was charged with not being loyal to the denomination's teachings and programs and for preaching too straight.

Looking back upon the experience of my first pastorate, I know if I had been more gracious and seasoned I perhaps could have held on another year or two, but the separation between me and the institutional church became more and more inevitable. I knew if I wanted to follow Jesus' voice, I would have to find my place of ministry outside man's religious systems, just as Jesus and the ancient prophets. The institution of the priesthood had no place for our Lord; it killed Him and the true prophets of old were in almost continual conflict with the priesthood as well. But oh, if religious institutions would only allow their men of God to obey God, how much help they could be to them.

However, before we left this first pastorate, Marcia and I had a marvelous experience that later led us to a freedom we have now experienced for thirty-six years of pastoral ministry. It began with the visit of that frail little evangelist, who came to us from the United States to preach at the weeklong revival meeting just before we were voted out. Rev. Robert Morgan became a great strength and a source of inspiration to us. After each church service, Marcia and I met with the evangelist and his sweet wife in our parsonage to share about the precious things of God, remaining there in fellowship until we were too tired to talk sense any more.

This went on night after night. While we shared together, this dear brother told me story after story about a man who was truly walking with God and whom he believed was a prophet or an apostle. I listened intently, for it seemed— though I had not been fully aware of it—that I had wanted to meet such a man since my conversion in 1952. These stories seemed too good to be false, rather than too good to be true.

Before long, Rev. Morgan and his wife called this prophet of the Lord, Rev. Loran Helm, who lived in Indiana, and told him about me. Immediately Rev. Helm, by the revelation of the Holy Spirit, said, "Rev. Schultze will be with us in the third meeting hence." Rev. Helm was a Methodist minister who, after having pastored several churches, was called by the Lord to forsake all institutional systems of man and to go only in the way the Lord would lead him. Of course, he made himself accountable to a number of men of God, but when churches asked Rev. Helm if he could come for a revival meeting, he did not go to his calendar or to his appointment book to see when he would have an opening. He simply prayed and asked the Lord to give him a witness whether it was to be in January, February, March, or April, etc. When he came to the right month, the Holy Spirit witnessed to him about it. Then he would pray and asked the Lord which week. Finally, Rev. Helm would pray as to what day the meeting was to begin.

For example, a certain congregation asked our evangelist friend, Rev. Morgan, to come to a meeting in Canada. The congregation suggested a certain date for his coming, so Rev. Morgan asked Brother Helm to pray about it. After praying, Brother Helm told Rev. Morgan, "You cannot go at the time the church wants you to come." Then the Lord gave Brother Helm the days when Brother Morgan was suppose to be there, and Rev. Morgan relayed this to the congregation up north. When the congregation received these new dates, they said there was no way they could have him come during that week because that was the week of wheat harvest. In Canada, the summers are very short, and the harvesting time is even shorter. If the wheat is not brought in within that short period of time, it will spoil. The dates the Lord gave Brother Helm for the meetings fell smack in the middle of this short harvest time. The congregation let Rev. Morgan know they wanted him to pray about another date to come and hold the meeting for them. Rev. Morgan replied that he could go only when the Holy Spirit led. As it turned out, on the appointed day that Rev. Morgan was to arrive, the day on which the Holy Spirit had led him to come, it began to rain, and it rained all week. Consequently, none of the farmers were able to get out into the fields to bring their harvest in. They all said to one another, "Oh, we surely should have had Rev. Morgan come during this week."

It was this type of praying and waiting on God, waiting for the voice of Jesus to speak, for which my heart yearned. God only works through persons who wait on Him. He cannot work through us as long as we make our own plans for our own convenience. My acquaintance with Rev. Helm turned out to be another step up on "Jacob's ladder" toward the perfect and acceptable will of God being fulfilled in my life.

CHAPTER TWENTY-ONE

Waiting upon God

In December of 1969, after being rejected by my first church, we rented a large truck and moved south across the U.S./Canadian border to our second pastorate in Billings, Montana. But now, instead of four in our family, we were five.

Marcia had miscarried with our third child on Christmas Day in 1968. Shortly after, we became part of a planning committee for a citywide revival, meeting with two of our sister churches in Edmonton. One of the ladies on the committee was in charge of a home for handicapped orphans, or half-orphans. When she found out Marcia had miscarried, she told her she had a black-haired, black-eyed boy just for her. In addition, because Marcia was a nurse, the lady offered to give her a tour of the home.

One day soon after, Marcia went and took the tour, as the lady gave her a short history of each of the fifty children who lived there. She did not tell Marcia which was the black-haired, black-eyed boy she had mentioned, but when they got back to the lady's office, Marcia asked if it was the little boy named Camron. Sure enough, he was the one. It had been love at first sight, and Marcia knew God had brought little Camron to us.

Camron's father was a Cree Indian from Northern Alberta, and his mother was of German descent. He was born with

Hirschsprung's Disease, a condition in which the large bowel will not contract and move the stool out through the rectum. As a result, the bowel continues to enlarge. When Camron was two weeks old, the doctors had removed two-thirds of his large bowel and given him a colostomy. When he was a year old, they were able to close the colostomy. Camron had diarrhea for many years after that. In fact, the doctors didn't know if he would ever gain control of his bowels, but at about four years of age, God performed a miracle and our son was healed.

Camron was eighteen months old when we got him, and he had spent his entire life in a hospital. At first he had trouble connecting with me because the only men he knew were doctors who hurt him, but over time he got past his fear and we were able to bond. It was fun to watch him explore his new world, as he was very expressive about all the new things he saw and experienced. Camron eventually grew up to become a very gifted tool and die machinist, and it was a joy and privilege to have him in our family.

Billings, the site of our new pastorate, is a beautiful little town in the foothills of the Rockies, only about one hour from Bear Tooth Pass. This pass is one of the most spectacular in the world, rising to an altitude of about 12,000 feet on switchback roads with incredible sights of mountains and valleys, and leading to the north entrance of Yellowstone National Park. While we were in Billings, we had the opportunity to take this scenic drive a number of times to enjoy God's wonderful handiwork and to marvel at His breathtaking creation.

The congregation at Billings consisted of about seventy regulars, who welcomed us with open arms. And much like the previous congregation, they were well organized.

From then on, Marcia and I attended many Bible conferences, seminars, and conventions, but we nearly always returned home feeling disappointed and saying to each other, "This is not it. There has to be something else." The sermons were good and the singing was fine, but something was missing, and we just could not put our finger on it. We later learned it was the leadership of the Holy Spirit, for it is only by the Holy Spirit that we can be fed. Not knowing that at the time, we continued to cry out to God for help, though we had no idea where it would come from or how long it would take to arrive. Through it all, however, we never gave up hope.

Then we drove about 1,500 miles to visit our denomination's international camp meeting. Approximately 20,000 people attended that week of meetings, so imagine my surprise, as I set up our tent in the camping area, to look up and see Rev. Robert Morgan.

"Now, children," he said, "you are going to come to the Waiting on God in a couple of months, aren't you?" I told him I knew nothing about it. Brother Morgan then told us there had been a death in his family and he had received a little inheritance money, so he gave us $100 to help us get to our first Waiting on God meeting.

We were so humbled and excited at the prospect. Eight weeks later, after another 1,500-mile, three-day trip from Billings, we arrived at the Holiday Inn in Indianapolis.

We soon learned that the Waiting on God meetings originated after Rev. Loran Helm, the wonderful Methodist minister we had heard about from Rev. Morgan, gave up everything to follow God. At that time the Lord instructed him to wait on Him for the next twenty years. Throughout that time, Rev. Helm and his wife and three daughters lived entirely by faith, without salary, as the Lord prepared him for his ministry. Only rarely did he go out to hold a meeting. After this twenty-year period of waiting, the Lord instructed Rev. Helm to find the people who wanted to be all for God. He was then to gather them together, at the Holy Spirit's direction, for three days at a time in some hotel to wait on the Lord with him, to be instructed and prepared for a worldwide revival.

In His high-priestly prayer, prior to His crucifixion, Jesus prayed for a worldwide revival: *"That they all may be one; as thou, Father, art in me, and I in thee, that they also may be one in us: that the world may believe that thou hast sent me"* (John 17:21).

The first Pentecost—the first outpouring of the Holy Spirit upon the Church—occurred when all of God's children came to oneness. Dr. Luke wrote in the book of Acts, *"And when the day of Pentecost was fully come, they were all with one accord in one place.... And they were all filled with the Holy Ghost"* (2:1, 4).

God wants to give the world another outpouring of His presence, and it will occur when He can find a people somewhere in the world who will pay the price to come to oneness—the kind of oneness that exists between the Father and the Son. God wants a holy, spotless bride. Jesus said when this occurs, as stated above, the world will believe. The impediment to oneness is the self-life, which the Apostle Paul referred to as the carnal nature that must be crucified out of us.

When Marcia and I arrived at the Waiting on God meeting, we found we were not quite prepared for what was in store. As we entered the lobby of that hotel, we saw people everywhere, talking and sharing with each other. The father of one of Rev. Helm's staff members, recognizing me from Brother Morgan's description, came up and welcomed us. He introduced me to his son, who shook my hand and immediately tried to embrace me in love. I in turn used our handclasp to hold him back. In all my thirty-five years of life, I had never been hugged by anyone other than my wife. I cannot even recall being hugged by my parents. It simply wasn't done in my German culture or heritage, and I considered it effeminate. Then, while I was still in a group with this young staff member, he remarked that he felt the power of the Holy Spirit flowing like electricity from my hand to his. I told him I hadn't felt anything, but he said, "I sure did!" This was something else I had never heard of before, and I stored it away in the back of my mind.

The meeting was about to begin, so we made our way into the main room and found seats in the middle of the left-hand section. As the prelude music played, the congregation stood. I looked to my right, and just above the heads of the congregation I glimpsed Rev. Helm moving down the aisle, with his staff following. I had never seen the man before, not even in a picture, but in that very moment, the Holy Spirit revealed his identity to me.

When Rev. Helm and his staff arrived on the platform, he smiled at the congregation and said, "The Holy Spirit wants us to praise Jesus." Then he lifted up his hands, and 700 people—minus two—did the same, and together they began to praise God—out loud. Marcia and I, of course, were the minus two. We had never lifted our hands to praise the Lord or praised God out loud. In fact, it was against my theology to do so. After all, I reasoned, Jesus had instructed His disciples, *"But thou, when thou prayest, enter into thy closet, and when thou hast shut thy door, pray to thy Father which is in secret; and thy Father which seeth in secret shall reward thee openly"* (Matthew 6:6).

What made things even more difficult was that the people were being so repetitive in their praises, using such phrases as, "We praise You, Jesus; Thank You for Your mercy; Glory be to the Father, the Son, and the Holy Spirit; Holy, Holy, Holy is the Lord; Thank You, Jesus," and so on. I had some negative thoughts about that, too, as it seemed the greatest imaginable insult to my intelligence—and to God's intelligence as well. I was thoroughly convinced you never had to tell God anything twice. Furthermore, I had been indoctrinated to believe we ought to use our brains.

Isn't it amazing that often, when we are in a prolonged search for something real and beautiful, just as we are about to grasp it we find a big wall looming in front of us, threatening any further progress. We had finally come to the place where the very thing we had been longing and praying for was right in front of us, but we would have to scale that wall of personal prejudices to get to the blessing God had for us.

After this praise had gone on for fifteen to twenty minutes, I was becoming more and more negative and miserable. Finally, I decided to look around at the faces of these poor, "uneducated" people. Being tall, I could easily see almost everyone in the room. As I looked at them, I saw their faces shining with the glory of God. Obviously, they were all having a wonderful time praising God, and I thought to myself, *If I looked into a mirror right now, what would my countenance reveal to me?* I concluded I would probably look as if I had just eaten some sour pickles. Then I said to Jesus, *If lifting up my hands and praising God out loud is all it takes for me to look like they do, it is worth the effort.*

So I swallowed my pride, and with a great deal of self-denial and will power, I lifted up one hand. Immediately I sensed the Lord say, "Use two hands. Put them all the way up and start praising Me," and I did. Instantly, something that had bound me for a long time—call it pride, if you will—began to break within me, and I knew I was free.

Once I began to praise the Lord out loud with raised hands, I remembered all the scriptures that command us to praise God out loud and to praise Him together in unison: *"Make a joyful noise unto the LORD...Enter into his gates with thanksgiving"* (Psalm 100:1, 4); *"O magnify the LORD with me, and let us exalt his name together.... lift up your hands in the sanctuary, and bless the LORD"* (Psalm 34:3, 134:2). We were certainly making a joyful noise that day, and we were definitely thankful, as we lifted up holy hands together. You certainly cannot be a praiser and complainer at the same time.

God wants his people to pray and praise, not only alone, but also in unison with other believers. Jesus, upon entering Jerusalem, found the multitude praising the Lord *together.* Indeed, thousands of voices praised God at the same time (see Luke 19:37).

This pattern of praising God together was repeated over and over in Israel wherever Jesus performed a miracle. This was not a practice the believers began when Jesus came, but it had its roots in Old Testament worship and was carried over into the Christian era. If you would look for the first description of a prayer meeting in the history of the church, you would find this, *"they lifted up their voice to God with one accord"* (Acts 4:24). Paul said to Timothy: *"I will therefore that men pray every where, lifting up holy hands"* (1 Timothy 2:8). This tells us that praising God in unison with uplifted hands was to become an ordinance of the New Testament Church, as it was with Old Testament believers. Someone may object that if we do so, we cannot hear each other's praises. But we are not doing this to be heard by men, but by God. He is worthy of our praise, and He can hear all of us at the same time. This archetype of worship is the main occupation of all the angels and saints in heaven: *"Let every thing that hath breath praise the LORD"* (Psalm 150:6). Someone once said, "When we pray, we act like men; when we praise, we act like angels."

God wants praise. God longs for praise. Jesus is addicted to praise. He had it continually before He came to earth, and He wants it here on earth. God will not be found in the company of skeptics, complainers, and faultfinders. If the multitude would not have praised Jesus out loud when He rode into Jerusalem, He would have had the stones cry out in exaltation and adoration (see Luke 19:40). Yet in many churches, if the pastor called for this kind of praise, he would be voted out immediately.

As you can see, this practice of audible, hearty praise with lifted hands was the norm in Old Testament days when the church was at her best. Here are further references: Psalm 63:4, 1 Chronicles 16:4, 23:30 and 2 Chronicles 20:21.

This praise session went on for forty-five minutes, longer than any praise session I ever experienced in any Waiting upon God gatherings I attended after that day. Perhaps God wanted to break me in by emphasizing the importance of such a spiritual exercise, and to prepare me for that unending praise session at the throne of God. After all, if we don't like strong and fervent praise here on earth, what are we going to do in heaven?

After the praise session ended, Rev. Helm sat down and said, "Now we need to pray about what the Holy Spirit wants us to do next. The Holy Spirit is telling me that we are to sing a congregational song. Now, Lord, is it in the red book or the black book?" He paused, then went on. "It is in the red book. Is the song in the first hundred pages, the second hundred, or the third?" He paused again. "It is in the second hundred. Lord, is the song in the tens, twenties, or thirties? And, Lord, which number in that group is it?" That was the way Rev. Helm found the hymn the Holy Spirit wanted us to sing. When he came to the right number each time, he would state, "The Holy Spirit is witnessing in my heart about this number." Others at times would have the same witness.

Of course, I was utterly amazed at this whole process, and frankly speaking, I was overjoyed with this part of the service. I had never been in a meeting where the minister in charge prayed in such a way in order to find the hymn God wanted us to sing together.

Ministers are taught in seminary that when you have a worship service, you should start with a hymn familiar to the people, meaning we were taught to get our hymns by the choice of men and not by the choice of God. In most church services I had attended, the order of service was planned by well-meaning men and women who tried their best to make the congregation happy.

Rev. Helm later addressed this issue in his book, *A Voice in the Wilderness*:

> *The average church person believes that the program of the church is to be handled like any other business, and should proceed along the path of least conflicts and most beneficial results.*
>
> *Quite to the contrary, any time a church works out a program or a religious plan in themselves, it is not pleasing to God. This is not a popular statement to declare, but I must give the truth in love or be held responsible at Judgment. I know that we dare not devise our own church systems and programs because our ideas, at their very best, can only come from our human minds and insights. They originate from the wisdom of the earth and cannot satisfy heavenly requirements, for God's Word plainly states: "...they that are in the flesh cannot please God." (Romans 8:8)*
>
> *I am not seeking to find fault with any church, but Jesus has revealed to me that unless our singing, our preaching, our Sunday schools, Bible schools, and revivals are led by the Holy Spirit, the fruit of these activities will not survive. Jesus tells us that "Every plant, which my heavenly Father hath not planted, shall be rooted up." (Matthew 15:13) This strongly*

indicates to me that the Holy Spirit must not only lead,
but must be the Author of all that I do. He must be the
One to plan my life; He must originate my programs or
I will be living a life which is powerless and ineffectual.
It is as I am submissive, broken, waiting on God, and
loving everybody, that Jesus is able to lead me into a
life of divine vigor and eternal glory.[1]

For Marcia and me, this was a very unusual meeting.
The Holy Spirit sometimes led us to a song that few in the
congregation had ever sung before, but because it was the
song God wanted, the anointing was so powerful and beautiful
that the Holy Spirit worked in the people as they sang: some
were touched with encouragement and blessing; others were
healed; some were convicted; others were delivered from
spiritual bondages. This was all because the choice of the
hymn was made by God and not by man.

I recall in one of the "afterglow" luncheons—a meeting
after the meetings—Rev. Helm sensed the Holy Spirit telling
him someone in the gathering had a severe sore throat. He
moved his arm from the left side around the room until it
pointed toward the right section. When he stated what the
need was on the right, a little lady from India arose. She
was so short she could not be seen from the platform. With
uplifted hands and tears streaming down her face, she cried
out, "It's me! It's me! I've been praying to Jesus that He
would deliver me from this terrible sore throat." Rev. Helm
prayed, and to God's glory, the sore throat was healed. In
this manner, by the pinpoint accuracy of the Holy Spirit
working through this servant, many needs were met over
and over again.

Of course, there was much corporate praise for every
deliverance. I assume it was something like the days when
Jesus was on the earth.

With the Lord leading and helping in this way during

each session, no one wanted to leave. It was as if Jesus Himself were literally directing the services. Services often lasted three, four, even five hours, yet at times seemed to have lasted less than an hour.

It had been sixteen years since I had come to the United States, and at last I had attended a church meeting so enjoyable I didn't want it to end. However, despite all the wonderful corporate praise and miraculous workings of God, there were certain things that bothered Marcia and me, things we just could not accept at the time. Again, the devil often puts up a wall before we reach the very blessing our heart has been yearning for. Consequently, Marcia and I planned to leave after the first session and go back to Montana, even though we had witnessed such amazing things.

Before leaving town, we decided to eat at McDonald's. Of course, there were hundreds of people at the meetings trying to find someplace to eat, and there were many restaurants nearby. And yet, with all the possibilities, as Marcia and I sat there at McDonald's, in walked Rev. Morgan—alone. He immediately came over to our table and asked how we were getting along. Being a well-known evangelist, he could have gone out to eat with many ministers or laymen who would have treasured his company, but here he was at McDonald's, asking how we were doing. We told him we were just about ready to go back to Montana, and we gave him some reasons for our departure. His response was, "Dear children, why don't you just take the things that help you, and leave the rest alone." In other words, don't eat the whole fish; leave the bones alone. We could not have thought of any wiser counsel than that.

The Lord sent Rev. Morgan to McDonald's at just the right time to tell us what we needed to know to keep us where we would learn to walk by the voice of God. Because of Rev. Morgan's encouragement, we went back for the second session and felt much more comfortable as we focused only on the things that would help us.

Isn't this what the Apostle Paul instructed us to do? *"Finally, brethren, whatsoever things are true, whatsoever things are honest, whatsoever things are just, whatsoever things are pure, whatsoever things are lovely, whatsoever things are of good report; if there be any virtue, and if there be any praise, think on these things"* (Philippians 4:8). This is an important point to remember when entering a church service or any such meeting. We may hear or see things that are not to our liking, everything may not be done in divine order, or we may not be ready for them. But if we can focus on the positives, we will receive help. Sometimes, after the service is over, through the help we have received we may be able to encourage others who are struggling along the highway to heaven.

The most positive aspect of this Waiting upon God was the powerful presence of the Lord and the leadership of His Holy Spirit. In the afternoon session, I was asked to share my life story. After relating my early life experiences from birth until the time I was saved, I returned to the back of the large, ornate meeting room. There at the end of the center aisle was a man nearly as tall as I and weighing almost 300 pounds. His name was Joseph Bishop, and he was a fairly new convert. During his adolescence, he had become so angry at the church and its people—as well as everybody else— that he was about to enter the Mafia. In fact, the Mafia had already accepted him.

But that all began to change the day Rev. Helm visited Joseph's parents' church. At his parents' home after the service, Joseph heard Rev. Helm share story after story of how Jesus had helped him, leading here and directing there. When Brother Helm was ready to leave, he turned to Joseph and told him how much he loved him, put his arms around him, and prayed for him. That act so affected the young man that he came to church that night for the first time in a long while, just to hear Rev. Helm preach. Before he returned home, Joseph had entered into the Kingdom of God.

Joseph had an alarm business, and he had a way of getting along with everybody. No one was a stranger to him, and after just a few minutes of meeting someone, he would talk to them about his wonderful Savior. Just as he was angry at everyone before he was converted, now the love of God flowed out of Joseph's heart toward everybody he met.

That day, after I finished sharing my story at the Holiday Inn, as I came down the aisle toward the back wall, there stood Joseph, whom I had never met, looking straight at me. Without my expecting or wanting him to, he took a step forward and put his arms around me. Now me being a rather thin man, and because Joseph was so much bigger and stronger, I couldn't easily escape his grip. "Brother," he said, " I want you to know that I love you and that you are precious in Jesus' sight." He was the first man who ever put his arms around me, and in that moment God broke something else that had bound me for years. From then on, I was able to begin to love people in a new and special way. I learned to love the elder men as if they were my fathers, men of my own age as brothers, and young men and boys as if I were their father or grandfather. However, I never put my arms around a woman to express love for her, except with my wife and daughters. It is very dangerous for a man to put his arms around another woman. Many times, something gets started that leads down a terrible path of heartache and broken marriage.

Because the Lord had changed some things in my heart that day, all the negatives in my life began to turn into positives, little by little. As we follow the Lord Jesus in love and as we have love toward all men, God begins to open our understanding to many things that otherwise we would never comprehend. Someone once said, "If you love something enough, it will reveal itself to you." Love is a great door to the hidden treasures of Christ's glorious Kingdom. The depth of our love for God will determine the depth of our revelation and knowledge about Him.

At the end of the third day of Waiting upon God, Brother Helm felt led by the Holy Spirit to have an offering taken to help us get back home to Montana. The generosity of those people was amazing. I don't know exactly how many others received an offering during those three days, but I do know there were dozens who received financial help. Because God was leading through those meetings, everyone's need was met: the many ministers who lived on a shoestring, college students who had little or nothing, and elderly people who were short on funds. In some way, it was like being in the early Church, when everyone laid what they had at the apostles' feet, and then distribution was made to everyone who had a need.

Discovering and meeting people's specific needs was one of Rev. Helm's outstanding characteristics, and I have seen him do exactly that for over thirty years now.

When Marcia and I left Billings to go to that first Waiting upon God meeting, we had only enough money to travel those three days to Indianapolis. No one knew we did not have enough money to make it back home again. But there, at the end of the meetings, the Lord made ample provision for us to return home with our hearts satisfied at last. We left those meetings knowing that if the Holy Spirit leads, God's will is done and His Kingdom is come among us.

Back home in Billings, a year later, we were soon surprised with a visit from Thomas Harman, our good friend and print shop manager from Indiana. As Thomas and I stood in front of our beautiful white stucco church building, he asked, "Reimar, are you going to the next Waiting upon

God?"

"I had not planned on it," I answered.

"Well," he said, "Jesus tells me in my heart that He wants you to go."

Instantly I followed up with, "Then I am going!"

We took our two daughters with us to the next Waiting upon God, and when those memorable sessions ended, my then ten-year-old daughter, Esther, remarked, "Daddy, don't you ever leave me home when there is another Waiting upon God like that."

And indeed, she and her family have been at every one of them since.

Reimar

"There must be a God!"

CHAPTER TWENTY-TWO

"Start Packing..."

Upon returning to Billings from our first Waiting upon God, we shared with our congregation how the Lord blessed and helped us in Indiana. We thought surely the next time these dear people would want to go with us for this liberating adventure in Christ Jesus. To our surprise, the opposite was the case. The congregation, which had previously been so loving toward us, suddenly cooled. We were no longer on the same wavelength. Shortly after, for the first and last time in my life, I considered quitting the ministry.

I went to my office and wrote a letter to the US government, asking to be reinstated in the Public Health Service where I had worked before I entered the ministry. But before I dropped the letter into the mailbox, I went up the Rims, the mountains surrounding that lovely city, to seek and receive a word from the Lord. As I sat on a boulder, overlooking the city and smelling the pungent odor of the majestic pines, the Lord told me, "This is not your church. You can't build a church; only I can. Take your hands off the church, and just walk with me." In Matthew 16:18, Jesus said, *"I will build my church; and the gates of hell shall not prevail against it."* Oh, how the tension drained from my shoulders as I came to perfect peace about the issue. It wasn't up to me to build a church. All I had to do was walk with God. It sounded wonderful—so simple and do-able by the grace of God.

What are we preachers doing meddling in the church-building business? We say we know Jesus is the One who builds the Church, but do we really believe it? If we build a church, then it is ours and not God's, and He has little to do with it. If we build it, it is only a religious organization and not part of His body. But if we let Him build the church, then it is His doing and He will dwell in it. He will anoint, protect, bless, and sustain it—provided we allow Him to continue to be the Head of the church, working in and through His precious Holy Spirit *"to will and to do of his good pleasure"* (Philippians 2:13). Pastors must let the Holy Spirit lead them in all church services and activities. Nothing in the church must come out of men's desires, preferences, or pressures from certain groups or individuals. We must also remember Jesus warned the Pharisees against allowing their traditions to imprison them. Everything that is done in the church must come from the Holy Spirit. If not, the church is a headless body, and souls are not fed.

Jesus said, *"Every plant, which my heavenly Father has not planted, shall be rooted up"* (Matthew 15:13). This is serious. I am so thankful that in my fifth year of ministry the Lord told me, "Take your hands off the church, whether it was built by the hands of men or by Me. Just follow Me step by step in holy trust." Regretfully, most churches are not started by the Holy Spirit, nor are they sustained by Him. Yet, in many of them God has a few precious souls who need a loving shepherd.

After serving this congregation in Billings for about three years, the Lord told me to move on. I had several calls from a congregation in Coeur d'Alene, Idaho, and they sounded like a wonderful group of people with a great vision for missions, and they were located right in the middle of the picturesque Rocky Mountains. But every time they called or wrote to me,

Jesus said, "No, this is not for you." Then I was contacted by a church in Lincoln, Nebraska. Lincoln is situated in the middle of the Great Plains, where the ground is as flat as a pancake and you can travel hundreds of miles without seeing anything but cornfields, silos, and a few houses scattered among the golden grain. There was nothing that attracted me to Lincoln. Also, this congregation was only half the size of my current one. But as I meditated upon it, I decided to call another pastor who I knew walked with God. As we talked about the situation, the Lord began to witness in our hearts that Lincoln was the place to go. I immediately went to the public library to find out the pollen count of Lincoln. I had hay fever in Billings, a mountain city, and I was concerned about how much higher the pollen count would be in Nebraska. To my dismay, I discovered the count in Lincoln was a thousand times higher than in Billings. I don't recall what book I used to obtain these figures or whether they represented the average for that year or just for a season. Nonetheless, I prayed, "Lord, are you sending me to Lincoln to die of hay fever?" As far as I could see, there were only negatives on this prospect: flat ground, lots of strong wind, a much smaller congregation, and far too much pollen.

I made a telephone call to the chairman of the pulpit committee in Lincoln and made arrangements to fly down to the city and "try out." This meant I would meet with the church leaders on Saturday afternoon for questions, preach on Sunday morning and evening, and then the church would vote on whether or not they wanted me as their pastor. When I arrived in Lincoln, I was told there was an important football game going on and some of the leaders wanted to attend, so my meeting with the leaders that afternoon had been cancelled. This was another negative. But Jesus said, "Go. This is where you belong." After I preached on Sunday morning and evening, the words from Jesus were confirmed when the church members voted 100 percent in my favor.

A few weeks later, with the temperature hovering at twenty degrees below zero, we loaded a U-Haul truck to move to our third pastorate. It began to look like we would average a new church every three years, and it got to the point that whenever Marcia and I passed a U-Haul on the Interstate, we tried to get a look at the driver and then asked each other, "Does he look like a preacher?"

Again, as we left Edmonton with a new family member, so we left Billings with yet another addition to our family. We had contacted the welfare system in Billings about adopting a brother for Camron and the girls. When they found out we had taken one handicapped boy, they asked if we would consider taking another. Marcia told them we would, as long as it was not such a serious or permanent disability that we would be tied down for the rest of our lives. That is when they introduced us to Chester, who had a congenital hip condition. He was four years old at the time, only four months younger than Camron. He was blonde and blue-eyed, and had been raised by a ten-year-old sister before welfare found him. He was presently in a foster home. His mother never wanted or accepted him, even to this day, and his speech was limited to about ten words, which were difficult to understand. Chester was also far behind in coordination and motor skills, but we felt we were to take this boy into our home and make him part of our family. Welfare paid for the correction of his congenital hip defect shortly after we got him, and he was in a body cast for six weeks. As time progressed, God began to heal Chester's other problems, and despite his negative medical history, Chester has learned to carry his own weight. He now lives near us in Kokomo and works in a factory.

We arrived in Lincoln to find our new parsonage painted a bright yellow and located only one block north of the little stone church, which was hugged by fifteen-foot juniper trees. This was another well-organized church with a lot of talented and intelligent, well-educated people. A young man by the name of Robert Morey always sat close to the back of the sanctuary. Robert was six-foot-two, slender, with dark wavy hair. He had a brilliant mind, and though he was still in high school at the time, he was already taking courses in astronomy at the University. As time went on, Robert began to inch his way closer to the front, bench by bench, until finally he was sitting on the platform with me, leading singing. When I asked him why he had moved from the back to the very front of the sanctuary, he replied, "I had been able to figure out every one of the many preachers we've had over the years, but you were different." What Robert did not yet know was that by then I had gone to two Waiting upon God meetings. When I announced the next one, Robert was interested.

Upon arriving at the meetings in Indianapolis, Robert was thrilled with what he found, and he immediately got right in line with the work of the Holy Spirit. And that was just the beginning. Little did we know, when Marcia and I first considered the move to Lincoln, with its small congregation, the pollen, the wind, the flat ground, and the football games, that we were going to find our son-in-law in that church, and that he would have the calling of an evangelist. What a treasure we found hidden among all those negatives! And how often do we miss God's treasures because we are so caught up in the negatives? Jesus had told me to go to Lincoln and not to look at the circumstances, but rather to look only to Him and believe. Circumstances can deceive, frighten, and mislead us, but if we will keep our eyes fixed on Jesus, we will never go wrong. As the Bible says, we are not to go by sight, but by faith. Didn't God send Abraham from the fertile plains of the Euphrates to the rocks and a pagan people in Canaan? Yet, it is here in Canaan that God revealed Himself to mankind and sent His Son Jesus into the world.

In Lincoln we also discovered Robert's sister, one of the finest soprano voices in the country, who eventually followed us to our present pastoral ministry, where she has been with us now for twenty-three years. In addition, we became acquainted with a lovely teenage girl named Ruth, who had long, straight, red hair and came from a broken home. When we moved from the Lincoln congregation, Ruth followed us to our present pastorate, where Jesus found her a wonderful husband.

Soon after arriving in Lincoln, I began to visit our people, and while some were glad to see me, others seemed to consider my visits an interruption to their television programs. I asked the Lord what to do about this, and He told me, "Stop visiting the people. Visit with Me. You are the one who has the biggest need in this church." And so I heeded His directive. Every morning I prayed and waited on God in the sanctuary from seven to eight. I then returned home to eat breakfast with my family and see the children off to school. By nine I was back in the sanctuary, where I remained in prayer until about noon. Throughout the afternoon I returned to the sanctuary periodically to meet with God again, praying and waiting on the Lord to speak to me and teach me. And that is exactly what He did. He told me of the many things He wanted removed from my heart. He would love me and chasten me, and then love me and chasten me some more, to make me a vessel fit for the Master's use.

As I read *A Voice in the Wilderness* by Rev. Loran Helm, the Lord showed me the ugliness of my heart. He revealed to me that I needed to be sanctified. We need to understand that when we are born again, Jesus removes all our sins we have committed as far as the east is from the west. But after the rebirth we still have to deal with the carnal nature. This evil nature entered man through Adam's disobedience and every man is born with it. The process by which the carnal nature is dethroned to be replaced by God's own nature is called sanctification. It is this carnal nature which refuses the Lordship of Jesus Christ over our lives.

Therefore Jesus prayed concerning his disciples, "*Sanctify them through thy truth*" (John 17:17). Paul prayed for the born again Christians at Thessalonica, "*And the very God of peace sanctify you wholly; and I pray God your whole spirit and soul and body be preserved blameless unto the coming of our Lord Jesus Christ. Faithful is he that calleth you, who also will do it*" (1 Thessalonians 5:23, 24). God wants us to be sanctified so that he might fill us with his Holy Spirit.

We become candidates for sanctification once we seek first the kingdom of God and strive to obey God in everything. As I was waiting upon God I discovered that because of my carnality I had been robbed of intimate unbroken fellowship with Jesus the first nineteen years of my Christian life.

The carnal nature must cease to rule in our lives. This carnal nature, the Adamic nature or the old man, as it is also called in the Bible is the cause of all adultery, fornication, criticism, resentment, hate, anger, murder, greed, bitterness, impatience, harshness, pride, grudges, pouting, deception, foolishness, jesting, backbiting, lying, cheating, exaggerations, lust and self-assertion. It will plot, plan, reason and figure, but it will neither trust nor obey. It has filled our prisons and divorce courts, divided our churches and driven thousands of ministers out of their pulpits. It has emptied our church prayer meetings, and it has brought worldliness into our sanctuaries.

Carnality is blind to the things of God, it opposes everything that is of God, and it will never follow Jesus. Carnality put Jesus on the cross. Carnality is a killer. Paul warns us that *"to be carnally minded is death,"* and that *"the carnal mind is enmity against God"* (Romans 8:6, 7). Carnality has done more damage to the church than all the evil forces of the world put together. Jesus and all the great men of God have taught us that our worst enemy is within us. Carnality has made the professing church sick. Someone said that if our bodies were as sick as the professing church we would all be in an intensive care unit of a hospital.

Carnality has to be dealt with. Carnality has to be slain out of us. This is why Jesus said, *"If any man will come after me, let him deny himself, and take up his cross daily, and follow me"* (Luke 9:23). Jesus died on His cross to save us, but we must die on our cross to follow him.

It is a sobering fact that all Christians are carnal until they are sanctified, cleansed of this carnal nature. To maintain the state of sanctification we must remain on the cross through continual self-denial, by the Word and the blood of Jesus. Many believers think they are sanctified because they have spiritual gifts, but Paul tells us that although the Corinthian believers came *"behind in no gift,"* they were yet carnal, unsanctified (1 Corinthians 1:7, 3:1-3).

As I sat in the pews of that little church in Lincoln sometimes the Lord would say to me, "Do you remember how you responded to your wife yesterday?" And, oh yes, did I ever remember. It seemed in those days of waiting upon God nothing ungodly in my life remained uncovered. Then the Lord revealed to me the seriousness of criticism and judging our brothers. I had been in the habit of analyzing, criticizing, and judging other preachers on their lifestyles and sermons in the presence of my wife. I did not realize that in doing so that I had violated the law of love over and over again. We cannot walk with God if we violate the law of love. The law of love is the queen of all laws pertaining to God and man. If we violate this law it prevents us from hearing the inner voice of Jesus. Jesus said, *"my sheep hear my voice, and I know them, and they follow me"* (John 10:27). How can we follow if we can't hear? Paul said, *"as many as are led by the Spirit of God, they are the sons of God"* (Romans 8:14).

As I was responding to God in repentance, self-denial, and obedience, He began to cleanse my heart and simultaneously take the wax out of my spiritual ears so that I began to be led by the Holy Spirit. Oh, what a wonder that was and still is. In addition to that I began to experience the joy of obedience. The joy of obedience is a gift from God to every obedient heart. This joy far surpasses the joy of conversion, which peaked on the day of our salvation. As I continued to wait upon God, I received my spiritual "pilot's instrument rating" by which I could fly through the dark overcast of spiritual gloom and doom into the sunshine of God's splendor. I was being baptized in His love. Oh, yes, at last I came into joy unspeakable and full of glory! I suddenly had love for everyone, for friends and enemies alike: for those who helped me and for those who damaged my ministry. Suddenly I found myself in the kingdom of God which is *"righteousness, and peace, and joy in the Holy Ghost"* (Romans 14:17).

This process of concentrated waiting on God, of inner cleansing, lasted about two years. I know God can do this work in a day, but there was so much within me that was not pleasing to the Lord, and there was so much unlearning that had to be done. All these nineteen years well meaning religious men had taught me, but now I was being taught of God. I was in an extended process of relearning. I received a powerful revelation of the depth and ugliness of sin and of the effervescent brightness of God's holiness.

I had attended man's seminary, but I was now in God's seminary. He was preparing me so that His spiritual lifeblood would pulse through my spiritual veins so that I might be one with Him, which is what abiding in Christ means. It is coming to oneness with our Lord, just as a branch is one with the vine.

Occasionally during the afternoon, as I sought God in the sanctuary, I thought I heard what appeared to be a door opening and closing, but since I heard no footsteps in the vestibule, I dismissed it. To my surprise, I found out years later that while I was waiting upon God and praying, Ruth, the red-haired teenage girl I mentioned earlier, would slip into the front door. Instead of going through the sanctuary doors where I was praying, she slipped into the basement to hear me pray. Several months later she met Jesus in a youth revival meeting in Omaha, and her sister also came to Jesus soon after. Oh, what do we miss when God calls us to Nineveh and we instead go to Tarshish! What if Marcia and I had ignored God's directive and gone to Idaho instead of Nebraska? God wants us to go by revelation, not by reason.

I have heard of pastors who have gone to bigger churches because of personal ambition or outside pressures, only to get involved in an ungodly relationship with a secretary or someone else in the congregation and end up losing family and ministry. It is essential to wait on God until we hear His voice, and then obey His directive, instead of listening to the signs and signals of the world and yielding to the pressures of men.

Shortly after this, the church in Lincoln had sold its building and parsonage, and we had moved out of the yellow parsonage into a beautiful home in suburban South Lincoln. We were surrounded by professional people: a surgeon, a lawyer, a gas company executive, a university professor, and others of equal standing. Our house was only one block from a golf course and a huge park with bicycle trails and a lake for sailing.

At that time the church had been thinking about expansion and had bought ten acres of land on which to erect the new building. Since the old church had been sold, we were meeting in a school in the interim. During those first three years at the Lincoln church, I found myself thinking I could be happy there for the rest of my life. But before our fourth year in Lincoln was over, I began to get restless, tensions developed once again in the church, and I knew some people in leadership would prefer I leave. By then, I had come to the conclusion that I wasn't worth a whole lot in the pastoral ministry.

And then, after thousands of hours of waiting upon God, on Monday, August 15, 1977, at eight o'clock in the morning, I heard the Lord speak within me: "Start packing. You are leaving next week, Tuesday afternoon." That was the first revelation I had received from the Holy Spirit in a very long time. I immediately called out to my wife, who was upstairs, "Honey, the Lord just spoke to me."

"Praise the Lord," she called back. "What did He say?"

"He said, 'Start packing. You are leaving next week, Tuesday afternoon.'"

"Praise the Lord!" she repeated. "Where are we going?"

"He didn't tell me," I answered truthfully, "but I believe when the time comes to leave, Jesus will help us know where we are to go."

Many wives in such a situation would have said, "Now, honey, just wait a minute..." But our marriage had been put together by the Holy Spirit, and He had given me a wonderful wife, so there was no "wait a minute," only a "praise the Lord!"

Indeed, glory to God! It looked like a great adventure lay ahead of us. By this time, besides our own four children, we had Ruth. Since her home life was not what it should be, she lived with us for a while. About the same age as our two daughters, Ruth wanted to be with them as much as possible. Back before seatbelt laws, we often went places together in our Volkswagen Beetle: the black labrador, Marcia, and I in front, the three girls in the backseat, and the two boys behind the backseat in the baggage compartment under the slanted glass—all packed in like sardines.

Immediately after the Lord told us to start packing, I knew my time of waiting on God was over for the day, so I got into my car and drove to a truck rental place and told the manager, "I would like to reserve the biggest truck you have because we are moving next week, and I plan to pick up the truck next Monday." He asked me where I was going, and I told him I didn't know. He asked me to repeat my answer, probably thinking he had heard me wrong. After all, there I was, reserving a truck with a ten-dollar deposit and a signed contract, without knowing where this truck would take us.

On the way back to the parsonage, I stopped at various grocery stores and loaded my car with empty boxes. The packing began immediately. As the boxes filled up and began to pile up in our driveway, the neighbors came over to ask where we were going. I gave them all the same answer: "I don't know." Most of them had the same perplexed response as the rental truck manager. "You don't know?"

We packed all day Monday and Tuesday and into Wednesday. On Wednesday, I met for lunch with the president of the state church organization to which I belonged. This brother, a kind and successful businessman, was also a member of my congregation. While we were eating and sharing, he came to the point where he said to me, "Pastor, you have no future in the church." Before either of us could say another word, a voice came over the loudspeaker, calling me to the phone. I excused myself from this dear brother who had just told me I had no future in the church and went to the phone.

Marcia was on the line, and I could tell by the tone of her voice she was thrilled about something. "Honey, Brother

Helm just called from Indiana. He was in the garage with his son-in-law, and all of a sudden Jesus spoke to him and told him to call Rev. Schultze and tell him the Lord has revealed a place for him to go. Rev. Helm has been trying to get hold of you, but he will call back tonight in order to share with both of us where God wants us."

I went back to the table, with the words of my lunch partner ringing in my ears: "Pastor, you have no future in the church." But the word I heard from the Lord while talking on the telephone with Marcia told me otherwise: "God has a place for you, and He will be with you there." Only a few seconds had separated one message from the other. The first was the voice of man, the second, the voice of God. Rev. Helm was 750 miles from us, and I do not recall having informed him of our current situation.

As evening approached, my wife and I anxiously awaited the call. We did not quite know how to juggle the timing of this call because we had a church board meeting in our parsonage that evening. But, praise the Lord, just before the board meeting began, the phone rang. Marcia and I each picked up a phone, ready to hear what God had in store for us. Brother Helm began to share with Marcia and me that there was a handful of people in a little town near Kokomo, Indiana, that the Lord wanted us to shepherd. The group was so small that perhaps either Marcia or I would have to work to sustain our income. Of course, we were both professionals—she is a nurse, and I was a machinist. Obviously, though, if someone had to work, it should be me, as I wanted my sweetheart to be able to stay home and be a fulltime mother.

From the moment that phone call began, Marcia and I felt the presence of the Lord more strongly than we had for many years. It seemed like the joy of the Lord flooded our hearts like never before. We felt as if we were on our way to freedom and that we had stepped onto a glorious highway of "His Kingdom come, His will be done" that we had never known existed. As God personally called Abraham out of the land of the Chaldees, He was calling us out of Lincoln, out of the restraints of men and manmade programs, to bring us into His perfect will.

The call was short, and we were able to start our board meeting on time. As we came to the close of that meeting, I told the board members we would be leaving the following Tuesday. I had already informed them several weeks before that I was praying about leaving the Lincoln pastorate, and they had been most gracious not to push me, giving us all the time we needed to find another place of service. To my amazement, when I announced we were leaving on Tuesday, nobody asked where we were going.

Before the meeting's closing prayer, Robert's sister, Marilyn, suggested that since I was leaving so soon, perhaps the church could give us the next two weeks' salary in advance. Everyone agreed, and this was surely of the Lord because Marcia and I were nearly penniless after paying the $10 deposit for the truck rental. With the assurance of these additional funds, we received confirmation that God was with us in this move.

On Friday, the Lord sent another pastor, his wife, and two boys to our home. They were passing through from the West to return to their home in Michigan and decided to stay and help us pack. We so appreciated their gracious offer and much-needed assistance, as we raced the clock to be ready to leave our home in the next few days.

Fortunately, by this time we had two cars—the Volkswagen and a Cadillac. A few months before the Lord directed us to move to Kokomo, I was on the telephone with Thomas, my print shop friend from Indiana. While we talked business, I mentioned our need for a second car. Instantly, he said, "Your car is a 1974 Cadillac on the east side of town."

Thomas had come through Lincoln only once, and that was on the Interstate. He certainly did not know that I didn't have an extra dollar to put down on a vehicle. He also didn't know if there was a Cadillac dealer on the east side of town, but it was obvious he was speaking by revelation of the Holy Spirit, and I believed that revelation.

I quickly located a Cadillac dealer on the eastside and talked to the salesman, telling him I wanted a 1974 Cadillac. When he insisted they did not have one, I assured him they did. He even got out his inventory sheet and showed me there was no '74 Cadillac on the lot. But I knew what God had promised, and I continued to believe the revelation of the Holy Spirit.

Next, he tried to sell me an Oldsmobile or a Pontiac. I said no, it had to be a '74 Cadillac. When he continued to insist they didn't have one, I went home, but when I came back the next day he said, "I just remembered. We do have a '74 Cadillac. It's sitting against the back wall, but it's not for sale. It's marked to be auctioned off at Kansas City in a few weeks." The salesman in Lincoln did not know he had my Cadillac on his lot, but a man of God 750 miles away knew by the revelation of the Holy Spirit that my car was there. Oh, what we miss by not being connected with God!

Now we were getting somewhere, so I said, "Tell your boss I'd like to have that car, and ask him how much he would sell it for." Hallelujah! I was on my way. When God gives us a revelation, we are likely to meet all kinds of obstacles before we see it fulfilled. When God gives us a yes, the devil gives us a no. But we must not turn back; we must trust, pray, and press on until we have what the Lord has said is ours.

When the salesman returned he said, "The boss will sell it to you for $4,000."

"I'll take it," I said, though I had nothing to put down toward its purchase. The Cadillac had been owned by a veterinarian, and occasionally he had used it to haul piglets in the trunk. But you would never have known, for the car was clean throughout, and there was no odor anywhere, not even in the trunk. It was a '74 Cadillac Fleetwood, the largest passenger car Cadillac ever made and the largest car sold at that time. (As I said, this was before seatbelts were required, so at times we had four adults sitting on the front bench.) I left the dealership and headed to the Allstate insurance office to inquire about a loan. They looked up the value and told me I got the car far below the retail price and they could give me a loan for $4,000—just what I needed without a down payment.

Going from a '65 Volkswagen Beetle to a '74 Cadillac Fleetwood was quite an improvement in the ride, space, and amenities. This car was fancy—the backseat even had footrests—and this was quite a learning experience for me. Although I had adjusted earlier to driving larger cars, that was before I was in the ministry. Now I was a pastor, and I had not yet adjusted to pastors with a vision for missions driving luxury cars. The whole idea was running 100% against my grain. But Jesus had told me to buy this vehicle, so there was nothing left to do but obey and be happy about it. I thought I had looked so good, so holy, so sacrificial driving to missions meetings and church meetings in my old Volkswagen Beetle. But can you imagine how I felt and what a reception I got when I showed up in a three-year-old Fleetwood? Oh, how we all need to understand and remember that so we will not judge any man by his outward appearance.

If you want to be popular with everyone, you must conform to their ideas and become a prisoner of their value system. But if you want to be free and be popular with God, then be prepared for a lot of criticism and be willing to be a blessed fool for Christ's sake. Because of God's great love for us, He will continually attack our ego until there is nothing left of it. In fact, if God would really have His way with us, many would have to trade Cadillacs for Volkswagens, while others would have to trade Volkswagens for Cadillacs.

And so we were ready for our move to Indiana, with all the vehicles we needed. Since our phone call telling us about this little group of believers near Kokomo, we had learned a little more about them. There were six adults and a few children who had previously been in traditional churches where they had experienced a spiritual void. They felt there needed to be more than just repeated preaching on salvation. These few individuals were yearning for a closer walk with God, but they did not know how or where to begin. Some years before, they had come under the teachings of Rev. Helm, and now they had a desire to reach "higher ground." They shared this longing with their pastors and some other Christians in their previous churches, but their opinion was not appreciated. Already feeling they didn't belong, they decided to leave their churches and meet together on a weekly basis to pray, praise God, read the Word, and encourage each other. They asked God to send a pastor who would take them beyond their salvation experience, beyond the wilderness to the Promised Land itself. For two years, they waited and prayed, "God, send us a servant." When they first began to pray this way, the servant God had for them was not ready yet—God was still working with him, cleansing him and teaching him. Of course, that servant was me.

I cannot adequately stress the importance of a congregation getting the right pastor. I believe many congregations have the wrong pastor, and therefore the sheep are not fed. If a pastor is called by God to minister in a village that has a little congregation, but he chooses to go to a large city church because of the opportunity and the greater prestige, neither congregation—the one in the little village or the one in the larger city—will be adequately fed by the precious Holy

Spirit. I believe sheep and shepherds not matched by God is a contributing factor to 18,000 pastors leaving the ministry in our country every year.

That same evening after we received the call from Rev. Helm telling us about the little fellowship near Kokomo, we got another call, this time from one of the two men in this fellowship. He told us how glad he was that we were coming to visit, as that was the impression he had gotten from talking with Rev. Helm. I tried to explain we were not coming just to visit; we were coming to stay, to live there. It was difficult for him to imagine that a pastor of my background and education would actually be willing to come and shepherd this little group of six adults and a few children, but we assured him that was what we were doing. And so we continued to pack on Thursday, Friday, and Saturday, resting, of course, on Sunday. I've seen many Christian families move into a new home on a Friday or Saturday, and then not come to church on Sunday because they wanted to arrange the furniture. Sundays belong to the Lord Jesus. We must not violate the day He has set aside for worship and rest. We need to keep the Sabbath day holy—not just part of the day, but all of it.

When Monday came, we started loading the truck, and we finished loading it on Tuesday. We were ready to leave about eleven in the morning, but Jesus had told me to leave on Tuesday afternoon. Since the afternoon begins at twelve, we left at 12:01 and headed for our new home near Kokomo. I drove the truck, towing the 1965 Beetle behind it, and Marcia drove the Cadillac.

The first night on the road, we stayed in the motor home of our friends from Michigan who traveled part of the way with us. The next morning, I was impressed to look under the Cadillac. When I looked at the inside of the two new front tires, it appeared someone had taken a utility knife and slit them all around. I praised the Lord as I had been taught, and then immediately found out that the service station next to us had the replacement tires we needed. God never fails! *"Praise the LORD for his goodness, and for his wonderful works to the children of men!"* (Psalm 107:8).

The second night Esther and I stayed in a motel, while Marcia and the other children went on to Kokomo. For our final day of travel, the day I was to meet my new congregation of two men, four women, and four children, I decided to dress in old blue jeans and a flannel shirt. I did not want them to think I considered myself "somebody." I just wanted to be a servant. Of course, because I was towing a big load of stuff behind me, it was practical to wear that kind of clothing.

When I crossed the Iowa-Illinois state line on our way to Kokomo, something unusual happened in my heart. I remembered my homiletics (preaching) professor, Dr. Lewis, from Asbury Seminary, who said, "Schultze, you will preach to thousands," and here I was, in the prime of my life, headed for six adults and four children. As I thought about it, for the first time ever, I began to shout. I was in a great Holy Ghost shouting time! I had never shouted in my entire life— Germans simply do not do that. I had studied science at the University of Wisconsin, and scientists don't shout either. I had a minor in philosophy, and philosophers don't shout. I studied theology, and theologians don't shout. I had been in a denomination where they no longer shouted, although they did at one time. But there I was, in spite of all this background to the contrary, shouting uncontrollably. The joy of the Lord in my heart was so great I just couldn't hold it in anymore.

From within myself, I had this realization from the Lord: "You are now walking with God, free of all restraints of any institution, and of the many rules and regulations of man. You are on a journey to obey the Master's every command. You are getting into what I brought you into the world for!"

Of course, when my homiletics professor told me I would preach to thousands, it didn't mean anything to me because all I wanted to do was love Jesus with all my heart. If all I did was help just one person on this earth, it would have made my life worthwhile. Furthermore, I never was a people-counter. I have never counted church attendance in all my years of ministry. I never asked the church treasurer who gave money or how much. I never counted how many souls I was able to pray with, to lead to Jesus, or how many were healed through my laying hands on them in prayer, or how many were sanctified.

And yet, unknown to me as I traveled to Kokomo, in a matter of two weeks after this shouting experience, I would indeed be preaching to thousands of people. Even before I arrived in Indiana, the Lord made it clear I was to go on the radio. So, in light of that revelation, my homiletics professor had not just said something out of his own thoughts but had given a prophecy of my future ministry: "You will preach to thousands."

With little effort, we found our way to the place we were to meet this little group of praying believers. We drove off the Interstate, onto a state highway, onto a county road, and then onto a gravel driveway that led us into the woods to a tri-level house, where this tiny congregation had been meeting and where a new church was born by the Holy Spirit. Jesus said, "I will build my Church," and my appointment to this new congregation was definitely of Him. I was forty-one years of age.

CHAPTER TWENTY-THREE
Coming Home at Last

O f the six adults in this little fellowship, three had jobs and three did not. As we pulled into the driveway of our host's home, half of the congregation—the three who were unemployed—came out to greet us. The other half was still at work, and there were tears in the eyes of our welcoming committee. What had seemed too good to be true had now become too good to be false, and they rejoiced in that realization.

As I assessed my finances, however, I realized I had only $15 left in my pocket. No salary had been discussed or even considered by this little group; they were too excited about our coming to think about money. I, on the other hand, had to think about money, as I had a family of six to support.

A few days prior to leaving Lincoln, I had been wondering where our family could stay when we arrived at our destination, since at that point I had received no promise of a salary. I considered the options: we could stay at the Rescue Mission, sleep under a bridge, or go to my in-laws' home, which was a two-hour drive to the north. Fortunately, Stephen, one of the men in our fledgling congregation, called us just before we left Lincoln and invited us to stay with him and his family. Besides their family of four, a sister and niece were also living with them, so we added six more people to the household of two families already living together.

As you can imagine, their furniture had to be rearranged to make room for some of the things we had brought along with us in the truck. Then, late in the afternoon, the rest of the congregation arrived, and were they ever excited. Not knowing what to do to start this church I simply said, "We need to get up and form a circle and just lift our hands and praise God. This church must begin with praise to Jesus." I believe that is the way the early Church started, with much praise. So as my custom had been in private for some time now, I lifted up my hands and began to praise the Lord.

I expected the six people present with me at the time to make some sort of feeble effort at lifting their hands and praising God because that is the response I got in our previous churches, but I was in for a great surprise. Their arms flew up into the air, and they began to praise, adore, and magnify the name of the Lord with such power and anointing they immediately drowned me out. I then thought it would last only a minute or two, but they went on and on as if they were already standing around the throne of God.

Finally, after quite some time, I reluctantly stopped them and soon discovered they had spent much time in praise together over the past two years. One of the ladies in the group told us that while we had been praising God, she had a vision of the angels of God all about us. It was a confirmation that Jesus was with us in this venture. This church was started by the Holy Spirit, and when God is in something, it will never end.

On Sundays, we set up the living room in a more formal way in order to have our church service. That first Sunday, Stephen's sister, Pam, and her husband, David, joined us. After I had finished preaching, David stood up from his chair, took about two steps forward, which brought him into the vicinity of our makeshift altar, and gave his heart back to Jesus. He was our first convert in Kokomo.

Our Sunday services were not much different from the other times we had spent together during the week. There was no morning service; church began at two o'clock in the afternoon. Since no one went home, after a couple of hours we just continued the service—fellowshipping, eating, and sharing together—until bedtime.

During the weekday mornings, I would go out into the woods to pray because there were just too many people in the house for me to have the freedom to cry out to God. Occasionally I was joined by Cricket, a German shepherd who perhaps enjoyed the prayer time as much as I did.

The third day after our arrival, one of the two laymen asked me, "Pastor, are we supposed to pay you a salary?" I thought it was very considerate of him to ask, though I can't recall exactly how I answered him. Then he said, "We know one thing for sure—we will not go by the wisdom or calculations of man as to how much we are going to pay you. We want to go by the witness of the Holy Spirit. We are going to ask Jesus what your salary should be." If all three factory workers had tithed or double-tithed, there would not have been adequate finances to take care of our needs. Still, it would have been a great help, and we would have been thankful.

Then this dear brother reiterated, "There is one thing we want to be sure of: everything that is done in this church is to be done by the leadership of the Holy Spirit, no matter what it is. Pastor, if the Lord would lead for you to go to Florida each year for three months or longer, then that is what we want you to do. The only thing that matters to this church is that it be led by the Holy Spirit because it belongs entirely to God." That was the decision made by that little church in its first week of existence, and that policy has never changed in the last 29 years.

To help them find God's will, the congregation met together

and decided to contact two men they knew were close to Jesus, and then ask them to pray with this group about the salary the Lord would want me to receive. First, they made up a list of salary figures. They told me, "We will not even consider a salary lower than your last fulltime pastorate. That will be at the bottom of the list." The next salary figure was to be in increments of $25 a week to a maximum of $125 per week above the previous salary.

They jumbled the figures by number and called Tom Harman at his print shop in northern Indiana, the same man God used to get the Cadillac for me in Lincoln. They did not tell Tom what the issue was about, but simply asked if the Holy Spirit witnessed to his heart on any one of the six numbers. I do not recall what number the Holy Spirit witnessed to this dear brother, but the men made note of it and then called a minister in Indianapolis who, in the same process, got the same witness. When my congregation looked at the matching numbers, they laughed and praised the Lord, and then laughed some more. As far as my wife and I recall, it was either the highest or second highest figure on that list. So our salary, with only three people working in this congregation, was to be either $100 or $125 more a week than at our previous fulltime pastorate.

On top of that, a few days later, the Holy Spirit witnessed that I was to go on the radio. So we now needed to trust God for money for both the salary and the radio. Isn't Jesus wonderful? For without Him, this would have been an impossible venture at best.

But with God, all things are possible. In a matter of days, the money started coming in. One man at the Chrysler factory in town heard about my story and said, "I'll give $50 a week for a few weeks." An Indianapolis business heard about it and sent a check for a couple thousand. Other churches heard about the beginning of our fellowship and began to send $50 a week. And the money continued to come in. The salary the Holy Spirit witnessed to was provided every week, and sometimes more. Oh, if only all church boards would inquire of the Holy Spirit what the salary of their pastors should be!

In the beginning of the second week, I went to the local FM radio station and talked to the sales manager, who was also a Christian. I said, "The Lord wants me to go on radio. Do you have any openings?"

"Well," he replied, "I just had two spots open up, both on Sunday mornings. One is at quarter to nine, and the other is at nine o'clock."

"I will take the nine o'clock slot," I told him.

It is amazing to me that the sales manager of this powerful radio station, heard throughout all of central Indiana, did not question my credentials and was not bothered by the size of my congregation. Neither was he concerned that I had just arrived in town and didn't have an address of my own. He just said, "I will put you on each Sunday morning at nine," and I've been on this station now for more than twenty-nine years, preaching the unsearchable riches of Christ.

Because of Jesus, the three families living together in one home worked out wonderfully each day, all of us blending together as one. Some nights, we prayed together for an hour, other nights for two or three. Even so, after a couple of weeks, I began to ask the Lord if there was somewhere else we should live. I did not want to wear out our welcome, even though it seemed as if they wanted us to stay with them forever—such was the love in this group. However, I continued to pray about a place for our own family of six, and God soon made a way. Now for the first time since I was born, after twenty-two years of feeling "homeless," I began to have a sense of coming home.

Rev. Robert Morgan

He found a hungry heart in Canada.

CHAPTER TWENTY-FOUR

"Go Buy a House Today"

After four weeks, Jesus spoke to me as clearly as when He had said, "Start packing. You are leaving next week, Tuesday afternoon." This time He said, "Go buy a house today." I was surprised because, by now, my total savings were only $100. I had never bought a house and was inexperienced at this sort of thing, though I did know realtors sold houses, so I picked one from the Yellow Pages and gave him a call.

"Sir, I would like to buy a house today," I said.

He seemed taken aback at first, but then asked, "What is your price range?"

"Oh, I don't know," I answered. "I only have $100."

All I heard was silence, a click, and then another voice. "What can I do for you?"

"I would like to buy a house today."

This time when I was asked about my price range, I didn't repeat my former mistake but instead answered by the guidance of the Holy Spirit. "Sir, money is no factor. Line me up six houses, and I would like to have at least 2,500 square feet in the house."

"That would be wonderful," he said. "I'll arrange for you to see six houses, and I'll call you back." And he did.

Can you imagine what kind of conversation ensued on the other end of the line when I hung up? Since I had told the first realtor I had only $100 and the second one that money was no problem, it is easy to understand why Marcia and I were shown houses that ranged from some of the best to some of the worst.

In my great need to go by the witness of the Lord and because of my inexperience in the real estate market, I called a man of God and said, "I am looking for a house to buy. Would you pray with me that I will know when I get to the right house?"

"The Lord is with you, brother," he told me, "and He will tell you when you come to the right place."

That was the end of the conversation. It took me a while to assimilate that, and then I said, "Well, that is a good answer, isn't it? I will have faith that God will do it."

Marcia and I looked at house number one, and it was very run down. It looked like it should have had a fence around it with a NO TRESPASSING sign. House number two was quite reasonable, while a doctor could have lived in house number three and been happy. And so it went from there, and I had no witness on any of these houses. When we came to the sixth and final house, we found ourselves looking at an old farmhouse built in 1870, making it 107 years old at the time. The two-story home with 3,000 square feet was sitting on two acres of land. It had a three-car garage, a huge barn standing thirty-two feet tall, and a couple of out-buildings, which at one time were used for chickens or farm machinery. It was obvious by the size of the house and the landscaping that, in the past, it had been owned and occupied by a very wealthy farmer.

My wife and I and another couple were not able to enter the house at that time. It was locked up, so we just walked around and evaluated the situation. Then I stood by an oak tree on the east side of the house and prayed quietly within my heart until I heard Jesus say, "This is your house."

In amazement, I said, "Lord, I only have $100, and they want $56,000." It was 1977, and that was quite a lot of money for a house in Indiana at that time, but in the Holy Spirit, I prayed, "Lord, if you want us to have this home, drop the price $6,000 by tomorrow." No one but Jesus heard my request. The prayer did not come out of my mind, but out of my heart, just as the words had come out of my heart in 1952 when I said to my atheist professor, "I will speak against evolution tomorrow."

That evening, at home with our precious friends, I received a phone call from the realtor, who said, "Reverend, I have good news for you. The people who own the home you are interested in had been shopping in town, and when they returned from the store, they decided to lower the price from $56,000 to $50,000."

I immediately exclaimed, "I'll take it!"

In His great love and mercy, and in order to help my faith, the Lord did what I asked, down to the exact amount and within the specified timeframe. Just as the Lord had revealed to Rev. Helm a few weeks before that I was to go to Kokomo and that the Lord would be with me there, certainly the Lord was with me as I bought my first home.

The next assignment was to get the money to purchase the house. The realtor told me I could get a 95 percent loan, but when the banker found out this old house had a gravity furnace, he took it down to 80 percent. Then the sweet, elderly, experienced banker asked me how much money we had. When I told him, he asked where we planned to get the rest of the money.

"That's the reason I am here in this bank," I told him.

He then asked if I had any money in savings. I told him we did not. Next, he asked if I had any stocks or bonds, and I told him I didn't even know what they were, which at the time was absolutely true. Then he asked if I had a church headquarters that would help me out. I told him, "My church headquarters is in heaven." Each time I answered a question, he lowered his head slightly. He asked the size of my congregation. I told him, "With all the children, we are now about twenty-six." Next he asked if we were well established in the community. "We have been here four weeks," I said. His head dropped again.

My wife and I were in his office for about one hour as he asked question after question. It was obvious he could not figure us out. Of course, all we could do was simply look to Jesus, and that is what we did. Finally, the banker said he had one more question. He wanted to know if we thought Jesus was coming soon. When I said, "Yes, I believe He is," that was the end of the questioning period. He said he would take the matter to the Board of Directors and let us know their decision later. The very moment he said that, the Holy Spirit witnessed to me that we would not get the loan from that bank. We shook hands with the banker and left, continuing to trust.

That night, after we had returned to our host's home, the Lord touched one person to loan us $5,000 without interest and without setting a time period for repayment. Another person gave us a gift of $5,000. So, during the course of one day, our assets went from $100 to $10,100, once again affirming the witness we'd had before coming to Kokomo: "The Lord will be with you there."

After two or three weeks, we received a letter from the bank telling us our request for the loan had been denied. We made application at another bank, but even with the increased amount in our bank account, they told us they could loan us only 50 percent of the money needed. We had never heard of such a thing, so when I called and asked the reason, I was told this particular senior loan officer did not like the house. Apparently it was personal. After a few days and a lot of prayer, I was told they would give us 66 percent, and I said I would take it. Of course, we still needed some help because 66 percent plus my $10,100 was still not enough to pay for the house. The answer came through my mother-in-law's bank in northern Indiana, where we were able to get a second mortgage to cover the difference.

On December 23, a blustery day with light snow blowing, we moved into our first home. Although I was forty-one years of age, in all my years of ministry I had never thought about owning a home. I assumed I would probably move every three or four years for the rest of my ministerial life. Because of the denomination's policy that congregations should provide a parsonage, it was unlikely we would ever own a home or build up any equity, so I figured we would end up in a trailer home at retirement.

But God, in His infinite mercy, provided us with one of the finest homes in the area. When we bought it someone told me that when the house was built, it was the showplace of the township. It has wide oak pocket doors that divide the rooms, and they still look marvelous after 136 years. Practically every bit of the woodwork is oak, and all the prior owners had left the beautiful woodwork intact and unpainted to keep showing the beautiful grain. There are three large, lovely bedrooms on the second floor, and the house has a slate roof that has been maintained through the years. With the little repair we did recently, that roof could last another hundred years.

How this home stayed on the market for so many weeks is still a wonder to me, except that I know the Lord Jesus held it for us. Two or three weeks after we moved in, a gentleman wearing a fur coat and driving a Jaguar came to our door and said, "I want to buy this house." Since he owned several oil wells in Texas, he had all the money in the world and could have given us double, triple, or beyond what the property was worth. But I told him Jesus had given us this house, and it was not for sale. He left disappointed, but there are some things that money just can't buy, aren't there?

There were, of course, some challenges. The previous owners had not taken care of everything quite as well as they could have. The day we moved in, there were about six inches of water in the basement. We were told this had never happened before. I had to buy a little pump and, with a garden hose siphon out the water which took several days. The outbuildings were also in dire need of repair, including roofing, painting, and new siding.

On the day we moved the furniture into our new house, Stephen, who had so graciously housed our family, began to feel sick and ended up lying down on the floor, his strength completely gone. Jim, Stephen's cousin, had heard about our fellowship and had decided to help us move. As six-foot five-inch Jim stood next to me, Jesus told me in my heart that Jim was to pray for Stephen. In my mind, I said, "Lord, he is not a Christian." I was thinking of the statement that says God does not hear the cries of the sinner, but in actuality there is no verse in the Bible that says that. How often we misuse and misinterpret the Holy Scriptures! And yet, convinced that there was indeed such a verse, I continued to argue with the Lord until He finally made it clear to me that the Bible does not say God does not hear the prayer of a sinner. What it does say is, *"If I regard iniquity in my heart, the LORD will not hear me"* (Psalm 66:18).

I could see that Jim was not regarding iniquity in his heart; he was, in fact, there to help me, so he was doing good by helping a man of God. I therefore asked Jim to pray, and as he did, Stephen was healed and raised up, and Jim was restored to Jesus. These first works of God within this home happened even before the furniture was settled in.

We moved into our new home and began to arrange the

furniture on December 23, continuing into the next day. On Christmas Day, the church people politely asked our entire family of six if we would please go upstairs at a certain time and not come down until we were told to do so. We complied and waited until the call came: "Pastor, you may come down now." When we went downstairs, there in our living room we saw a brand new refrigerator, a brand new washing machine, and a brand new dishwasher. Here we were only four months into our ministry in Kokomo, and the Lord had provided a good salary, a home, a radio ministry, and new appliances. Truly the scripture says, *"But seek ye first the kingdom of God, and his righteousness; and all these things shall be added unto you"* (Matthew 6:33). We were seeking His kingdom and His righteousness, and the things we needed started coming to us in abundance. Another verse that has been a blessing to us throughout the years is 1 Corinthians 2:9, which says, *"But as it is written, Eye hath not seen, nor ear heard, neither have entered into the heart of man, the things which God hath prepared for them that love him."* True Christianity works just the way the Bible says it should.

Throughout the years, Jesus really helped me die out to many things. Prior to my period of waiting upon God and learning to hear His voice, I had a mindset against material things and was accustomed to being happy with little; I was not trained to be happy with much. Because of my childhood background, I wanted to live a little below the average income for the rest of my life because that was where my comfort zone was.

In addition, in the early days of our marriage, Marcia and I had serious thoughts about going to the mission field. We even applied to go to Africa or Haiti, and we had also been thinking of India and China. We were and still are very much aware of the needs in underdeveloped countries, and it only made sense that we in America should live frugally and share our wealth with these nations. We especially want to support our Christian brothers and sisters in the work of evangelism in other parts of the world. But as noble as this may appear, it can lead to a mindset that can block God's purpose for us.

As I said, I had always wanted to be an example of prudence and moderation. I wanted to be known as a pastor of sacrificial giving who drove old cars, but Jesus ruined all that for me once He completely took over my life.

Isn't there an element of pride that can easily set in upon us when we play the great sacrificial saint who goes about with just two changes of clothes and lives in a little one-room apartment? Does that kind of living endear us to the heart of God? Or does it bless God more for us to simply do as He directs, whether it is up the ladder or down, whether it is living in the slums of Harlem or in a palace in the Hawaiian Islands?

Gradually I had to face the question whether I would be willing to live with an average or better than average income. The Apostle Paul said he had learned to be happy with little, and yet he had also learned to be happy with much. He had learned to be content in any state of material possession and circumstance. He said, *"Not that I speak in respect of want: for I have learned, in whatsoever state I am, therewith to be content. I know both how to be abased, and I know how to abound: every where and in all things I am instructed both to be full and to be hungry, both to abound and to suffer need"* (Philippians 4:11, 12). When I came to Kokomo, because of the dear saints here, I had to learn to be just as happy on the top as on the bottom.

In the first forty years of my life, in a larger sense, I had functioned as a servant, living with relatively little finance, and I delighted in doing so. Now, as I came to this little congregation, all of a sudden I had to deal with being served;

as a servant of God, that was a cross for me. I learned that there was pride at the bottom of my servanthood and that if God is in something, there is a cross in it as well. Of course, my own servanthood has continued since then, but now it seems people help me as much as I help them, and that enables me to press into new areas of grace and humility. You can tell now that even though the Lord did a great work in me before coming to Kokomo, He continued to refine me. And this refining is still going on today.

So through these years of transition from little to much, God had to shake me again and again. He had to deliver me from my preconceived ideas, my theological thinking, and my "spiritual" attitudes that I held so dear. Of course, God does that with each of us: once we yield to Him, He breaks and slays us, again and again, to take the "self" out of us. He pulverizes us by putting us in the refining fire to make us new, from the tips of our toes to the tops of our heads, and then uses us for His glory.

God had given us a palace for our home and a congregation whose love towards us was abounding and overflowing. That house would become a place of fellowship, love, healing, encouragement, and answered prayer. It was not our house, but it was Jesus' house, and it still is. In the first twenty years in this home, my wife, with the help of the ladies of the church, served over 3,000 meals from our dinner table. Each Sunday after the morning church service, we would invite five or six people—sometimes as many as ten—to our home for lunch. Most of the time, visitors on their first Sunday could count on eating at our dinner table. We were absolutely amazed when most of our visitors told us they had been in other churches for ten, twenty, thirty, or even forty years and had never eaten at the pastor's table or had a meal with their pastor in a restaurant.

In addition, the Lord directed us to have afterglow

services at our table after each Sunday morning service. And how enjoyable they were! However, after twenty years, the Lord said we needed to stop that particular hospitality. It was becoming too much for us, as we were getting older and needed more rest.

In the ensuing years, this little congregation has continued to kill me—with love. They were killing me and killing me, in order for me to be delivered from every remnant of my self-life, pride, and prejudice. Of course, in the real sense, it was not their doing, but God working through them. In addition to the wonderful new appliances, these gracious people gave us other items of love and care. During our second year in Kokomo, we were told once again to go upstairs and wait for the signal. This time, when we came down, they told us to go outside. We did, and to our amazement, there in our driveway sat a large, fully-equipped Buick station wagon. Trust me when I tell you that you can humble a minister by despising and rejecting him, but you can also humble him by loving him.

This sort of thing went on and on, and after a few more years, the station wagon was worn down, and automatically Marcia and I reverted back to another little Volkswagen. Soon afterward, following one of the mid-week church services, I was walking off the platform when two businessmen grabbed me by my arms, one on each side, and walked me out of the church. There in the driveway was a brand new Cadillac. "We got this for you," they announced, and then told me how it came about. They had bought themselves new Cadillacs, and their wives told them, "How do you dare buy yourselves new Cadillacs when your pastor drives a little Volkswagen Rabbit?" The men got the point.

Indeed, isn't there a very precious scripture that fits in here? *"Believe in the Lord your God, so shall ye be established; believe his prophets, so shall ye prosper"* (2 Chronicles 20:20).

And did those two businessmen ever prosper because of what they did!

Yet, I must inject a word of caution when we talk about prosperity. The prosperity God talks about is a prosperity that comes out of His wisdom, not from man trying to manipulate God or demand goods for the sake of self-indulgence. The latter is the heart of the popular, modern-day "prosperity theology," which had its birth in hedonistic materialism. It will not seek first the kingdom of God and His righteousness and let God in His wisdom add all other things as **He wills**. This prosperity theology is evil and deceitful, and causes people to seek prosperity for its own sake; therein lies its sin.

The reason so many are drawn to this theology is they are so impoverished in Christ they have to look for riches in the world. They are a far cry from the Apostle Paul's "contentment theology" expressed in several passages of his letters, such as:

- *"And having food and raiment let us be therewith content"* (1 Timothy 6:8).
- *"Not that I speak in respect of want: for I have learned, in whatsoever state I am, therewith to be content"* (Philippians 4:11).
- *"Let your conversation be without covetousness; and be content with such things as ye have: for he hath said, I will never leave thee, nor forsake thee"* (Hebrew 13:5).

Or consider this crowning statement of them all: *"But godliness with contentment is great gain"* (1 Timothy 6:6).

Many a modern Christian is a materialist at heart. He cannot find rest in what he already has, and he certainly has no idea of all the riches there are in our triune God. Even when Paul was physically poor and afflicted, he talked about the exceeding riches in Christ Jesus, and of the eternal weight of glory that is ours to experience. He was so rich in

Christ that when he was in his terminal prison in Rome, just a hole in the ground with a small opening on top, he led forty-seven Roman guards to Christ before he was beheaded. He continually prayed for souls, for the Church to be purified, and for God's will to be done, but how often did he pray for material things?

Oh, how we need to have a contentment theology like the Apostle Paul's! Don't seek prosperity in the things of the world, but in Jesus your Savior: *"Godliness with contentment is great gain."* A man is more than a trillion times richer on the day he receives our Lord than he was the day before. He just needs to go on a journey to start counting his blessings. John said, *"Love not the world, neither the things that are in the world. If any man love the world, the love of the Father is not in him"* (1 John 2:15.)

Again, some fall prey to the prosperity theology because they have not found enough of the riches of our Lord to be content. Others fall for it because, through their lack of discipline, they keep spending more than they take in. They want a God who serves them as a banker with a never-ending supply of funds. Friends, only the disciplined will become true disciples of Jesus, and discipline demands a cross: a crucifixion of all our passions, lusts, and cravings for earthly things. The prosperity theology offers no cross, it knows of no crown, and it is void of the glory of God.

No, I'm not promoting worldly prosperity. I am promoting absolute obedience to God as the only remedy to man's misery, endless cravings, and futile dreams.

CHAPTER TWENTY-FIVE

Go East, then South

The greatest numerical growth of our congregation came during the two years we moved ten times, despite the church growth specialists who say a church won't grow without a fixed location or building that is easy to find. Oh, really? How many good reasons do we put forth to justify all this church building business? There is so much of it that is not of the Lord. God can do absolutely anything, and it has nothing to do with what experts and specialists say. In our two years of wandering from building to building, our congregation doubled, and then doubled again—a 400 percent growth rate.

Now, here is the story of how we found our first permanent—or should I say, semi-permanent—building. The building was a classic, and it just happened to sit right in the middle of the city square.

We were worshipping in our tenth building when I received word that we had two weeks to vacate the basement of the insurance building in which we were meeting. A few days later, I was scheduled to fly to Florida to assist Loran Helm in his ministry, so I had little time to work on this next moving project. Needing a quick solution, I drove to the home of Dave and Pam and said to them, "Let's pray together and ask Jesus to help us find our next place of worship." When you have a great need, don't always try to pray through on your own. Gather some friends and pray together, for Jesus said, *"Again I say unto you, That if two of you shall agree on earth as touching any thing that they shall ask, it shall be done for them of my Father which is in heaven"* (Matthew 18:19).

After prayer, I left Dave and Pam's home. Instantly, I knew I was in the palm of my Lord's hand. I had never before had an experience quite like that, nor have I since. As I faced the main road, the Lord told me to turn right. After about four blocks, at the stoplight, Jesus said to turn right again. At the next intersection, He told me to turn left. When He told me to go straight east, my excitement grew. I knew that Jesus, the Creator of the universe, was directing me to our next building.

I drove a block and a half east, and the Lord told me I had gone too far. I turned around, and when I had gone back half a block, He told me to turn right and go north. At the end of the block, He said, "This is where I want you to park the car." I stepped out and found myself at the edge of the city square. I was still excited, yet when I looked at the shops and offices and all those parking meters around the massive courthouse building, my heart moved a few inches in the direction of my shoes. Having prayed with the saints a few minutes before, I thought surely, after moving ten times around the city, the Lord would move us outside the city to where the grass is greener—literally.

You see, I was thinking of a suburban church, and here the Lord Jesus not only led me to another building in the city, but right smack in the heart of the city. I looked to the left and spotted a building that had once housed a large electric store with a massive showroom that had been used for light fixtures. Now it sat empty and sported a "for lease" sign. As I looked through the dusty windows, there was no word from Jesus. Then I turned to the right. The second building from the corner of the square also had a "for lease" sign in the door, and the moment I saw it, Jesus said, "This is your place."

Suddenly, my heart bounced up from my shoes, back into my chest where it belongs. It wasn't the thought of becoming a storefront church that caused my heart to rebound, but realizing I was in the will of God—and, of course, there is no better place to be. When we are in the Lord's will, it is like experiencing a little bit of heaven right here on earth. Didn't Jesus teach us to pray, *"Thy will be done in earth, as it is in heaven"* (Matthew 6:10)? Of course, because this building was part of a city square, it did not stand alone. All the individual, narrow buildings were joined side-by-side, as if glued together. But I didn't care. God had led, and because of that, I knew He would meet with us in this place. How great is that?

Now came the interesting part: how would my congregation respond when I told them our new building was on the city square—that it was a storefront? The devil told me there was trouble ahead and I would disappoint this congregation that had done so much for Marcia and me. Of course, the devil is a liar, and the father of all lies. But the devil never comes to us with an introduction: "Hello. I am the devil, and I have come to tell you a lie." If so, life would be a lot easier. But no, the wicked one frequently places thoughts into our minds, and we often don't know where they came from. So we trust, we plead for God to apply the blood of Jesus to our hearts, and say, "I resist the devil" (see James 4:7). ("Plead the blood" is one of those odd church-speak phrases that baffles many when they first hear it, as it did me, but it is quite scriptural.)

At the next church meeting, I took the whole congregation on a ride with me—a story ride. I took them on the left turns and the right turns, going east, west, and north. I took them along to the square—not literally, of course, but in their imaginations. And when I had them before the storefront, when I told them how Jesus had said, "This is the place," they rose to their feet, raised their hands toward heaven, and praised the Lord from the depths of their souls. Oh, glory to God! Oh, I HATE THE DEVIL, I HATE THE DEVIL, I HATE HIM! He deserves to fry at high temperature in the fires of hell forever. How many joys does he steal from us? How many clouds does he hang over our heads, and how many wonderful Christians has he led astray?

I signed the lease for two years, and then I left for Florida. I told my associate, "It is all yours," and thank the Lord, Tony knew just what to do, as always. The church people came in and worked every day until late into the night—cleaning, decorating, and beautifying the building. Tony even painted a beautiful mural on the basement wall.

In a week or two, after dozens of hours of hard, sacrificial work, the building was ready for occupancy. By that time I had returned from Florida, and we were going to move into the new building the following Sunday. We had scheduled a special program of dedication with a dedicatory speaker, and had done everything else that goes along with such a great event. After all those ten moves, we finally were settling down.

Well, it's time for you to raise your eyebrows, if you haven't already done so. Just a few days before the dedication Sunday, I decided to check with City Hall to see if the congregation could meet in such a building. Was I ever in for a surprise! This building had to be approved by the planning commission and by building inspectors; it had to meet electrical code, health code, and fire code. Well, the city planning commissioners walked through the building and said it would not pass the required fire code for church meetings because it was too dangerous. But I had signed a two-year contract and put down the deposit, so I was stuck. We had to find another building immediately. The commissioners said, "It can't be done." The devil said, "It can't be done." And, yes, this time my heart also said, "It can't be done." This time, my heart not only sank in the direction of my shoes—it fell all the way into them.

But as I made my way to the fire station, I used my familiar weapons: I prayed, I trusted, I pled the blood of Jesus, I resisted the devil. Jesus had told me before and now told me again that this building was for us. Should I believe the commissioner or Jesus? Now, put your eyebrows back down. Are we supposed to do what Jesus tells us to do and stick with it no matter what, or should we quit when everything looks dark? As I was seated in the office of the Fire Chief—who, by the way, had already been through the building—he said to me, "Well, Pastor, there is only one thing left that I can do, and that is to call the State Fire Marshall in Indianapolis."

During the course of our conversation, I found out he was a believer. And so he believed with me. The building had a basement, a ground floor, a second floor, an attic, a huge freight elevator, and stairs to connect them. As this Christian brother spoke with the Indiana Fire Marshall, he told him about the building, discussing each floor individually and then giving me the okay signal. Finally, he came to the attic, the last space to be confirmed. Once that was done, he hung up and said, "You are in!"

Of course, Jesus was right again. He defied the odds against us. As I told you earlier, walking with God is thrills, romance, and adventure—never a dull moment!

And now we were in our new church building with a two-year lease. This building was significant to the growth of our church, as well as for a very special upcoming event. Because of our location on the city square, there were a number of families and individuals who found us and became a part of our fellowship. It was also in this building that our oldest daughter, Esther, was married—on a very, very short notice.

CHAPTER TWENTY-SIX

In Eleven Days

A t the time we moved into the building on the square, Robert Morey, the young man from our pastorate in Lincoln, had moved to Indiana to attend a seminary in Anderson some fifty miles to the southeast of Kokomo. During the weekends, he would come up and stay with us, and then help us in our church services. While he was there, he and our older daughter, Esther, began to enjoy each other's company quite a bit. Because they both liked music, they invited others to join them in songfests. Esther played the piano, and the rest sang along together.

Esther was in her last year of high school at the time, and Robert was preparing for the ministry. Part of that preparation was spending a significant year of waiting upon God to reveal his location of ministry and his life companion. During that year as Robert waited on God, Esther finished high school and began work as a nurse's aide. Because Robert was seven years older than Esther, it never entered our minds that they could possibly be meant for each other. However, Robert confessed the thought had occurred to him, but he always dismissed it because of what he saw as an age barrier and because he wanted to keep his heart pure and open to all options. Esther never even considered the possibility of marrying Robert; she simply enjoyed the fellowship in the Lord with him.

Both wanted nothing but God's will for their lives. Esther was raised watching her parents obey God without hesitation when His will was revealed, and that is what she wanted as well. She rarely missed her time alone with God in the morning and was in church every time the doors were open, except in the most unusual circumstances. And she had never dated. I had told her that if she kept her heart until God brought the right man to her, then it wouldn't be broken to pieces, and she believed me.

Robert came from a generation of godly people on both his mother's and father's side of the family. I can best describe the spiritual commitment of his heritage by telling you about his great-grandfather George Hatch. George was a partially deaf wheat farmer in Nebraska, who had seven sons. One weekend during haying season, George learned a devastating storm was on the way. Farmers had to go out immediately and work all day to save their crops. The problem was it was Sunday, but the hay crops were necessary to feed the cattle during the winter. The loss of even one crop could bring hardship later on. But George decided to honor the Sabbath and not work on Sunday. When his neighbor learned that George was not going out to bring in the hay, he was amazed.

"George," he asked, "aren't you going to bring in your hay?"

"I'm growing sons, not hay," he answered. "We're going to church today."

Indeed, George lost his hay crop, but he saved his sons. I cannot possibly tell you how many faithful men and women of God have come out of that consecrated decision from generation to generation: laymen, pastors, and missionaries. That family just never learned how not to go to church, how not to read their Bibles, how not to pray in the mornings, or how not to tithe their income.

I cannot adequately express the tremendous influence that comes out of a godly heritage, out of dedicated great-grandparents, grandparents, and parents. I can speak of this from my own experience. I was saved at sixteen but had no Christian heritage, so I groped around in my church life for many years, doing the best I could, without the example and support of a parent. As I look at my grandchildren now, who even in their childhood have won souls to Christ, I see what I missed by not having a godly heritage.

Had George made an exception that memorable day when the storm took his hay crop, no doubt one or several of his sons would have been introduced to that same exception-making business. Further, there is no telling what damage that spiritual cancer would have brought down on the generations that followed.

About a year after Robert finished seminary, he took his first pastoral position in Fayetteville, West Virginia. If any man ever needed a wife, it was Robert. He not only needed a wife for companionship and fellowship in the Lord, but also to help him with the most mundane tasks so he could make it through the day. Pastors need wives as surely as fish need water.

After Robert left for Fayetteville, Esther realized how much she missed him. She felt surprisingly lonely without him, even though she still had no interest or expectation that they were to be married. After all, she had known him since she was ten and he was seventeen. He was like a spiritual big brother to her.

I remember the noteworthy day Marcia and I received a phone call from a man who walked with God. This servant of Jesus told us the Lord had revealed to him that Robert and Esther were meant for each other. He contacted us as Esther's parents, out of a sense of good Christian ethics. When we heard the message, Marcia and I immediately rejoiced and knew instantly this was of God. The same revelation was also shared with the chief elder in the church Robert was pastoring. When Robert heard this news, the "it's too good to be true" turned into a jubilant "it's too good to be false." Esther also was delighted, knowing that her best friend on earth was now to be her husband.

Then, to add to the excitement, there was an interesting addendum to the revelation: the two were to be married in eleven days. That is what the Lord wanted, and because God was in it, Robert and Esther rejoiced.

For Robert, eleven days sounded long enough once he heard God speak on the matter. Esther, however, was overwhelmed with everyone's questions about all the details of the wedding. She was still trying to get used to the idea of getting married so soon and didn't really care about all the thousand details that came with it. But she settled down as soon as I told her, "Give it all to Pastor Tony, everything from A to Z. Just show up at 6:30 on Friday night, everything will be taken care of." Tony was known as my associate who could do everything, so that settled it. Someone in our church had a gorgeous wedding dress that fit Esther perfectly, and all the rest just fell out of heaven for her.

It didn't take long, once Robert had received the revelation, for him to drive from West Virginia to our home in Kokomo. Esther and I were standing in our lovely living room when he pulled in—or rather, crashed into our driveway. Being of European extraction, my imagination was running full speed. I thought Robert would come in, we would all sit down and chat a little, and then Robert would ask for my daughter's hand. I couldn't have been more wrong. Instead of Robert coming inside, Esther ran out the door the moment she heard him squeal into the driveway. She didn't even say goodbye. Robert opened the door on the passenger side of his car, Esther jumped in with a "let's get out of here!" and away they went.

After a few seconds of emotional adjustment, I shouted, "One gone, three to go! Praise the Lord!"

Early on, Marcia and I had prayed that God would give our children mates of His choice. That day, the prayer was answered for child number one, and a great burden lifted off me. My responsibility for this child was gone, and I knew she was in good hands.

The wedding, of course, was wonderful. It was not so stuffy you dared not sneeze. It was like a church service, in a way, or a "singspiration," a banquet, a homecoming, or a touch of revival. All those words describe Robert and Esther's wedding. There were hymns, gospel songs, prayers and praises, a review of what God had done, and more. Later, someone said, "We've never seen it like this before. It was the most wonderful wedding we ever attended." It was not expensive either—a few hundred dollars at most.

This all happened in the storefront church on the city square, of which Jesus had said, "I will be with you there." When we obey God, He will be there for us when we need to hear His voice. Do you remember when God said to me years ago, "Go to that little church in Nebraska"? Had we not obeyed, we would have missed Robert.

I will never forget when Esther called me from West Virginia a few weeks later. She had been raised by a father who practically made himself unavailable each Saturday so he could pray and prepare his sermon. So, after the second or third Sunday with her unique husband, she said to me, "Daddy, I don't know what to do with Robert. He goes hiking on Saturdays, or he visits the sick, or he prays with people, or he goes to the store. He doesn't pray like you do. He doesn't prepare like you do."

"Well, Esther," I said, "when he preaches, does he have the anointing?"

"Oh, yes! Oh, yes," she assured me. "He has a great

anointing, and he preaches powerful sermons."

"Then leave him alone," I said.

The fact of the matter is Robert has the habit of reading six chapters of the Bible daily. He also prays for hours on a daily basis, and he has tremendous retention of what he reads. Did not Jesus say that the Holy Spirit can bring all things to our remembrance (see John 14:26)? So, although sometimes Robert prepares the way I do, frequently when he gets into the pulpit, the Holy Spirit weaves the things he has read into a beautiful fabric of love, forgiveness, and encouragement toward holy living.

My second daughter, Karin, was also married by the revelation of the Holy Spirit. In 1983 Marcia and I attended a revival meeting in Muskegon, Michigan, where a male trio ministered in song. On our way back home, just before we entered our city of Kokomo, I said to Marcia, "Do you feel what I feel?"

"Yes, I do," she answered.

When we got home we related to each other how we both felt the Lord meant for Don Litchfield, one of the men in the trio, to be Karin's spouse. The following day I called a few men of God to see if they had a confirmation on our witness on this relationship. All confirmed what was on our hearts was truly of the Lord.

The next assignment was to relay this information to our daughter. By this time the Lord had already witnessed I was to get a new fulltime associate, so within a few days Don, coming out of Asbury Seminary, arrived at our home to help us in the ministry.

I called Karin at work and asked her to meet me at the Long John Silver's restaurant, where I planned to break the news to her. As we sat at the table together, I slowly and carefully began to share with Karin the background of what I was about to tell her. It wasn't long before this straightforward young lady, who is so much like me, said, "Dad, I know exactly what you're going to tell me. The Lord already revealed to me that Don would be my husband."

Oh, praise the Lord! Now we had the Lord's witness in Mom and Dad's heart, in the hearts of several men of God, and in Karin's heart as well. The only thing left was to pray that Don would also get the word of the Lord that our daughter was for him.

Something happened when Don first saw our beautiful Karin. He immediately began trying to "keep his heart" and put all thoughts of marriage to her out of his mind. However, he was quite happy and relieved when another man of God called him and confirmed that Karin was to be his beloved wife. They were married about two months later and have since given us four wonderful grandchildren who love Jesus very much.

Let me inject here that just because a marriage is made in heaven does not mean there is no need for both partners to embrace the daily cross and deny self continually. Many marriages are made in heaven, but if either of the spouses is not willing to humble self and continue to live at the foot of the cross, those marriages can turn out to be as disastrous as if God had never brought them together in the first place.

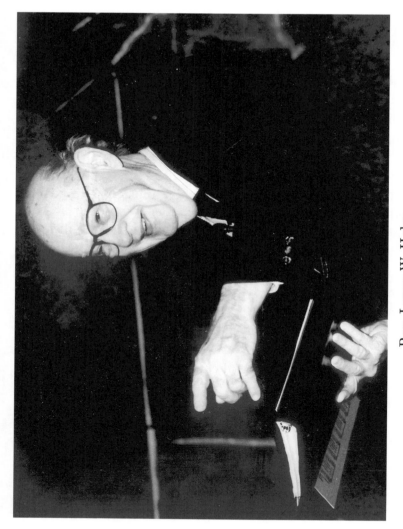

Rev. Loran W. Helm
"Only by the Holy Spirit can we be fed."

CHAPTER TWENTY-SEVEN

A Call to the Mayor

Even though our congregation moved ten times in four years before leasing the building on the city square, I'm not sure if any of us ever thought seriously about putting up a permanent church building of our own. We had a strong desire to give to missions and to help Rev. Helm in his calling instead of putting our money into bricks, stained glass, and beautiful pews. Consequently, the money went to help others, and no money went into a building fund.

When I drove from my home to our leased facility at the square each day, I passed a building that formerly had been the Social Security Office and the State Unemployment Agency. In one of the windows was a piece of plywood with the words "For Lease or Sale" printed on it. After several months I began to have an operation of the Holy Spirit in my heart about the place, and so I inquired about the price of the property. The owner was asking $247,000. Without a building fund and no further leading to proceed, I did nothing more to pursue it, but the work of God in my heart continued for a whole year.

Then, while Marcia and I were visiting a man of God in Florida, the Lord dropped the revelation into my heart that we were to offer $95,000 for that building. That less than half the asking price. I called the owner, a Jewish man named Mr. Andich, and made my offer. To my surprise, he was interested and wanted to meet with me right away.

When we returned from our trip, Mr. Andich called to nudge me along on the project, but I sensed the Lord's Spirit telling me it was not yet time. Because the man was anxious to sell the building, he checked around and learned the names of some of my key laymen and then asked them to persuade me to proceed with the purchase. But since I had no green light from heaven, I continued to wait. After several weeks, I was surprised to receive another call from the owner. He again said he wanted to talk to me about his property. Immediately Jesus spoke to my heart and said, "This is the right time."

We met for lunch at the Elks Club and talked for a while. He then invited me to go to the Jewish synagogue, his house of worship, about a block away from the property under consideration. We sat down in the back pew of the synagogue, which had also been built by this Jewish gentleman, and then he said to me, "My wife and I talked it over, and we would like to offer the building to you for $90,000." I immediately clasped his hand and said, "It's a deal." Have you ever heard of someone deciding to purchase a $247,000 building, offering only $95,000, and getting a counter offer from the owner for $90,000? But that is exactly what happened in this case. Mr. Andich then said, "I need $20,000 down, and we can handle the rest on a land contract."

I stood before my congregation the following Sunday and said, "I need $20,000 by Tuesday noon for a down payment on the new building." With no building fund and only a few hundred dollars in savings, I made no financial appeal to the congregation, nor did I ask for pledges. I simply told them I needed $20,000 by Tuesday noon, and anyone who wanted to help was to give their money to my associate, Pastor Tony.

On Monday evening, Tony came to my home with a check for $22,000. We gave $20,000 to our Jewish friend and used

$1,000 to clean up the building because it had been vacant for a while and had mildew growing inside it. Then we took the remaining $1,000 and put it into the mission fund.

After I signed all the papers for the land contract, I handed $20,000 to the owner. Then I had the bright idea to contact City Hall to see if there was any problem with the zoning, the fire code, or the building code. Yes, haven't we gone through this before?

Within hours, one of the inspectors came to the building, looked things over, and said, "You can't use this building as a church because you only have two off-street parking spots, and it is an ordinance that for every three persons you have attending the church, you must have one off-street parking spot." With just two off-street parking spots, which amounted to a little driveway next to the building, the maximum seating for our church would be six people. That would be just enough for the Schultze family.

How do you think I felt when I discovered I had given that dear Jewish man $20,000 in cash and had signed away the church for $70,000 in a land contract, only to find we could not get into the building? Do you think I prayed? Do you think I cried out to God and went to the altar? Do you think I was in a hard place? Most definitely! But after I prayed for a while, the Lord began to show me what I needed to do. Oh, what would we do without being able to pray to a prayer-answering God?

About two years prior to the purchase of this building, Pastor Tony had called me and said, "Pastor, do you know the mayor of our city is cutting his own grass? I saw him with a little lawn mower cutting the grass around his house." When I told him I was not aware of it, he said, "Do you think the mayor should do that?"

"No, he shouldn't," I admitted, reasoning that the mayor had the highest position in the city government and should not have to cut his own grass. Then I said goodbye to Pastor Tony and called the mayor. "Sir, I would like to ask you a favor," I said.

"Go ahead," he answered.

"I'd like to ask permission for our church's young people to cut your grass."

There was a long pause, and then he asked me to repeat my offer. I did, and he was utterly amazed. Then he wholeheartedly agreed to my proposition. By the time we purchased the new building, our young people had been cutting the mayor's grass faithfully for about two years, and shoveling his snowy sidewalks as well.

And so, as I cried out to God in prayer, the Lord told me to call the mayor, so I did. "Sir," I told him, "I have a dilemma, and I was wondering if you can help me."

I explained the circumstances, and when I was done he said, "Pastor Schultze, you are in. Go ahead and move into the building, and I will take care of everything else."

How do you think I felt then? I guarantee you the intensity with which I had been praying and interceding just minutes before was the same intensity with which I now began to praise God and rejoice. The city soon granted us a waiver to use the building in spite of the parking regulations, and we now had a building of our own. Oh, how it pays to trust and obey God! After moving into the building, we were able to develop a close relationship with the Rescue Mission a few blocks away, and they felt free to send their clients to us for services and counseling. Had we not been in that location, we would never have been able to help those people from the Mission.

Some may think I should have let the Board of Directors or a businessman in our congregation take care of purchasing the building, but if the transaction had been done traditionally, we would never have gotten the building Jesus had for us.

The traditional manner would first have involved checking all the legal aspects of the matter; we would then have been told the building was not appropriate for church use, and we would have backed off. What God intended for us would never have become ours. Reason or sound judgment would not have given us that property any more than reason and sound judgment would have made it possible for Israel to cross the Red Sea into a desert land.

I found my wife by the Holy Spirit's leading; we came to Kokomo by the Holy Spirit's leading; I purchased our house by the Holy Spirit's leading; I went on radio by the Holy Spirit's leading; I started my writing ministry by the Holy Spirit's leading. Marcia and I assisted a man of God for fifteen years by that same leadership of the Holy Spirit. We crossed the ocean forty-eight times by the witness of the Holy Spirit. We found our building on the city square by the Holy Spirit's leading, and now this building as well. The Apostle Paul said, *"For as many as are led by the Spirit of God, they are the sons of God"* (Romans 8:14). May we never settle for less than hearing and obeying the voice of God, for without it we suffer the consequences of our choices made in the flesh.

Eckart, Wolfram, Reimar, Renate

The Schultzes 50 Years Later.

Jean Skaife

She met a need across the ocean.

CHAPTER TWENTY-EIGHT
Follow Me as I Follow Christ

A rather significant event occurred in the years of our ministry following our move to the new church building on 500 West Superior Street in Kokomo. The Lord revealed to me that I was to give up the agenda of my own personal ministry and become a servant to Rev. Loran Helm. The Lord also showed me that Rev. Helm's calling and ministry were greater than mine, and far more important at that time.

I am called to be a teacher, but Rev. Helm had an apostolic calling, with a message the Church desperately needs to hear. The Lord told me to assist Brother Helm in any way I could, and to learn from him. I was to become his apprentice. Consequently, I offered my assistance and made it my priority to be available when he needed me. And apparently he definitely needed me because for nearly fifteen years, I became a "baggage carrier" for a modern-day prophet on his travels to serve the Lord.

These travels took Marcia and me to various churches for revival meetings throughout the United States. We also traveled to some foreign countries as the Lord led us: to Israel eighteen times, as well as to Egypt, Germany, Italy, Austria, and Nigeria. Besides his ministry trips, Rev. Helm spent some time each year in Florida, to rest and to help a fledging church. To assist him in these situations, I carried his luggage, made his flight arrangements, did trouble-shooting, and handled complex situations for him. Marcia and I took his laundry to the dry cleaners, bought groceries for him, prayed with him, washed and kept his car in good repair, and dined with him every day.

Actually, for a few years, nearly one-third of our time was given in assistance to this servant. Many weeks we were unable to be home with our congregation except to preach on some weekends. Providentially, the Lord sent two associates to our fellowship who were quite able to shepherd the congregation in my absence, and of course, He had provided us with a congregation who supported us completely in this season of our lives.

While we spent time with Brother Helm and his wife, we learned about walking with God. We felt like little Elishas, pouring water on the hands of an Elijah. Every hour with this couple was a learning experience in abiding in Christ, whether observing how they reacted when people spoke evil of them or if our party was about to be left behind because the plane was overbooked. We watched their response when there was no hot water in the hotel room, when the room was saturated with cigarette smoke, when we were last in line to be served or forgotten altogether in a restaurant. It is our reactions more than our actions that reveal our character.

By observing their daily lives, we saw that it was possible to live a sanctified and godly life. We learned how to respond in all circumstances as Jesus would have responded 2,000 years ago. We learned how to love and take care of the maids, the college students, the widows, the orphans, and those who are usually forgotten. Before Brother Helm would leave a men's restroom, he would clean up around the sinks and pick up the paper towels from the floor. In those fifteen years, we were with a couple who never said a negative thing about anyone at any time. To them, all people were precious.

I became a disciple of Brother Helm. When we become disciples, we make disciples of others. In general, only disciples beget disciples. One of the greatest needs in our churches is for those who will be like Matthew who, when called, dropped everything to follow Jesus. The Church is desperately lacking in understanding discipleship.

In those fifteen years, we saw a man of God who, upon entering a motel room, immediately knelt down and prayed to sanctify the room and then, with his wife at his side, read some scriptures. Before leaving that hotel, after all the luggage had been packed, Rev. Helm would again read some scriptures and pray with those present. In the fifteen years we were with this couple, we heard them engage only fleetingly in any conversation concerning the things of the earth. Their conversation was nearly always about Jesus—what He had done, what He was doing, and about His precious holy Word.

In the sixth chapter of the book of Deuteronomy, we are told the people of God should review in the morning, at noontime, and in the evening all that God has done. The Helms did this consistently, just as the scripture admonishes us all to do.

Rev. and Mrs. Helm, in my estimation and that of many others, were one of the rarest and most godly couples who ever entered the stream of human history. Most every profitable thing Marcia and I have learned in our spiritual walk we owe to their teaching and example—and, of course, to our dear Savior, Jesus. As Paul said, *"Be ye followers of me, even as I also am of Christ"* (1 Corinthians 11:1), so we followed in the footsteps of these choice servants as the Holy Spirit granted them grace and direction.

The Helm's beautiful pilgrimage is documented in Rev. Helm's autobiography, *A Voice in the Wilderness*. The very heart of Rev. Helm's apostolic message is that self-denial is the missing link in contemporary Christianity. Self-denial is what connects the believer to the victorious Christian life. Self-will never takes one step after Jesus. It must be crucified moment by moment. Therefore Jesus said, *"If any man will come after me, let him deny himself, and take up his cross daily, and follow me"* (Luke 9:23). It is by self-denial that we follow Jesus; as we follow Him, we hear His voice (see John 10:27, 16). Rev. Helm wrote that God "will send a mighty World Wide Revival that is truly of the Holy Ghost, once He can find a body of believers who will truly begin to wait upon Him and put Him absolutely first above everything of earth."[1] I am convinced that had we not given fifteen years in the prime of our lives as apprentices in God's kingdom, in loving servanthood for this godly couple, our current ministry would have been very limited.

There are many who say we should never follow a man; follow Jesus only. There is nothing in the Scriptures that tells us not to follow a man. Throughout the Word of God we are admonished to follow our parents, our teachers, our government officials, and the men that God has chosen for us to follow in our spiritual lives as they follow Christ. It was when Israel did not follow God's appointed leaders that the nation went into idolatry, adultery, witchcraft, and apostasy. God sent apostles, prophets, evangelists, pastors, and teachers for us to follow. Hence Jesus said, *"He that receiveth you receiveth me, and he that receiveth me receiveth him that sent me"* (Matthew 10:40).

Can you see the seriousness of this? Jesus said if we reject the man He sends us, we reject Him! Men sent by Jesus are neither to be ignored nor rejected. They are our Lord's ambassadors, whom He holds in His right hand of government (see Revelation 1:20). If we aren't following a man of God, it is likely we are not following Jesus either. Indeed, doesn't Jesus suggest in Matthew 10:41-42 that there ought to be a man of God to whom each of us should give a cup of cold water in order to receive a prophet's reward? When Paul said, *"Be ye followers of me, even as I also am of Christ,"* he gave us not only sound doctrine but also advice that is sound and profitable for our souls.

Furthermore, all of us must always see our ministry in the context of the universal family of God. Jesus did not teach us to pray, *"My* father which art in heaven," nor did He teach us to pray, "give *me* this day *my* daily bread." No, lest we become isolated in our ministry and independent of one another, in our Christian pursuits Jesus taught us to pray, *"Our* father which art in heaven," and "give *us* this day *our* daily bread." We must always think of ourselves as being a part of the whole, and not the whole in ourselves. The anointing is in the whole body working together, preferring one another in love.

Following a man of God can lead to some interesting, even uncomfortable places. After all, didn't Jesus tell Peter to get out of the boat and walk on the water? Because of my commitment to serve Rev. Helm, I had to miss two important events, but Jesus has greatly repaid me the price of yielding up my own wishes.

Both of those missed events occurred during the spring of 1983, when Rev. Helm called Marcia and me from his condo in Florida and asked if we would come down to be with them for a week or so. Since the Lord had already revealed to us that we were to help this couple whenever needed, we gave them an immediate yes. But when we got off the telephone, Marcia and I looked at each other and simultaneously announced, "That means we will miss Karin's high school graduation." The graduation was scheduled for the next week. Our second daughter was an excellent student and would be receiving recognition during the graduation ceremony. Of course, having lived with us all her life, Karin knew nothing mattered but doing God's will. Even though she would miss us at her graduation, we knew she would understand. Consequently, our second daughter attended her graduation without us, and few from her school understood why her parents were not there—but God did. Most of our congregation showed up to love and support her, while her parents assisted the servants of the Lord in Florida. Now did we lose our daughter over this? Well, here are Karin's own words about the event:

My parents had been preparing me for moments like this for as long as I could remember. The "main thrust" to our childhood training was to do God's will foremost and utmost. I simply knew I was still loved, valued, and cared for, even when my parents had to upset my plans to do what the Holy Spirit was leading them to do. In fact, I even felt honored when I could sacrifice a little something for the sake of the kingdom.

But my teachers and fellow students simply couldn't comprehend that God would lead parents to miss their child's graduation. They couldn't imagine why God couldn't accomplish His will some other way—not to mention I had the highest grade point average of my small class and would receive special mention. Added to this were all the other strange ideas they remembered my father having about dating, rock music, and "keeping the heart." However, despite their indignation, I had learned that the events that mark the pathway of man take second place to the events God wants to use to orchestrate our spiritual journey.

Rather than losing Karin through missing her graduation, we gained one of the most dedicated, uncompromising disciples of Jesus you could find anywhere in the world. We missed our daughter's graduation by obeying God, but by obeying God we have the greatest hope to save our children and to lead them to higher ground.

Has it ever occurred to you that nobody in all of time ever lost anything worth losing by obeying God?

During the period of time our church was worshipping on the city square in Kokomo, a shy, well dressed, pleasant-looking lady walked into our storefront sanctuary and came back into my little office. And what an office it was! It was probably about ten feet square, and the furniture consisted of an old school desk, an office chair with one spring and a broken seat, and a wooden chair for any visitor who happened by. It was not much of a welcome to this visitor, whose name was Marilyn. (Unknown to me at the time of our meeting, Marilyn would later engage me in a worldwide Internet ministry.)

Marilyn has a double Master's degree in social work, and she had a few questions for me. After I answered them she left, and I thought I would never see her again. But as she was walking out the door, the Lord gave her quite a few revelations about me. She knew who I was, what I was on earth for, and that she was called to my ministry for life.

Understandably, Marilyn was at the next church service and nearly all of them since. Within a year of our meeting, Marilyn began to pray about leading a soul to Jesus. She began to cry out to God that He would save a soul on her behalf. Shortly after, she met an atheist engineer named Bruce, whom she invited to church. It seems he was the soul she was praying for, for not long after, the Lord began to work with Bruce, and he was miraculously saved out of deep sin. Soon after, God led Bruce and Marilyn to be married. When Bruce heard me preach for the first time, my topic was "There's room for you in the inner circle." Immediately Bruce knew the message was for him, and he entered into Marilyn's vision to stand with me and support me 100 percent.

These two souls have become one of the most wonderful

lay teams in our church, much like the husband-wife team of Aquila and Priscilla, who faithfully served and supported Paul in his ministry. Since Marcia and I first met Marilyn and Bruce, our plans have always been their plans, and there are other couples like this in our church. Bruce and Marilyn's understanding of discipleship, I believe, came mostly out of my refusal to do their wedding for them. Now that sounds harsh if taken out of context, so let me explain.

As I mentioned earlier, in the spring of 1983, Rev. Helm called Marcia and me from his condo in Florida and asked if we would come down for a week or two. After the first week, Rev. Helm said to us, "It would be wonderful if you could stay another week." Our "yes" came just as quickly as the previous one that affected Karin's graduation. But once again, after Marcia and I returned to our room, we looked at each other and said, "Now we have to miss Bruce and Marilyn's wedding."

It is only natural for a couple to want the senior pastor to do the wedding, so we had never even prayed about another possibility. They had told their relatives all about my story, and they were eager to meet Pastor Schultze. You can see that this was the more difficult of the two assignments. And yet, when Jesus calls, we either excuse ourselves from man or we excuse ourselves from God.

Brother Helm did not say, "The Lord has revealed for you to stay," but rather, "It would be wonderful if you could stay." He gave us a way out, yet he knew nothing about our circumstances. But why would we not want what is wonderful in the sight of God?

I prayed for a few days before I called Marilyn. When I finally did, the conversation went something like this: "Praise the Lord, Marilyn, this is Pastor." Then I shared with her that Brother Helm wanted us to stay longer.

She chuckled and said, "Pastor, the Lord already revealed to me you would not do the wedding. Pastor Jerry is supposed to do it." Pastor Jerry was one of my associates.

Can you imagine the burden that fell off my shoulders when I heard that the Lord Jesus, in His love and mercy, had already prepared Marilyn's heart and that she was excited because Jesus, the Son of God Himself, had the wedding under complete control? Jesus would be a guest at her wedding as He was at the wedding of Cana in Galilee 2,000 years before, where He changed water into wine. As Jesus took care of everything at that wedding of old, He would take care of all the needs in this wedding.

Before I go on, here is Marilyn's story, as she related it to me:

The Lord showed me that you would not be marrying us. So when you called, I was delighted. I already knew from the Lord that you were not returning for the wedding, and so your call cleared up any questions I had about God's revelation.

Remember that I had not been in this ministry for even one year. I wanted to walk with God like you and Rev. Helm. I wanted to hear from God, too. When God speaks, we are not always prepared, but I wasn't disappointed. It encouraged me that God cared about every detail of my wedding, which is one of the most important events to a woman. I was thrilled and there was joy in my heart for God had spoken.

I never thought to pray about who was to marry us. You would have thought I would have prayed about it, but for some reason, I just assumed that you, Pastor, would marry us. You can pray about things and sometimes overlook certain details, but if your heart is right before God, He will not let you miss any good thing. To me, this was like one of those moments in a Christian journey where God speaks, man obeys, and blessings flow!

As we came to the end of our second week in Florida, Brother Helm said it would be wonderful if we could stay a few more days, and that time we had nothing scheduled. We soon found out God had something on the books for us on the following Sunday—we were invited to what they called an "Ice Cream Pool Party" at a congregant's home. We reluctantly went, and I was asked to tell my life story. One of the young men in attendance had just graduated from Bible College. Gifted as he was, he was offered several outstanding positions in the ministry. He had also received a call from a minister in Indiana, who asked the young graduate to join him in ministry but could not promise him any income. Through something in my story, the Lord confirmed to him that Indiana was the place for him to go. Soon after his arrival at his new destination, all his needs were well taken care off .

So where are those who were affected by our extended stay in Florida? Where are they now some twenty years later? Our daughter Karin and her husband are heading up a high-standard, no-nonsense "Shadrach" discipleship program for youth, which can only be joined by meeting certain spiritual requirements. Karin's husband, Don, was my associate pastor for years, and I think he has the finest singing voice in the world. When he sings, the anointing is there. He and Karin now have four children, all lovers of Jesus and all praying about entering the ministry, either at home or on the mission field. And all of them play stringed instruments and piano as well.

Bruce and Marilyn are one of the most wonderful lay teams in our church. Marilyn quit her job as a social worker and is now my fulltime, unpaid, happy, worldwide missions coordinator, and she has engineered the publication of my first book, a devotional titled *Abiding in Christ*. She also handles all my correspondence and travel plans. These two people have become shining examples, illustrating that nothing matters but the will of God, regardless of the cost. The young preacher who went to Indiana had a flourishing ministry in Indianapolis for several years.

The man of God did not say years ago that I was to come down to be with him in Florida; he said it would be *wonderful* if I could. Now, was it wonderful or not, considering all that came out of it? Can you possibly tell me the number of souls that will be in eternity because my wife and I said yes in the face of great obstacles and even misunderstandings? What would we and the world have missed if we had taken the path of least resistance to appease many of our acquaintances? I cannot adequately express the need for absolute obedience to even the slightest prompting of the Holy Spirit.

Paul's words, *"Be ye followers of me, even as I am also of Christ,"* constitute such an important formula that leads to blessings untold—provided, of course, the *"as I am also of Christ"* stays in the formula.

The Schultzes with children and grandchildren visiting Munich, Germany 2005.

CHAPTER TWENTY-NINE
An Airplane! What For?

G od loves His children so much that, from time to time, He surprises them with the most unusual gifts.

While I was still a student at Asbury Seminary, there was a flying club whose members owned a little Cessna airplane. Several students, while receiving theological training, also got their pilot's licenses through that flight school. Marcia had urged me to take some flying courses, but I was not interested, nor did I see how we could afford it. I had my mind set on getting through school; flying was not on my agenda.

Years later, while living in Kokomo, we visited a friend in Alabama. This brother was an electrician, but on the side he was a crop duster. He owned a Comanche four-passenger airplane, and one day he took me for a ride. As we soared above the earth, he suddenly said, "Why don't you take the controls and see how you like it?" I did, and after I flew for a little while, he said, "Why don't you learn to fly?" I said I had never really thought about it, but after we landed, he gave me $200 for my first flying lessons.

As a pastor, I had learned to use the money people gave me only as it was designated, and there I was with $200 designated specifically for flying lessons, so I took my first lessons at a little airport about four miles directly south of our home. The grass landing strip was about 2,000 feet long and 100 feet wide, with a low spot in the middle that turned into a mud puddle every time it rained. There were some high tension wires on the north end of the runway, so when landing from the north, you had to clear those wires and then make a steep descent to ensure enough runway to come to a stop. Then, of course, if it had been raining, you had to try to leave as much mud puddle on one side of the airplane as you could. Learning to fly at that particular airport sometimes included plenty of adventure, and at other times nothing but, "Help me, Jesus!"

At six feet, four inches, I was an entire foot taller than my flight instructor. When we got into this little two-passenger Cessna 152, he would put his seat all the way up, and I would put mine all the way back. Even then, it was a tight fit.

Of course, I was in the pilot's seat, as was the custom during flight training. The first item of business was to learn take-offs and landings, as well as turns and climbs, climbing turns and descending turns, before moving on to more difficult maneuvers. It was a rather enjoyable experience, but it took a while to get used to having three wheels underneath me that did not touch the ground.

Little by little, as finances were available, I took more lessons till I obtained my pilot's liscence. I shall never forget my first landing at the Municipal Airport in Kokomo. Instead of having a 2,000 foot-long grass runway with a dip in the middle of it, this airport had two runways, each a mile long and paved. Oh, what a feeling I had when I got into this "big" airport! I felt like I was flying into Kennedy International in New York City, even though I was just landing in Kokomo with that little Cessna 152.

Occasionally, over the next few years, I rented an airplane to keep up the minimum requirements of the FAA— six takeoffs and landings every six months. Then, in 1984, something special happened. It was Thursday, May 10, my forty-eighth birthday and the day of our midweek church service. This service was a combination of sharing and prayer with the adults, while the children had their service in the Fellowship Hall.

Having pronounced the benediction, I was about to step off the platform when one of my associates said, "Pastor, you can't leave yet. We have something for you." So I remained up front while all the members came onto the platform and handed me birthday cards. I thanked them and was ready to step off the platform when, again, my associate said, "You can't go yet. We have something more for you." He opened a small cardboard box and handed it to me. I removed the crinkled paper and found a little wooden airplane with a tiny propeller that was turned by a rubber band. I again expressed my gratitude and was about to leave for the third time when I was stopped by my associate. Then a couple of youth rolled in a portable table, and on it was a large birthday cake, with a sugar airplane on top. Once again I expressed my thanks and tried to leave.

For the fourth time, my associate said to me, "You can't leave. We're not done yet." He was laughing and having a great time, as was the congregation. Of course, they all knew what was coming; I was the only one in the dark. At the associate's signal, the doors to the sanctuary opened, and in came a stream of children. The first one was inside a big cardboard box shaped like the fuselage of a Cessna airplane: a propeller up front, a wing sticking out each side, and a tail. The child had to hold it up with both hands. Another child followed behind, holding the tail. Attached to the tail of the "airplane" was a banner, similar to those pulled by planes for advertising. I still didn't understand what was going on until they "flew" the banner right in front of me and stopped. The banner was actually a huge check made out to Pastor Reimar Schultze. The notation line on this giant check read, "For an airplane," and on the dollar line was this amount: $3,512.

Then the associate said, "We have raised this money for an airplane for you, and we are going to raise the rest as needed. Now go find a plane. This is your birthday gift."

I believe the size of the congregation at that time—those attending the morning worship—may have been about sixty or seventy, including children. We had just bought a church building, we had a strong missions budget, and now an airplane for the pastor.

If we love Jesus only for Himself and seek nothing but His will, many times He gives us wonderful gifts, whether physical or spiritual, as we see in the Psalms: *"For the Lord God is as a sun and shield: the Lord will give grace and glory: no good thing will he withhold from them that walk uprightly"* (Psalm 84:11).

I never had a desire to fly. I never imagined getting a pilot's license. And it was certainly way beyond my imagination to own an aircraft, especially as a pastor of a relatively small congregation. But by the grace of God, I was seeking first God's kingdom and His righteousness, and as a result, experiencing the God who enjoys giving out of His abundance even more than we enjoy giving our all to Him.

Of course, now it became a matter of finding the airplane God wanted me to have. Rationally, I could have contacted aircraft brokers or looked at advertisements for used airplanes. But my choice was to let God lead me to the right plane, as He had led me to my wife, my house, my radio ministry, and to many precious people in my life.

After several weeks, I made reservations to rent a Cessna to fly to northern Indiana to deliver a $1,000 check to put toward the purchase of a car for an evangelist who lived in a trailer home. The day was perfect for flying—practically no wind and not a cloud in the sky. But one hour before departure, Jesus said, "You are not flying to see this evangelist; you are driving." I called the airport to cancel my rental and offered to pay them for the reserved time anyway. Graciously, they declined my offer.

Marcia accompanied me, and on our return trip, as we were about to pass the Rochester airport, she said, "Honey, why don't we stop at this airport? It just could be our airplane is here." Well, you know how it is with men when they have their schedules set and their wives make a suggestion. But, oh, dear men, we will never find out this side of eternity how much we missed because we had our schedules set and our plans fixed! Remember the story of the Good Samaritan (see Luke 10:30)? The preachers had their schedules set in stone, and so they missed what God had for them.

Expectantly, I turned the car into the airport and inquired if they happened to have a plane for sale. The manager replied, "Yes, that white-and-red striped Cessna 172 over there belongs to an osteopathic doctor. He would like to sell it, but it is not advertised."

At that moment Jesus said, "This is your airplane." A few days later on a rather windy day, I flew that aircraft out of the Rochester Airport to its new home in Kokomo.

One of the first responses I received regarding this purchase was from a lady of another church who had heard about my new plane. "Did you get a real one?" she asked. I assured her that, indeed, it was real. To the average church member, it is absolutely inconceivable that a church would waste money on such a thing for their pastor, even though the seven-year-old plane we purchased cost no more than a new car. Whatever God is in is never too little, never too much; it is always just right. *"For as the heavens are higher than the earth, so are my ways higher than your ways, and my thoughts than your thoughts"* (Isaiah 55:9).

Shortly afterward, I learned how it happened that I received an airplane for my forty-eighth birthday. While I was away traveling, the Board of Deacons met to discuss a gift for me. They had just heard a message from a visiting man of God about the importance of ministering to the pastor, so one of the board members suggested the church purchase a plane for my birthday. The discussion went back and forth, as they weighed the pros and cons, including the cost, and tried to discern whether or not this was God's will. Finally, one of the deacons, a very quiet widow, remarked, "How important is an airplane if we don't buy it and we miss what the Holy Spirit is planning to do?"

At that precise moment, the power of God descended into that room in such a manner that *all* the board members felt as if they were being thrown back against the walls behind them. They had never before experienced such a witness of the power of God in their lives, nor have they since. No one said any more about the plane, for no more discussion was needed. God had spoken! The next matter of business was, "Well, since that's now decided, how do we go about getting one?" I have to confess I do not have the slightest idea what all is contained in that revelation of the airplane. All I know is it was real, and I leave the rest in the hands of God.

Now you can see why they wanted me to have an airplane much more than I wanted to have one. After two years of flying the Cessna 172, which I had purchased with the money the church gave me, I decided I wanted to sell it, but the Board of Deacons was adamantly against it because of the powerful witness of the Holy Spirit.

You see, owning an airplane is more than just having a piece of equipment sitting in a hangar. The plane needs to be flown at least once a week or the engine may get rusty. If you are an instrument pilot, as I am, and you don't fly at least once a week, the pilot will also get rusty. On top of that, there is maintenance, repair, and insurance. So when I don't have a ministerial assignment to fly the aircraft to visit and encourage a pastor, I fly it just to maintain currency and proficiency. Most of the time, the Lord has me go somewhere about once a week to help someone.

So after two years, my thoughts of quitting flying altogether became quite strong. But after hearing from the Board of Deacons once again on how the Holy Spirit witnessed that the plane would be tied in somehow with the great work of God ahead, I began to pray earnestly about the matter. I also asked another man of God, who is very sensitive to the Holy Spirit's leadings, to pray about it with me. During the prayer, the Holy Spirit witnessed to my brother that I was not to quit flying, but to sell the airplane and get something better. I was shocked. Here I was looking to sell out and quit flying, and instead the Lord tells me to move up a notch! That Holy Spirit leading started us on a search for and the acquisition of a Cessna 182, my present aircraft. This is also a four-passenger aircraft, but it has a lot more room, more power, and more instruments. We bought this airplane for $32,500 nineteen years ago, and now it is valued at $100,000.

Because of the Lord's help, our church was birthed by the Holy Spirit. These events concerning my ministry in Kokomo did not come out of men's ideas—they came by the Spirit of God as Jesus spoke to me in 1977, saying, "Start packing. You are leaving next week, Tuesday afternoon," and then saying a few days later, "Go to Kokomo, Indiana. I will be with you there."

This wonderful congregation not only supplied me with one of the finest aircraft in its category, but they also continued to supply the financial help to keep it up and current with the newest advances in technology. The congregation recently bought me a panel GPS system that makes many more airports accessible to me in inclement weather.

"Eye hath not seen, nor ear heard, neither have entered

into the heart of man, the things which God hath prepared for them that love him" (1 Corinthians 2:9). "Things" here refers to things of the earth, as well as things of heaven. God does not care only about our spiritual needs, but also about our earthly needs.

Over the years, I have had three operations on my legs for varicose veins, a problem that started when I had to stand for prolonged times in the train in East Germany. Being able to fly a plane and get to places three times faster than I could driving a car has spared a lot of wear and tear on my legs. Surely, as the song says, "His eye is on the sparrow, and I know He watches me." That airplane has now carried me over 200,000 miles to many marvelous, divine assignments to help and encourage other believers, especially pastors—assignments I would have missed had I not received this wonderful gift from God's people.

We must let God be God. There are times He might take us through years or decades of great deprivation, and there are times when He will make up for what we have missed earlier. He knows our needs better than we do. It is not unusual that occasionally God puts His choicest servants into a bed of affliction or into a narrow place that will make them more like Him. At other times He lets his beloved experience some of the vast ocean of His infinite bounty.

The bottom line of this chapter is that our God is a God of extravagance, and if, out of His great love, He desires to share some of His extravagance in a more personal way with us, we should not reject it, for if we do, we reject Him. God wants us to enjoy all He has for us without feeling guilty about it.

CHAPTER THIRTY
God's Open Doors

While in a hotel in Anchorage, Alaska, one night Rev. Helm had someone slip a piece of paper under my door. On it was written a scripture that said, *"I have set before thee an open door, and no man can shut it"* (Revelation 3:8).

In this chapter I would like to tell you about a few doors that were opened for us shortly after this revelation. Keep in mind none of these doors were opened by me out of a sense of urgency or personal ambition. All of these doors were opened by the Lord; it was His doing, not mine. The Lord told me long ago to "walk with God," and that is all I have been trying to do since my pastorate in Montana.

Let's look first at my involvement in radio ministry, and then at my call to write in this next chapter. To refresh your memory, in 1977, before we arrived in Kokomo, the Lord revealed to Brother Helm in prayer that I was to preach on the radio. I had never desired to be on the radio, but I obeyed God and contacted a local country-western station, which had an open slot on Sunday morning, so I took it. The Lord provided the money, and since September 11, 1977, He has made a way for us to be on the radio every Sunday morning at 9 A.M., which is a primetime airing period. Although it would not have been my preferred type of radio station, it was what God wanted, and today, some twenty-eight years later, it reaches over 100,000 people in north-central Indiana. The Lord wants the message of self-denial and obedience, the missing links to victorious living, to reach the hearts of the multitudes, and this was one way He chose to do it.

The Lord also told me, "No music." So, for over twenty-seven years, I have had no music on my program except the one time soon after returning from Nigeria when I played a one-minute excerpt of the Nigerian believers in song. The reason for this no-music mandate was that the Lord had said, "There is enough Christian music on radio. There needs to be more Bible teaching."

But there was more to that initial revelation about speaking on the radio; the Lord had made it clear that I was to be on more than one station. For nearly nineteen years we waited for further revelation as to when we were to pursue the "other" station or stations. During those nineteen years, I could have contacted Christian radio brokers and asked them to put me on the air, but had I done that, it would have been my doing and not the Lord's. I also would have been ahead of God's schedule, and when we do that, we are on our own, and the consequences will be disappointing and even disastrous.

In August 1996, the Lord said to me, "Your ministry will start moving." Until then our ministry had been predominantly local. But after thirty years of pastoral ministry, at the age of sixty, it almost seemed the work I was brought into the world for was about to start in earnest. Someone has said the greater the preparation, the greater the harvest. Indeed the Lord was true to what he spoke to me. Things began to get into motion, and they have neither stopped nor slowed down since.

The next major step came the following summer, when Marcia and I were attending meetings in North Carolina. As I was leaving one of the sessions, a short, slender, elderly gentleman with a sweet demeanor, Don Powell, said to me, "I have listened to one of your radio tapes and would like to make a deal with you. If your church will fast and pray for our ministry, I'll give you free radio time each week so you can reach the whole world for Jesus." I was elated.

Don Powell had been a missionary in the Caribbean for many years. He was one of those men who could not be stopped. One day, while he and others, including his daughter, were on a boat he used to visit the various islands, a fire broke out and the fuel tanks exploded. Many were injured, and Don received third-degree burns over most of his body. Upon reaching shore, in excruciating pain, he ran back and forth on the sandy beach. There was no nurse or doctor on that island, so he and his daughter were taken to a hospital on a neighboring island. Shortly after, Don's daughter went to be with the Lord, but the Lord miraculously delivered Don through weeks of pain and multiple surgeries.

Not long after, the Lord impressed upon Don to use the radio to proclaim the gospel to the uttermost parts of the world. Through a series of miraculous events, God made it possible for him to buy land near Elizabethtown, Kentucky, to build a worldwide short-wave radio network, as well as an FM station. From there, my voice began to go out to over 150 nations. The Lord had said in 1977, "Go on radio," and now I was on two stations. The "Call to Obedience" message could now be heard in over one hundred countries and many islands of the sea. God said in Isaiah 60:9, *"Surely the isles shall wait for me."*

The following year, I received a call from a Christian station in Knoxville, Tennessee. The lady manager of the station said, "Someone sent me one of your tapes. I want you on our radio station." This became our third station. The lady in Knoxville sent a tape on to a clearinghouse of ministries for Christian radio stations. They then sent me a list of about thirty radio stations where they could place me. After prayer with another servant of God, I signed up for Florida, Alabama, and two other short wave stations broadcasting to India and China. What a privilege it is to reach the people of these two countries! English is the national language in India, and is now being taught in China as well, even in many elementary schools. The Indian program is broadcast out of Germany, and the Chinese program out of an island north of Siberia in Russia.

For nineteen years, though I had broadcast from a powerful radio station, it was still a local station, and my listeners were restricted to central Indiana. Suddenly, without my doing anything, there came an explosion of opportunities. I now receive requests nearly every month to go on the radio somewhere in the world. I never cared much for Christian radio because so little of it is truly anointed of the Lord. But in 1977, the Lord said, "You go on radio," and that is what I did.

As I mentioned earlier, from the time Marcia and I came to Christ, we have had a great vision for the multitudes of lost people in the world and wanted to go overseas as missionaries. Instead, the Lord put us together and sent us to Indiana, where we have since been able to reach more people around the world than if we had been foreign missionaries in a literal sense.

God had a plan for me even before he put the sun, the moon and the stars into the heavens. I still marvel at that fact. But just as He has a plan for me, He has one for you, too, as the Bible attests. Notice Paul's words, *"According as he hath chosen us in him before the foundation of the world, that we should be holy and without blame before him in love"* (Ephesians 1:4).

Had I allowed bitterness and resentment to come into my life because of the deprivations, hardships, and losses in my childhood and youth, I never would have been used by God; I would have stepped right out of God's foreordained plan for me. Do not allow bitterness, resentment, and disappointment to get into your heart. Do not allow the darkness of the past to overshadow and squelch you. Do not become a casualty. There is no future in the past. Instead, look to God in the middle of the storms and trust in Him; you will be surprised what He will do in and for you.

Think of it. Before God separated the land from the sea and the light from the darkness, He had you and me on His mind. He created you and me for a divine purpose: the most elementary purpose was that we should *"be holy and without blame before Him in love"* (Ephesians 1:4). That sounds like God, doesn't it? How can we possibly settle for less than that? But in addition to the basic purpose for which God created us, there is a specific work that He wants all of us to accomplish. We find this in the writings of the apostle Paul: *"For we are his workmanship, created in Christ Jesus unto good works, which God hath before ordained that we should walk in them"* (Ephesians 2:10).

There are many good works we could enter into. We could be an usher. We could be a missionary in Africa, or we could work in an orphanage. But if God has not *"before ordained"* any of these works, we labor in them without His anointing, strength, and blessing. We will bear no fruit for eternity.

Dairy farmers will tell you every cow has its own stall. All stalls look the same, but every morning and evening when the cows come into the barn, each goes to its own stall. They would not feel comfortable in any other place. So it is with us: once we enter into the work He has foreordained for us, we find rest; we will not find it anywhere else.

None of what I'm doing now is anything I would have chosen for myself. I had to die to all my choices and preferences in order to let God have His way with me. And I can surely testify today that it was best for Him to have his way with me. As I said earlier, I never wanted to be a pastor. I never wanted to go on radio. I never wanted to live in the state of Indiana. Each of these things contained a personal cross on which I had to be crucified, but thank God, where the cross is, there the glory will be also.

God's open doors can include almost anything we are involved with in this life, especially those things that have to do with our calling and life's mission. When we keep our eyes on Jesus, when we follow Him day-by-day and hour-by-hour, He will send the anointing and provisions we need to fulfill our earthly mission.

Oh, child of God, don't get discouraged; keep pressing on! Don't go man's way. Don't try to make things happen in the flesh. Don't push for success. Don't compete with others. Don't seek after the exalted places. Don't seek the honor of man. If you do, your faith will be destroyed. Jesus said, *"How can ye believe, which receive honour one of another, and seek not the honour that cometh from God only"* (John 5:44)? The passionate lover of Jesus always seeks the lowest places, and the Lord will be with you to call you up when the time is right.

When I was in my forties and fifties, the Lord revealed to me that my ministry would not really begin until I was in my sixties and seventies. Everything that preceded it would be preparation. But again, "The greater the preparation, the greater the harvest." Or as Brother Helm has stated, "The deeper our spiritual roots go downward, the higher our spiritual branches spring upward."

We must die out to our tendency to get in a hurry. God can indeed move quickly; He can do more in seconds than man can do in centuries. But most of the time He wants us to move slowly. One of my favorite hymns is "Not So in Haste, My Heart" by Bradford Torrey:

Not so in haste my heart!
Have faith in God and wait;
Although He linger long,
He never comes too late.

He never cometh late;
He knoweth what is best;
Vex not thyself in vain;
Until He cometh, rest.

Until he cometh, rest,
Nor grudge the hours that roll;
The feet that wait for God
Are soonest at the goal.

Are soonest at the goal
That is not gained by speed;
Then hold thee still, my heart,
For I shall wait His lead.[1]

That is what the Lord told me: "Go slow." For many years he led me to smaller and smaller churches, waiting on God for hours a day and pouring water on the hands of a prophet for fifteen years. Oh, my friend, if you go at the Master's speed you will get to feast on the riches of His good and perfect will too. He too will give you that promise: *"I have set before thee an open door, and no man can shut it"* (Revelation 3:8).

However, this promise is a conditional promise. It is reserved for those who have forsaken all to do their Master's will. We all come into the world the same: naked, having nothing. What we get in life is how we respond to our Creator. We certainly will be deprived of God's richest blessings if we complain. The questions people in trouble often ask are, "Why does God let this happen to me?" or "Why does God pick on me?" or "Where is God in all of this?" We must turn the question around to give it a bit of legitimacy. The issue is not whether God held up His end, but whether we held up ours. God already demonstrated His love to us by sacrificing his Son on a cruel cross. But how have we shown our love to him? Where is the evidence?

God is asking all of us, "Where have *you* been all this time since I brought you into this world? Have you loved Me with all your heart, soul, mind, and strength? Have you served Me? Have you won others to Christ? Have you regularly prayed for the needy, the lost, and the persecuted church? Have you worshiped Me, and given generously of your substance to the cause of Christ's kingdom? Have you denied self to do only My will? Have you lived a holy life? Where have *you* been all these years?"

Oh, my friend, God owes us nothing. We are but a pitiful, sin-stained people. We owe everything to our Holy God who, because of His great mercy, has not yet destroyed us for our rebellion and indifference toward Him.

"I have set before thee an open door." When I lay under those pine branches as a lonely thirteen-year-old in Germany, I had no idea what God was all about, or what He had in store for me. But as I responded to Him in self-denial over the years, I entered more and more into His glorious purposes for my life.

And so, by the grace of God, I have the right wife; I am in the right city, the right house, the right church, and the right ministry for now. That includes the pastoral care, the radio, the writing of Christian letters ("Call to Obedience") I send out once a month—all of these things that God had in store for me long before I ever called on His name.

CHAPTER THIRTY-ONE

The Call

In 1974, after thousands of hours of waiting upon God, the Lord revealed to me to start a monthly epistle titled "Call to Obedience." I still remember the day when I ran off the first twenty-two copies of that first edition on an old mimeograph machine and sent them out to a few key people. Now this monthly "Call to Obedience" goes out by the thousands, in print and via the Internet, to many countries around the world.

Let me share with you two beautiful stories of how this message, this "Call to Obedience," started in a few countries.

Inga Karnishauska, a Latvian evangelist's daughter, came to the United States several years ago and found the "Call to Obedience" letters in the home of a Nigerian pastor who was then living in South Bend, Indiana. As soon as she read them, she said, "This is what the Latvians and the Russians need."

During her first visit with us, Inga selected 100 different "Call to Obedience" messages to take with her back to Latvia, where she began to translate them into the Latvian language.

I soon discovered that right after the Berlin wall came down in 1991, American evangelists had traveled to Russia, Latvia, and the other Soviet bloc countries and brought the

gospel to them. Hundreds of thousands made professions of
faith, but then the Americans, with their noisy, high-tech
evangelistic campaigns, left these new converts to fend
for themselves. The evangelists did practically nothing to
establish a foundation to help these new believers grow in
the Lord. As a result, there was a multitude of believers
but practically no Bible Schools or Seminaries, no mature
Christians adequate for the task of spiritual nurturing.
There were practically no pastors to help these little lambs,
nor any biblical teaching literature in their own language.
Many of them had even received a false gospel, promising
if they would turn to Jesus, they would prosper financially;
months or even years later, they still lived in poverty and
soon gave up the faith as a hoax. Others heard the message
of faith, and only of faith, without any teaching on obedience,
love, or how to follow the Lord Jesus on a daily basis.

Through my writings, people began to find the Lord,
while others began to be established in discipleship. First
there were only one or two impacted by these letters, then
three or four, and so on as the letters were passed around.
In order to study the messages more deeply, these believers
formed "Call to Obedience" Bible studies. Since most people
in these former communist countries are still too poor to
own their own Bibles, they were grateful to have the "Call
to Obedience" letters for their studies. As these believers
met on a weekly basis and invited others to join them, many
found the Lord in these studies, and the fruit of these home
groups led to the establishing of churches.

In 2002, when Inga visited with us, she invited me to
come to her country to share with her people who had been
blessed by the "Call to Obedience" letter.

"I don't think I have the strength for such an obviously
long journey," I told her, "but I believe the Lord may send my
children on my behalf."

Shortly thereafter, Jesus said to me, "The church needs to send Don, Karin, and their four children to Latvia." When I announced this to the church, the congregation was so excited that in one single service over $7,000 was raised for this missionary venture. Before long the family was on their way, with all four children taking their stringed instruments with them. Oh, what a blessing they were to the Latvians, who had just recently come out of communism and had so little materially speaking!

At sixty-eight years of age my health improved, and Marcia and I were soon on our way to Riga, the capital of Latvia, via Munich, Germany. When we arrived in Riga, Inga and her father were waiting there to greet us with open arms.

On the first full day in Riga, I was wonderfully surprised at how the Christians had been nurtured by the "Call to Obedience" letters. I was driving a nine-passenger van full of youth leaders to a conference, where I was scheduled to speak. Finally I turned to the young man sitting next to me and said, "All of you have been totally silent now for the first half hour of the drive. Are you always that way?"

This young man, who was only nineteen years old and had just been saved six months earlier, said, "The Bible says we need to be slow to speak, and we should refrain from all idle words." I was stunned, as I realized I was with youth who actually took Christianity seriously, right down to the core.

Upon arrival at an old palace that was in renovation, I began by sharing two sessions with the youth in the afternoon. That evening, at our regular bedtime, Marcia and I went to our room to rest. The next morning, Inga told me the youth had stayed up until 3:30 in the morning, praying and going over everything I had taught them. With only three hours of rest, these youth were back in the first session the next morning. Oh, my friend, those young people truly sought fellowship with God with all their hearts!

Inga also had the vision to translate this humble letter into the Russian language. Many Russians had been moved into Latvia by the Soviet government during the communist years, and so these letters went to the Russian-speaking people there. Inga's father had a contact in Kaliningrad, Russia, who was an overseer of many churches throughout that country, and they felt the messages needed to be distributed there as well. Even though communism had fallen, the situation in Russia was different than that of most former Soviet bloc countries, and Inga still needed permission from the Religious Department of the Russian government to distribute these letters.

By now, Russia had developed a somewhat anti-Western attitude, and that included the rejection of the wild, noisy evangelism of our churches, the immodesty of our gospel groups, and the many confusing doctrines we tried to bring to them. One of the most offensive things American people brought to Russia was Christian rock music. One of the Russian Christians who had served many years in prison said, "Don't play this music to us; this is what the communists piped into our cells to torture us."

Finally, the Russian Orthodox priests went to Moscow and asked for legislation to protect them from Western Christianity. The message of these formerly beaten-up and scarred priests was basically this: "Let us have our churches back. These people are our people; we suffered and bled with them. All these Westerners come in and confuse our people. The Baptists say they have the truth, as well as the Methodists, the Church of God, the Church of Christ, the Assemblies of God, the Pentecostal groups, the Jehovah's Witnesses, and all the rest. They come in with their high-tech evangelism and take the people away from us, and we can't compete with them. Give us time to heal. Give us time to get our sheep back." Consequently, Western Christian influences were greatly restricted by the Department of Religious Affairs, so at this time, when Inga had her vision to distribute the "Call to Obedience" in Russia, Christian literature could not be distributed except by permission from Moscow.

Some seasoned believers said, "Inga, it does not look like you can get a Russian permit from Moscow for Pastor Schultze's writings." But Inga, a tall, slender, blonde package of human dynamite with unshakable faith, got on a train to Moscow with a few Russian "Call to Obedience" letters. Two days later, this Latvian girl, one of the first students to graduate from a Bible school in Latvia after communism was thrown out of her country, arrived in the glamorous city of Moscow.

Immediately, Inga made her way to the Department of Religious Affairs, where she was told that the head man in that department was out of town but the associate would look at the articles. She was to return to the office in two days. When Inga showed up two days later, the clerk said, "You have a two-and-one-half year permit to distribute the Russian 'Call to Obedience' letters everywhere in Russia, except for two cities. By the way, when you send them out, put us on the list also." Not only was it remarkable that Inga received the permit, but that its duration was five times longer than normal.

While I was still in Alaska, Jesus said to me, *"I have set before thee an open door, and no man can shut it."* God's promises are always faithful and true, far beyond anything we could ever imagine. The "Call to Obedience" now goes into Latvia, the Ukraine, and Russia, all the way from St. Petersburg in the west to Siberia in the east. It even goes into a number of prisons. In fact, I learned there is a prison in Russia where every prisoner is required to join a "Call to Obedience" Bible study. Prisoners are getting saved, set free from drugs and alcohol, and discipled. When released, they return home to lead their wives and children to Christ, and to become outstanding, hard-working citizens.

In March of 1945, the Soviet troops drove my family out of our home in East Germany and almost put us at the bottom of the Baltic Sea. My Uncle Rudi fought the Soviets in the German army at Leningrad, which is now St. Petersburg. Now, some fifty years later, Uncle Rudi's nephew is reaching into that vast, beautiful country with the gospel of Jesus Christ. For you see, God always has the last word, and how wonderful these Russians are, so appreciative and full of passion and vigor! They are hungry for the "Call to Obedience" message, as are so many around the world. Now let me give you a beautiful story from the continent of Africa.

On one occasion, a pastor's son from Nigeria, West Africa, then a medical student at the University of West Virginia, met another student whose brother was a pastor in Charleston, West Virginia. As they got to know each other, this Nigerian told his friend about a vision his aging father had experienced while in Nigeria. He had seen a certain sanctuary and a certain man of God who had a message for his people. When the old patriarch came out of this vision, he told it to his son, admonishing him to look for such a man of God in the United States. When the Nigerian student visited his friend's brother's church, he said, "This is the place my father saw in the vision." Later, Rev. Helm visited that church to hold some meetings. The Nigerian student said, "This is the man my father saw in the vision." He begged Rev. Helm to come to Nigeria, but Rev. Helm told him he could only go when the Holy Spirit led him.

For over thirty-seven years, I have observed many wonderful evangelists, but I have never met one who, when asked if he could come and hold meetings, would not pull out his date book and look for the next available opening. The typical response from pastors and evangelists was always, "My next opening is on such and such a date. I can be with you then." But in twenty years of travel with Rev. Helm, I never saw him pull out a date book. It was always, "I can be with you only when the Holy Spirit leads."

For two years the Nigerian medical student pressed Rev. Helm to come to his country. Finally, in 1982, the Lord gave Brother Helm the dates to travel to that country, though he was to be in Nigeria only three days. Can you imagine traveling all the way from Indianapolis through New York City and Frankfurt, Germany, all the way down to Lagos to be in two meetings in three days in a remote village? But that is how the Lord led, and so it was what Rev. Helm did.

About sixty-five persons, including myself, accompanied Rev. Helm on this journey. Because of my previous varicose vein operations and because I was so tall and had such long legs, sitting in those little airplane seats during the overseas trip from New York to Frankfurt to Lagos was a mild form of torture. Then, upon arriving in Nigeria, we were jammed into little buses, even filling up the fold-out seats in the aisle, but we prayed and worshipped throughout the trip to the village. I sat on the left wheel-well behind the driver. One time, the tire under me started losing air, and it went down fast. As the bus driver stopped and looked at the tire, it filled back up. Jesus had told us to go to Nigeria; He had even told us when to go. We had obeyed, and when you are on God's schedule, He takes care of everything, including flat tires.

The Nigerians are beautiful people, and I immediately fell in love with them. They are dark complected, with narrow faces, fine features, and perfect posture. You would be hard-pressed to find a slouch among them. And, oh, how they dress! Hallelujah! Even in their poverty, African women dress like queens. Their garments are colorful and reach down to their ankles, and they walk with dignity and grace.

In Nigeria I did not see faucets with running water anywhere, except in our hotel, so I marveled at how they kept their clothing so clean. Their hair is also very neat. You see them walking along the highway in their flowing garbs, carrying gas cans, fruit baskets, and boxes on their heads, often without using their hands for support or balance.

While on the last stretch of the road, we saw one of the most beautiful sights on both sides of the palm tree-lined thoroughfare. On either side of the road were Nigerians, dressed like angels in white robes, waving palm branches, holding signs of greeting, and singing the praises of Jehovah with jubilant voices to welcome us.

Several of us wondered what message Brother Helm would preach to these people here at the edge of the jungle. What word would he give to them? Well, the answer is the same as for any people anywhere. The heart of man is no different, regardless of where he lives; man has the same needs in every country and clime.

Rev. Helm began by saying, "Hundreds of years ago, the white man put you into chains of slavery, but there are chains worse than the chains of slavery. They are the chains of the carnal nature. It is the carnal nature that imprisons man so he cannot have fellowship with God." I believe by now you can imagine the rest of the sermon.

This first service was an outdoor meeting and, although we stood under shade trees and structures with thatched roofs, it was still very, very hot. It was a primitive area, without running water, and electricity. The interpreter, though well educated, was very slow in his interpretation because, while he interpreted, he also ran a little commentary on what was being said. This made the meeting very long and hard on every one of us, but the people were touched and helped anyhow.

The next day, we all went back to the village, but instead of meeting outdoors, we jammed into a little cinder block building. On the way to the village that morning, the group in the other bus began praying and praising and exhorting one another from the Word of God. After a little while in that packed Mitsubishi bus, the "glory fell," as the old timers used to say, and the presence of God became so sweet and powerful that everyone on the bus was affected. Some who had never shouted before did so for the first time. Some just had tears running down their cheeks, while others laid their faces on their knees and repeated, "Glory! Glory! Glory!" Some tried to run, but there was no space, so they just ran in place. This may sound like strange behavior to you if you have never run or shouted with excitement to the Lord, but one of these days the glory of the Lord may come upon you, and then you will shout and run whether you had planned to or not.

As the busload of happy folk entered the building, they brought the "glory" of the Lord with them into the sanctuary. The fire of God and His love and holiness now fell upon everyone. Of course, with the Nigerians not having running water and the weather having been hot for several days, there was a lot of sweating going on in there. So we had both glory and sweat, and every face reflected the countenance of Jesus. We all were one in the Spirit, as if we had always been together. Oh, what will heaven be like!

There were no hymnbooks or chorus sheets as we sang. One of the locals went to the front and made up a song, blasting it out on his bullhorn. When the congregation began to catch the words and the melody and the drummer caught on to the rhythm and began to pound away on his goatskin, the meeting was on.

As Rev. Helm began to speak, he prayed, "Jesus, where is the interpreter? Who is the interpreter for this meeting?"

Then Brother Helm raised his hand and pointed to one of the precious black men and said, "You are the interpreter." None of us had ever met this man before, but Rev. Helm knew the interpreter by the Holy Spirit. Jesus had told me long ago that too many of us just want Him for salvation; few are willing to pay the price for true intimacy with our Lord so God can speak to us as he spoke to Moses. This was certainly not the case in Nigeria that day.

It turned out the interpreter, whose name was Joseph, was not part of that congregation or village. No one present knew him, but he had heard about the meeting in Lagos and had traveled 400 miles to get there. Although he was a bank teller, it immediately became obvious he was the Lord's choice for this assignment. He spoke perfect English and was perfect in the local dialect as well. Best of all, he interpreted no more and no less than what the preacher said. Just occasionally, he asked Rev. Helm, "May I say, praise the Lord?" Joseph was a man of the finest of etiquette, dressed like a gentleman. Truly, he was God-sent.

How does all this fit into the topic of God's open doors? Remember I told you how the Lord opened worldwide radio for me; how He opened up Latvia, Russia, the Ukraine; and here is how He opened Africa.

After the second meeting ended, I was privileged to meet Joseph. We spoke for less than a minute, but he gave me his calling card. Those few seconds with him opened Africa for the "Call to Obedience" letter. Had the Lord not specifically led for Joseph to be the interpreter, I would never have met him. The whole African connection was contingent on Joseph's being there and on the pinpoint accuracy of the leading of the Spirit of God.

Our group, at great expense and sacrifice, traveled 8,000 miles to hold two meetings in a remote village, to deliver two messages, and to return home with only one calling card.

When I arrived home, I sent Joseph a copy of the "Call to Obedience," and he immediately wanted more. He sent me a list of pastors, and these pastors also wanted more and sent me lists of others, and so it went on and on. Soon the letter began to move into the Christian community in that needy country. Now this message on how the chains of carnality imprison us and how we can be delivered from them is going into libraries, Bible colleges, seminaries, and pulpits in Nigeria, and into some other African countries as well. In a number of places, these letters are read from the pulpit or translated into a local dialect.

The Lord said, *"I have set before thee an open door, and no man can shut it."* In His grace and mercy, God took this formerly shy and bashful fellow from a far country and put him onto a journey of light and glory, and has now given him a little section of the world in which to share God's treasures. You may recall the old chorus that says, "Brighten the corner where you are." God has given me a few little corners, and I need to be faithful in those corners. He has also given you a little corner to shine your light in as well. It may be in your church, your home or factory, or somewhere beyond our verdant shores in some far-off valley or city. However, don't go seeking your corners, but seek only to follow Jesus, and in His time He will take you where He wants you to be. Keep focusing only on Him. Let Him be your life, your peace, your joy, your fellowship, your all-in-all. He must mean more than anything in the world to us, for when he becomes less, we are stepping out of fellowship with Him. If we do not love Jesus more than everything else, we cannot be his disciples. As disobedience took man out of fellowship with God, obedience to the Holy Spirit takes him back again. As long as we have Him, we have everything we need; if we lose Him, we come to the loss of all things.

Jesus died on the cross to save us, but we must die daily

to our self-will if we are to become true disciples. Take up your cross and follow Him. Determine with your heart never to let the flesh or your self-will make another choice. We must not only be saved from our sins, but also from ourselves.

Again I plead with you: forsake the world's pleasures; give yourself over entirely to your Creator. As you do, the light of His sweetness and majesty will take you right through the door into the glorious chamber of "His kingdom come and His will be done." As Jesus saw me hidden under pine branches in a forest of Germany at thirteen years of age and called me to go with Him on a wonderful journey of light, so Jesus sees where you are. He is waiting on you with open arms, saying to you now, "Come with me."

Will you please answer Him with a resounding "Yes, Lord, I come"?

Notes

Chapter 3: I Always Wanted to Marry a Jew

1. Jerry Silverman, *"Ani Ma-amin (I Believe),"* *The Undying Flame: Ballads and Songs of the Holocaust.* Judiac Traditions in Literature, Music, and Art series (Syracuse, NY: Syracuse University Press, 2002), pp. 116-117. Used by permission.

Chapter 5: East Germany

1. See also Alan Abrams, *Special Treatment* (Secaucus, N.J.: Lyle Stuart, Inc., 1985), p.11.

Chapter 13: Coming to America

1. Adelaide Plumptre, *"Keep Thyself Pure,"* 1908. Public Domain.

2. Emma Lazarus, *"The New Colossus,"* 1883. Public Domain.

3. Katherine Lee Bates, *"O Beautiful for Spacious Skies,"* 1904. Public Domain.

Chapter 16: Why Don't You Start Obeying God?

1. Loran W. Helm, *A Voice in the Wilderness* (Bourbon, IN: Evangel Voice Publications, 1973), p. 80.

2. John H. Sammis, *"When We Walk With The Lord,"* 1887. Public Domain.

Chapter 21: Waiting Upon God

1. Helm, *Wilderness*, pp. 158-159.

Chapter 28: Follow Me as I Follow Christ

1. Ibid., p. 172.

Chapter 30: God's Open Doors

1. Bradford Torrey, *"Not So in Haste, My Heart,"* 1875. Public Domain.

Additional Resources
by Reimar A. C. Schultze

Discipleship Training (www.schultze.org) has additional resources and materials that will help you walk with God.

- The "Call to Obedience" newsletter, a monthly sermon written by Pastor Schultze, can be received free by subscribing online.

- Abiding in Christ: The Essence of Christianity: A Daily Devotional which was published by CTO Books in 2002. This book reveals the secrets to discovering a life of unbroken fellowship with Jesus Christ.

- Spanish website: www.discipuladohoy.org

To order additional copies of Pastor Schultze's books, I AM Love and Abiding in Christ, contact:

BookMasters, Inc.
Ashland, Ohio 44805
USA Toll Free- 1-800-247-6553
or
Your Local Bookstore